D1087614

Dangerous Decisions

Problem Solving in Tomorrow's World

Dangerous Decisions

Problem Solving in Tomorrow's World

Enid Mumford
University of Manchester
Manchester, England

KLUWER ACADEMIC / PLENUM PUBLISHERS
NEW YORK, BOSTON, DORDRECHT, LONDON, MOSCOW

ISBN 0-306-46142-0 (Hardbound)
ISBN 0-306-46143-9 (Paperback)

233 Spring Street, New York, N.Y. 10013

10 9 8 7 6 5 4 3 2 1

A C.I.P. record for this book is available from the Library of Congress

Printed in the United States of America

Contents

Foreword

The new millennium is just around the corner and much is being speculated about tomorrow's world. A world where individuals will lead longer and healthier lives; where disease will be banished through new medical drug treatments and better sanitation; where leisure will become an increasing part of everyone's existence; where overall wealth will increase; and where, in general, the quality of life will improve for all. The so-called "information technology" revolution is responsible for this brave new world, providing an environment in which everyone will be "connected" via computer networks to virtually everyone else. We will be able to work anywhere, anytime, any place. We will be able to communicate with anyone and everyone. Indeed, much of this belief is already a reality. I can sit in front of a computer in Melbourne, Australia, and hold my classes in Houston over the Internet. With video-conferencing software, some basic hardware, and the Internet, it is possible to lecture to and interact with any students with virtually no cost. Believe me, it works. Communicating with anyone via E-mail is simply a mouse-click away. The world has indeed shrunk. But is this new world all that it is cracked up to be? Many people feel such positive—almost euphoric—views on technology are misguided. There are significant problems that simply are ignored by such a view.

A number of years ago I wrote an essay entitled "The Effect of A Priori Views on the Social Implications of Computing,"[1] which outlined three alternative positions—optimist, pessimist, and pluralist—that the role of new information technology could play for society. The optimist took the view that new technology would improve society through enhancements in worker productivity, the development of new jobs and skills, improved communications, increased leisure time, and better medical care, entertainment, travel, and education. The pessimist, on the other hand, saw none of these values, instead focusing on the erosion of privacy, loss of jobs and job skills, lower job satisfaction, and the further concentralization of power to those already in control. However, I argued for a third position—that of the pluralist. This position noted that new technology could be positive or negative depending on the way the technology was put to use. The pluralist concentrated on the development of criteria for social and technological acceptance and the application of "acceptable" technologies in appropriate circumstances. Professor Mumford's book takes such a pluralistic stance. She argues for problem solving that is not naive and simplistic. She shuns easy notions that complex problems can be solved by merely throwing more resources at them. Indeed, complex problems such as illegal drugs and cyber crime defy simple solutions. Consider some of the statistics Professor Mumford offers about drugs.

It is a well-known fact that today illegal drugs are controlled by large-scale organizations that cross national and international boundaries. Today's drug-trafficking industry is worth approximately $500 billion a year. She states that "the illegal drug industry is now believed to be the second-largest industry in the world, second only to the arms industry and larger than the oil industry. The U.S. government has spent in excess of $20 billion during the past ten years on international drug control problems with hardly any effect. United States and Mexican interdiction efforts have made little difference to the overall flow of drugs though Mexico to the United States. In the United States alone, eighty-five million people have tried illegal drugs and, across the globe, there are an estimated forty-five million people addicted to illegal drugs."

More than one-half of all fifteen- to sixteen-year-olds in the United Kingdom have taken illegal drugs. At Oxford University, it has been reported that 34% of the undergraduates have tried hard drugs. Russian Mafia groups that have historically controlled the illicit drug-trafficking business in Russia have now used their profits to control an estimated 40% of private industry, 50% of the banks, and 60% of state-owned companies. Two-thirds of the economy is criminalized. The average heroin user commits two hundred crimes per year to feed his or her habit. Gang warfare among drug dealers in major urban areas is out of control and threatens the stability of urban life. Efforts, both nationally and internationally, to quell the drug problem have failed. Without question drugs have become a major headache to our global society. It is an intractable problem that requires new strategies.

Professor Mumford notes that for a solution to be found there must be a "rational reconstruction" of the problem. Solutions can only be implemented if they are socially, psychologically, and culturally acceptable. This is exactly the position of the pluralist. What I find so appealing in this book is that Professor Mumford proposes a solution to complex problems such as drugs. The model requires problem-solving behavior to be analyzed in terms of "competencies, capabilities, and coordination." Effective problem solving requires individuals and groups with appropriate knowledge competence, organizations with the capabilities to support and deploy this knowledge, and structures that enable excellent coordination to take place between groups that are contributing to the problem-solving process.

In addition to addressing one of society's most thorny problems—drugs—Mumford goes on to warn us of another more subdued problem: cyber crime. While it does not garner the attention of the press or society to the extent that drugs do, cyber crime is nonetheless worrying. Here are some of the statistics she presents about cyber crime. In Europe alone, cross-border frauds totaled $69.3 billion in 1996. A large proportion of these were electronic frauds, i.e., cyber crime. By the year 2000, $1.7 trillion in transactions will be done over computer networks, and a significant proportion of these will be over the Internet.

Two high-profile cases of cyber crime have caught our collective attention this past decade: the infamous Nick Leeson case, which led to the collapse of Baring's Bank, and the German Markus Hess, who hacked into U.S. military sites and sold the information he gathered to the Russians. These cases are suggestive of how much damage cyber crime can do not only to companies but to countries as well. A worrisome figure produced by the U.S. Department of Defense was that in 1995 the department was attacked 250,000 times by hackers.

If cyber crime is not enough, Professor Mumford warns of yet another major concern for society—money laundering. Money laundering is where cyber crime and drugs meet since both need to find ways to take illicit money and turn it into "clean" money. Law enforcement agencies now use the term "narco dollars" to refer to money obtained from illicit drug trafficking. In the United States alone, this amount is somewhere between $300–$500 billion annually.

To show just how bad things have become, one commentator has proclaimed that "the 1990s are in danger of becoming the decade when international crime becomes Europe's leading business." But take heart. The good news is that this book provides a vehicle whereby we can start to seriously think about how we as a society can address these complex problems. They will not be easy to solve, but at least there will be a way forward. I encourage everyone to read Professor Mumford's suggestions for solving complex problems. They are thought provoking and exciting. They are, to me, a way of implementing a pluralist position.

Reference

1. R. Hirschheim, "The Effect of A Priori Views on the Social Implications of Computing," *ACM Computing Surveys* 18 (June 1986), pp. 165–195.

RUDI HIRSCHHEIM
Professor of Information Systems
University of Houston
Houston, Texas

Acknowledgments

This book could not have been written without the help of many experts in the fields of problem solving, drugs, and cyber crime. I wish to acknowledge my debt to these and to thank them for their kindness and invaluable assistance. Most important were Plenum editors Ken Derham and Elizabeth Pryde, who provided valuable advice on how to structure the book so as to improve its flow and logic.

In England, the West Yorkshire Police provided excellent information on their problem-solving approaches and on how a police force can be organized and motivated to become first-class problem solvers. In particular I would like to thank Keith Hellawell the then chief constable and Ian Newsome, David Lloyd, and Eileen Hunton from management support. They provided great assistance in suggesting and organizing meetings with police officers who had relevant experience in my areas of interest. Their knowledge was invaluable, and they freely gave up valuable time to talk with me.

My thanks go also to the Brighton Police Force in Colorado. They provided a great deal of important information on the philosophy and management of their very successful community-relations program, together with a video showing how it was put into practice. Two major companies, ICI and Shell, were also of great assistance in describing their strategies for preventing cyber crime. At ICI I would like to thank Brian Baister and at Shell, Chris Gillies and John O'Connor.

Many other people gave freely of their time and knowledge and I thank them all most sincerely. Kevin Gaston of the Manchester Business School provided much good advice and useful contacts in the early stages of the project and I am in his debt.

INTRODUCTION

Problem Solving and Uncertainty

MANAGERS AS PROBLEM SOLVERS

Problems are difficult questions that require time and thought to answer. All managers are problem solvers. They spend their days handling the problems of providing goods and services to markets that they believe are, or can become, interested in purchasing what they have to offer. This demanding activity is not simple; it requires setting up appropriate production systems, introducing new technology, handling employee relations, developing marketing strategies, and many other critical activities related to meeting the needs of the communities or countries in which they operate. These problems are usually tackled on the basis of experience or with guidance from experts. They may not always be straightforward; however, they are part of what most managers regard as "their job."

But, today, there is another set of challenging problems that managers are confronted with. These are new, complex, and often very threatening. They are outside the manager's normal day-to-day experience, and there may be few experts available to give advice; but the consequence of not tackling them may send a company on a route to commercial disaster. Some problems are so serious that despite our lack of knowledge we must make major efforts to remove or reduce them, even though the likelihood of success in doing so is poor.

Many of these very difficult problems arise from activities or changes that are taking place in the social and economic environments in which we live and work. They are events or circumstances that cause us stress and anxiety. For example, the challenges of a new global market environment may place competitive pressures on companies that they may be unable to handle. New products or processes may present novel and unanticipated health or environmental problems, and political, economic, or financial disturbances may suddenly change a viable market situation into a volatile and unstable one. Anticipating problems of this kind requires an ability to analyze the present and forecast the future, always difficult and uncertain tasks.

Managers hope that by understanding and tackling problems that confront them they will achieve a degree of personal and organizational stability and regain a sense of control and well-being. Unfortunately, a factor making success difficult is today's rate of change. Events that affect managers are occurring at greater speed and with more impact on industry and society than ever before. This influences the ease or difficulty with which problems can be solved. This is not a new situation. In the 1960s a political commentator stated in the *New York Times* magazine that "so much is moving and shifting that it is hard to catch more than a glance of the action as it passes by. Events tumble upon one another like theatrical happenings, and the sequence of things is lost."[1]

The philosopher Zygmunt Baumann suggests that one of today's great divides is that between order and chaos. The regular, predictable, controllable, and relatively problem-free world that many of us cherish is increasingly becoming separate from a contingent, erratic, unpredictable, and hard-to-control world that we increasingly experience but dislike, even fear.[2]

COMPLEX PROBLEMS

This book is about complex problem solving in conditions of uncertainty. The question it tries to address is how can managers make effective decisions in these kinds of situations, and, once these decisions have been taken and implemented, how can they live with the consequences. Making decisions requires making choices, and this always involves taking risks. We are never certain of the consequences of a particular decision because we never know what the future is going to bring. A solution that may seem logical and appropriate at one moment in time may turn out to have disastrous consequences when totally new sets of circumstances unfold.

We can never tackle all the problems that present themselves, and judgments have to be made on which problems we will address and which we will postpone for a future solution. This choice will require an assessment of the gravity of the problem—how serious are its consequences? And of its probability—how likely is it to happen? Both of these decisions require knowledge and sound judgment, attributes that may be in short supply.

Many problems are not well defined and contain sets of events. They more usually consist of a series of actions and reactions with the final result, which may be a disaster, a product of the interaction of the different parts. This leads us into one of today's popular areas of research—chaos theory. Chaos theory suggests that much of what looks complex, confused, and random is the product of an underlying order that we do not recognize. In this concealed but sensitive set of relationships, small perturbations can have a multiplying effect. The flap of a butterfly's wing in Hawaii that leads to a hurricane in the Caribbean is an example often given of how insignificant events can create major consequences. It is hoped that this book will contribute to a better understanding of problem complexity and how this can be addressed.[3]

For some groups, in particular scientists, problem solving often follows precise rules and treads well-worn paths. But for other groups, such as managers, there are no firm rules, although there are principles and approaches that can be helpful. Some of the most used of these will be described in the chapters that follow.

How problems are solved depends to a large extent, but not entirely, on the nature of the problem. Other factors that can exert a major influence are the environment containing the problem and the pressures and constraints exerted by this, together with the personality, interests, values, and assumptions of the problem solver on what will produce a satisfactory solution. All of these will influence whether the solutions should be ethical, expedient, easily obtainable, produce fast results or short or long term?

Problem-solving approaches are also likely to be related to a manager's role and status. A senior manager will have considerable power and authority. This will assist the collection of accurate information and help provide a correct understanding of the nature of the problem, but it can also lead to political pressures and selective vision. These may push the manager toward a particular definition of the problem and to a particular kind of solution. Even though the manager as problem solver gives priority to his or her company role, he or she also occupies other roles—those of friend or colleague, for example. These may cloud decision making and lead to conflicting loyalties. The manager's own personality will also be a factor, with strong, confident managers being willing to make tough decisions while weaker souls are avoiding anything contentious.

In contrast, while an external consultant hired to investigate an internal problem may take a more objective view, he or she can find that certain investigation routes are closed for confidentiality reasons, and that relevant information is difficult or impossible to obtain because he or she is an outsider.

Another factor that can cause uncertainty is who the problem is seen as belonging to. If the problem is the manager's own and is directly related to future career prospects in the company, it will usually be addressed with clarity, speed, and authority. However, if the problem is viewed as belonging to the company as a whole and affects a number of established activities, then a different strategy will be used. A longer-term structural solution may now be preferred. This will focus on reorganization, the redefinition of roles, and the reallocation of responsibilities. If the problem affects the company, but originates outside, then great attention will be paid to tracing its cause, intention, and location.

Problem solving is never simple and, irrespective of whose problem it is or where it is located, uncertainty is always likely to be a factor in decision making. Great attention will have to be paid to what is possible, acceptable, desirable, and ethical, with no guarantee that the right decision is being made. Today's and tomorrow's challenge is that the working life of most managers is likely to be a series of problems, each calling for different kinds of experience and approaches.

Problem solving will always have intended and unintended consequences and is directed at changing situations. If nothing changes then the problem has not been solved. If the changes that occur were not intended then the problem may or may not have been solved, but the result has nothing to do with the problem solver. Successful problem solving occurs when a carefully planned and executed change achieves a desired result with a direct link between what is intended and what has happened.

THE PROBLEMS OF DRUGS AND CYBER CRIME

There are many situations where the possibility, or need, for effective action coincides with the absence of precise rules or knowledge to help change the situation. This applies to the two problem areas chosen to provide specific examples in this book—illegal drug use and cyber crime. They have been chosen for three reasons. First, they are likely to be major problems for the start of the millennium and the foreseeable future. Neither shows any signs of being diminished or controlled. If anything, the evidence suggests that they will increase in severity.

Second, managers will be affected by both illegal drugs and cyber crime. There are no figures available on the scale of the problem of drug misuse at work, but it is believed to be considerable. Keith Hellawell, the antidrugs coordinator for the United Kingdom, suggests that employers should now begin setting up antidrugs policies in the workplace as a preventive measure.[4] He stresses that absenteeism, loss of concentration, unusual irritability, or a tendency to become confused could all indicate drug abuse and be a company hazard. Certain industries, in particular fashion and finance, are particularly susceptible. There are also no figures for the losses due to cyber crime—defined as fraud that is a product of illegal activity involving computers. This can be criminal activity by employees or due to external criminals breaking into confidential electronic files. It is seen by industry as a very serious threat that is difficult, even impossible, to prevent.

The third argument for using these examples is that illegal drug use and cyber crime, although equally serious in their effects, take very different forms. The former requires complex organizational networks to enable drugs to travel across the world from their source to their eventual market. In contrast, the latter can either be carried out by a single individual or a small group within a company or located many thousands of miles away. Distance is no problem to the cyber criminal because his or her communication links are electronic, and physical movement is not necessary. The only requirement is appropriate skill and knowledge and access to a computer network.

Cyber crime, is new, little understood, technology-based and rapidly accelerating as electronic communication assists the movement of cash and sends information at lightning speed around the world. Each protection device that is installed to prevent crime is rapidly confronted by a technique for circumventing it. Overcoming security barriers provides an exciting and lucrative challenge for criminals who wish to access sensitive commercial data, to damage competitors, or to launder money. These are the cyber criminals of today and tomorrow. They regard the drug barons as "old fashioned" and out of date.

Cyber crime activities have consequences for all managers. Alvin Toffler, extrapolating from changes in industrial structures, sees conflict as moving from the traditional background of killing and war, to the equally destabilizing battleground of bitter economic competition. Here the weaponry will be technology, particularly electronic communication and intelligence. He suggests that we are now in a period of what he calls "info-wars" in which industry fights industry throughout the globe. As in military wars, espionage will be a major factor, and this will not be only a passive collection of intelligence. There will be "commercial covert action" in which attempts are made to destabilize rivals through feeding false information into their computer systems. This misinformation may induce them to produce the wrong goods for current market needs, and in this way lose the edge over their competitors.[5]

An interesting feature of both illegal drugs and cyber crime is that they both eventually end up as part of the same process. This is money laundering. Both drug and cyber criminals need to turn their profits into a legal form of finance so that they can spend their ill-gotten gains. Without the availability of money laundering this would be difficult if not impossible.

We do not yet know what the future will hold, but we badly need some theories and tools to help us manage the very complex problems that we are certain to face. The two addressed in this book have been chosen for their intractability and complexity. They appear almost insoluble and their inviolability is increased by the fact that their control is largely in the hands of criminals. Our challenge in this book is to learn how to understand and address old and new problems with this degree of complexity. In the future there are likely to be many more of a similar kind.

THEORY AS AN AID TO UNDERSTANDING

Most books are based on some kind of theoretical model. The author has a particular view of the world, is influenced by a historical tradition, or is following some current popular belief. Simple models can be useful in clarifying problems and enabling them to be studied from different perspectives. They can also help simplify difficult concepts.

The theoretical models chosen to assist an understanding of the approach and discussion in the chapters that follow are the notions of "capability," "competence," and "coordination." By capability I mean having the power, capacity, and knowledge to achieve desired objectives. Capability is also an economic concept, as developed by John Kay and other economists.[6] It is a product of a resource-based theory of strategy that argues that firms and other organizations are essentially collections of capabilities, and that their effectiveness depends on the match between these capabilities and the market they serve. In this book the notion is related to effective problem solving by suggesting that this is also related to capabilities and that the success of a problem-solving process depends on the match between these capabilities and the problems it has to tackle.

This concept is very similar to the Law of Requisite Variety developed by W. Ross Ashby in 1956 and used extensively by Stafford Beer in his cybernetic models.[7] This concept maintains that complex problems that contain many different variables require problem-solving techniques with an equivalent amount of variety if they are to be solved or controlled.

In this book *capability* is applied to the problem-solving ability of organizations and focuses particularly on providing necessary and appropriate support for the problem solvers. The problem-solving ability of individuals is called *competence*. We might also call it skill. Competence has been defined by the philosopher Gilbert Ryle as "knowing how."[8] He argues that in ordinary life we are much more concerned with people's competencies than with their intellectual brilliance or their beliefs. What they can do is usually more important than what they know, for knowledge is only useful if it is applied. Competence implies that a person presented with a problem knows what to do. He or she can think things through logically and get results.

John Kay suggests that capabilities can be viewed as assets or contracts. It is important for them to be identified and their relationship to successful strategy formulation or problem solving recognized. Some may be rare and difficult for others to imitate. When this is the case the organization possessing them has a considerable competitive advantage. Three capabilities that Kay sees as important are reputation, innovation, and what he calls "architecture." By this he means the system of relationships within a firm and between it and its suppliers.[9] We shall call this social *coordination* or social partnership and define it as the ability to collaborate successfully with others.

Capabilities in the problem-solving areas addressed in this book—such as the identification and control of certain kinds of crime—will include the following:

- *Knowledge capability*. The ability to learn from the experience of problem solving and, as a result, to continually improve problem-solving techniques.

- *Resource capability.* An understanding of the resources required to produce effective problem solving in the selected areas. This will include staff numbers and expertise, and material resources such as transport and backup.
- *Psychological capability.* An emphasis on the importance of leadership, teamwork, trust, and good social relationships within the problem-solving team, in order to create and maintain morale.
- *Organizational capability.* An ability to plan and think strategically, to set objectives, to deploy resources effectively, to manage complex situations.
- *Innovative capability.* An encouragement of creative thinking.
- *Ethical capability.* An ability to create and sustain a set of ethical values regarding working practices and relations with other groups.

John Kay maintains that an important success criteria is establishing a match between the challenges faced by the organization and its capabilities. This will also be true of crime prevention and solution. A particular challenge with problem solving in these areas is appreciating that criminal activity exists and is a problem waiting to be tackled. These capabilities can also be translated into the individual competencies of problem solvers in the following ways:

- *Knowledge competence.* The ability of an individual to learn from the experience of problem solving and, as a result, to continually improve personal problem-solving techniques.
- *Resource competence.* An understanding of the personal resources required to produce effective problem solving in the selected areas. These will include time and skills.
- *Psychological competence.* An ability to work with others, to maintain personal morale, and to persevere through difficult problems.
- *Organizational competence.* An ability to plan and think strategically about ones personal contribution and how this fits with the needs of the total situation.
- *Innovative competence.* An ability to think creatively, to approach problems from different angles.
- *Ethical competence.* An understanding of, and willingness to accept, organizational values if these do not contravene important personal values.

Another simpler way of describing competencies is as task competencies—the knowledge and skills required to do a particular job, personal competencies—the ability to use judgment and to communicate effectively, and management competencies—providing vision, leadership, and effective control.

John Harvey Jones, in his book *Making It Happen*, describes the competencies he required as managing director of ICI.[10] These included ensuring that his board of directors worked effectively. To achieve this he had to:

- Increase the board's knowledge by allocating responsibilities and tasks that helped to fill gaps in this knowledge.
- Be able to manage his colleagues on the board, and to manage the company through the board.
- Develop the board as an effective team that could work together, collaborate, grow, develop, and provide an example to the rest of the company.
- Ensure that the board was the right size and composition, and that the succession to his job, and to the top jobs in the company, was under control.
- Ensure that the board was providing a clear, strategic direction to the company and that he, as managing director, was successfully communicating this, and the values of the company, to the outside world.

Coordination is the third concept addressed by this book. By this I mean the ability to collaborate creatively and productively with other groups, both inside and outside the parent organization. This attribute, sometimes called "networking," is seen by some management gurus as the one attribute most related to organizational success in today's complex world.[11] Solving the problem of getting high-quality products to customers quickly requires effective internal coordination and also excellent external coordination with suppliers and with purchasers. Just-in-time programs in manufacturing plants, which require suppliers to respond immediately to production demands, are attempts to achieve this. Similarly, national and local governments, companies, and security forces must coordinate their activities with many different community groups if they are to make an impact on the very difficult problems of drug misuse and computer fraud.

Capabilities, competencies, and coordination are group and individual attributes related to increasing knowledge and improving relationships, but other characteristics are required for successful problem solving. *Teamwork* is also very important. With large, complex problems good teamwork is essential. Information will need to be shared, strategies agreed to, and individual competencies used effectively. Lastly, *motivation* for both the group and the individual is essential. The problem solvers must actively want to understand and solve the problem or make a contribution to its future solution.

THE CHAPTERS THAT FOLLOW

The first two chapters of this book discuss the capabilities, competencies, and coordination skills that will contribute to the solution of difficult problems and examine some of the methods and tools that have been used by different groups to help analysis and strategy formulation when these kinds of problems are being tackled. They also open the discussion on the two problems selected for detailed examination—illegal drugs and cyber crime. Chapter 3 examines the problem-solving approaches of three professional groups—scientists, lawyers, and doctors. These are compared in terms of values, objectives, and the methods each uses to arrive at a solution. Chapter 4 focuses on the police as problem solvers and examines how they tackle different kinds of problems. These include the day-to-day problems of the man or woman on the beat, the general management problems of running a very large organization, and the specialized problems of a group such as the drug squad, which has to work on a very complex problem in a specific area. Chapter 5 looks at problems from the point of view of a drug dealer and a drug baron. It describes the management challenges in getting drugs from the peasant farmers into American and European markets.

Next the general problems of drugs and cyber crime are addressed. Chapter 6 provides a big picture analysis of the drug scene, showing its complexity and describing the different groups involved. Chapter 7 examines the role of governments in developing strategies to tackle the drug problem. Chapter 8 offers some approaches for addressing different aspects of the problem. These are not seen as producing a solution, but as assisting a degree of control in certain areas. Chapter 9 examines the problems of the various groups affected by drugs. Chapters 10 and 11 focus on the problems of cyber crime. Chapter 12 looks at money laundering, a facility that both illegal drugs and cyber crime require. The last chapter draws some general conclusions on complex problem solving and how this can be improved to cope with the new kinds of problems that may be experienced in the future.

This book makes no attempts to provide solutions to the illegal drug and cyber crime problem areas. In fact both of these may be insoluble if the objective is to remove them completely. Its aim is to provide a helpful approach to difficult problem solving, showing ways in which complexity can be understood and addressed.

CHAPTER 1

The Problems of Problem Solving

PROBLEM SOLVING—SOME DEFINITIONS

Before embarking on a discussion of the problems of complex problem solving we need to clarify how we are defining the word "problem." There are many definitions. David Bayley, a well-known writer on the police force and its future, describes problem solving by the police as a study of the conditions that leads to calls for their services, the drawing up of plans to correct these conditions, and the evaluation and implementation of remedial actions.[1] This is in contrast to what he sees as the usual practice of handling crimes as if they were isolated events.

Margot Constanzo, a lawyer who teaches problem solving to other lawyers, also takes a broad definition. She criticizes approaches that see problem solving as dealing with situations in which something has already gone wrong. She argues that these are situations to be managed, not problems to be solved. Her definition includes something that has happened in the past that leads to a problem, or something that can happen in the future and have the same effect. More controversially she suggests that problem solving is not creative thinking. She believes that problem solving is the application of established professional knowledge and methodologies to the solution of a problem. Creative thinking, in contrast, is the search for new knowledge and new methodologies, and it is more risky because it is venturing into the novel and the unknown.[2]

Donald Schon, an American academic, has an even broader definition. He sees most professional practice as a process of problem solving.

He argues that the first task is to understand the nature of the problem. This requires a process of what he calls "problem setting" and involves decisions on what the problem is, what kind of a solution is required, and a selection of the best means for achieving this.[3] Problems do not always present themselves as givens, they are often complex and uncertain. They have to be analyzed and defined before a possible solution can be identified and applied. There also has to be an assessment of the likely consequences of the proposed remedial action.

My definition is that problem solving is the application of knowledge with the intention of changing a dysfunctional or undesirable situation. This sees problem solving as an extension of the present, restoring order to situations that are moving out of control. A different kind of problem solving is related to the future. This sees it as the application of knowledge to influence events that have yet to happen but are seen as likely or possible to happen. These events may be negative or positive in their consequences. They may bring new problems or offer new opportunities. One of the objectives of this book will be to discover how both managers and the police define the problems they have to deal with. Are they interested in causes or only in effects? Do they take account of the consequences of failure, or even of success, when they are investigating problems or is this seen as the provenance of government and judges? There are many questions to be answered.

The problems we are concerned with in this book are likely to be both continuous and critical. None can be solved independently of others, and strategies will need to be constantly reviewed, updated, or abandoned to meet changing conditions. Our problem-solving approaches are also likely to be restricted. Any decisions that we make will be influenced by our ability to recognize alternatives. These will be dictated by the dominant values of the present time. Another time in another age could produce solutions we are unable to imagine.

PROBLEM-SOLVING QUESTIONS

Problem-solving approaches will always be handicapped by difficulties and ambiguities, many of which have to be accepted as they cannot be removed. A number of questions have been raised by West Churchman, a distinguished American academic. He asks: How does the problem solver decide what problems and aspects of the problem should be given most attention? If a problem has many aspects, which is the most relevant to pursue? The aim of the problem solver is to find a pathway from the problem to the solution: Should any pathway be acceptable or should the easiest and quickest route be the one chosen, even if this means redefining the problem? How can a problem solver tell if information is correct or distorted? How do we know when a problem has been solved? Can complex problems ever be seen as solved or is the problem solving process a continuing one? If it is continuous, how do we know when to stop? Finally, is the problem solver ever separate from the problem or is he or she a part of it?[4] Many of these questions are unanswerable, but being aware of them will give the manager who is tackling difficult problems an understanding of the difficulty of the task and perhaps a degree of humility.

The kinds of conditions that many companies are faced with today require fast, appropriate, and imaginative problem-solving responses. The modern firm has to be very aware of the different environments that surround it. These will be social, economic, political, and market influences that may be local, national, international, or global. The modern firm has to have an excellent intelligence facility to appreciate what is happening in each area and a recognition of the amount of urgency required in making an appropriate response. It must be able to understand and address the new problems it encounters and to develop strategies that, even if they do not solve the problem, will make a contribution to maintaining the firm's equilibrium in a volatile world. This means that most companies are continually searching for effective ways of responding to pervasive, complex, and rapid change in order to maintain a degree of internal stability in a potentially threatening environment.

I believe that excellent ideas for problem solving in volatile environments can be obtained from professions such as law, medicine, science, and law enforcement, and from organizations that are not profit oriented yet have considerable experience in dealing with extremely complex problems. In this book I have selected these groups as experts to learn from. All have to be first-class problem solvers even though they use very different approaches. All have to learn continuously from their experience so that their problem-solving ability increases, and all have to constantly rethink strategies for action as the problems they tackle grow and take new forms.

PROBLEMS AND RISKS

Complex problems have a considerable similarity to risks and can easily become risks. They often have a large subjective element, for what one person considers to be a problem or a risk, another will see as an opportunity. They can be threatening and some can be so threatening that they make people afraid, causing a fear component. This fear may be realistic and related to something that is actually happening or it may be based on hypothesis and related to events that may or may not occur in the future.

Experts tell us that today we are living in a "risk society."[5] Our environment has more negative than positive aspects and that, instead of choosing between desirable futures, we are more likely to be faced with a proliferation of different risks. Some of these risks will require individual choices, for example, whether or not to smoke, and others will be group or organizational choices. If we manage a factory they may include whether to downsize, outsource, introduce new technology, or embark on other popular, but risky innovations. There may also be risks that we cannot escape and have little choice over, for example, recent increases in e-coli food poisoning or phenomena such as global warming.

The risks managers face are worsened by increasing competition. There is a likelihood of company bankruptcy if they cannot cope with the new pressures and problems that this presents. The police force has an environment of ever-increasing crime. Some of this, such as the drug market, is difficult if not impossible to control effectively and some, like financial fraud, is aided by new, sophisticated electronic communication systems such as the Internet. How can we remove or reduce risks of this kind? Given the proliferation of today's problems, how do we decide which to give the most attention to?

MANAGING COMPLEXITY

Many problems that result from crime are simple and affect only a single or a small group of individuals. These can often be reduced in number through preventive action so that undesirable social behavior, such as theft, can become difficult to undertake. These problems can also be solved through removing the criminal from society and putting him or her in prison, although this may only be a short-term solution. Other problems, such as the development of a drug culture and the criminal activity that stems from this, are tremendously complex. The problems that then have to be tackled may be international in scope, affecting the functioning of society. They may be associated with wealthy and clever entrepreneurs. They are likely to be efficiently organized and have considerable rewards for the lower-level participants. From the point of view of the victims, which can be society as a whole, this type of crime can be seen as virtually insoluble. The groups and networks that surround criminal activity will be hard to penetrate because they are shifting and impermanent, with many hidden structures and boundaries. They can be similar to the structures described by mathematicians as "chaotic." They are prone to instability and breakdown if one of the connecting linkages is broken.

These very complex systems may have far-reaching effects. At one end of the drug market the BMW stolen from someone's driveway may be sold to fund the drugs an addict must have. At the other end, the poppy crop grown by a poor village in the Andes may start the long spiral of relationships that snakes across the world and eventually leads to the car theft.

As problems that have to be solved or controlled, these systems have major obstacles. We have to work hard to find a route that can lead us to a solution. It is usually not too difficult to identify and influence the outer networks of the system. But the controlling core, which receives most of the profits, can be very well hidden, protected by a system of bribes, rewards, and threats, which make information about its whereabouts and its controllers almost impossible to obtain. For these illegal systems to work effectively and avoid breakdown they too require organization, regulation, people in facilitating and managing roles, and large, protected, and accessible markets. They also require information, feedback, and the ability to make rapid responses to unanticipated, destabilizing events.

Both legal and illegal systems can become chaotic and unstable when small changes have major consequences, when problems are amplified not reduced, a state known as positive feedback, when behavior becomes unpredictable and when controls cease to work. Many groups have an interest in regulating these systems. These include the drug barons who require a degree of stability to manage effectively, those who stand to profit financially, such as growers, chemists, and dealers, the citizens of recipient countries who want drug addiction and associated crime reduced or eliminated, and groups such as police and customs officers who have the responsibility for assisting this reduction and handling the often violent consequences of a continuation of the problem.

Drugs are one example of a complex problem in today's society but experts with an interest in "risk" tell us that many serious problems are likely to arise from events that we cannot yet foresee. These can be local disturbances due to changes in human behavior and a growing tolerance for aggression, or they can be global disasters due to changes in our environment. These destabilizing occurrences will be encountered by every class in society, although their nature and impact may vary. Burglary may be experienced more by the very rich and the very poor than by the middle classes, whereas atmospheric pollution is likely to be everyone's problem. Solving these problems requires information and knowledge, and it also requires the ability to integrate the information we already have. Tomorrow's problem solving requires not only the ability to address existing problems but the ability to anticipate new problems and to take preventive action before they occur.

WHAT DOES EFFECTIVE PROBLEM SOLVING REQUIRE?

Stafford Beer, a well-known cybernetician, can provide some guidance when we are looking for a problem-solving strategy. He tells us that the solving of complex problems that contain a great deal of variety requires an equivalent amount of variety in the problem-solving process.[6] If the police want to solve a simple, small-scale burglary carried out by a single burglar they need only one police officer, providing he or she has experience handling burglaries and knows the local community and its small-time criminals. This officer will have the requisite knowledge to handle the crime. However, if the crime is large and complex, such as cross-border smuggling, then a variety of knowledge will be required that is unlikely to be possessed by one person or group alone. Police officers will have to collaborate with the customs officials of the countries the criminals pass through, and a knowledge of border crossings, custom tariffs, and available markets will be required.

Problem solving, particularly that associated with major crime, also requires a great deal of information, and this information must come at the right time and be accurate. This raises the question of how we know that it is accurate. It will have to be obtained from many different sources. Both victims and the police will make use of newspaper reports and have discussions with experts, colleagues, witnesses, and other interested groups. There may, however, be other more hidden sources of information. Industrial espionage, or the less illegitimate practice of having an informant in a rival firm, is not unknown, while the police both treasure and carefully conceal the network of informants they rely on for inside intelligence on specific crimes. Information is usually judged to be accurate if it comes from experts, if it comes from carefully controlled systems like computerized accounts, or if it is of a kind with which none disagrees—the state of the weather or the prosecution of a war, for example—although experts are not infallible.

One of today's major problems is too much rather than too little information, and electronic aids such as computers can assist the management of this by sorting, matching, categorizing, and printing only what is considered relevant. Communication networks are also very important. Today's police must be able to communicate electronically with many other police forces if national and international crimes are to be solved.

Managers also need to be aware of what is going on in different parts of the world, both within their own organizations and in the factories of competitors. To be of value this information needs control and order, in other words, a degree of systemization. If this does not exist then it becomes fragmented, discontinuous, and of little value. For the police the beginning of a valid information system is the reporting of crime. If they do not know that a crime has taken place, or is about to take place, no action will be taken. This is also true of industry. If managers are not aware that a new risk or set of risks is approaching then they will not take steps to avoid these.

Information does not just arrive; it often has to be searched for, and this requires an understanding of where it is located and how it can be accessed. Industry, and this may also be true of the police, has a tendency to focus on information that is quantifiable. This can be an unwise strategy as the most significant information relating to risks or crime may be subjective attitudes and experiences. The brilliant detective superintendent or managing director may have this reputation because his or her hunches are often correct. These hunches may result from an ability to bring together seemingly unconnected, qualitative information and turn this into a valid hypothesis or conclusion.

Problem solving, as we have seen, is dependent on information. It requires the ability to search for, analyze, and synthesize this information and to relate it to past, current, and future events. This in turn will produce the learning and knowledge that contribute to improved problem-solving skills. Effective problem solving requires a capacity to combine information with considered action, often on the spot and under stress. This is no easy task. Yet if certain problems are not solved within a given period of time, it may not be possible to solve them at all.

Effective problem solving also requires feedback. Events must be monitored so that their impact is noted and understood. In volatile situations effective feedback will provide the information to facilitate a constant adjustment of plans and actions. This adjustment will require creative responses in order to cope with new, unanticipated situations. If this does not take place the problem-solving process may break down and end in failure. Ideally, fast, effective problem solving requires a regular, orderly world situated in an environment that changes little. Today, this comfortable situation is very hard to find.

PROBLEM-SOLVING RELATIONSHIPS

The problem solvers of today and tomorrow must be able to operate in complex and volatile environments that contain many other interested groups. They have to be good at facilitating cooperation. Strategies likely to be effective, whether problems are organizational or criminal, will require networks of partners and contacts. The wider and more diverse these networks, the richer the flow of new ideas. There are often many different groups with an interest in the same problem. With crime these will include the police, community groups, the direct victims of the crime, and others who have suffered because the crime was committed. These will all have to develop relationships with each other and these relationships will, in turn, change over time with new expectations, demands, and solutions becoming of critical interest to each of the different parties. Because of this complexity few problems will have a single, specific solution. Most of these will require a range of activities directed at achieving a number of different objectives. Many are likely to be seen as continuous, and investigation will be halted only when resources such as money are no longer available.

There will be the additional challenge that the problem environment will be changing all the time. It will be dynamic not static. This means that the problem being investigated will also change and the rate of change will be important. Rapid changes make problems more difficult to solve and control. Problem solvers must have clear objectives and a good understanding of what they are trying to achieve. This may be either prevention, reduction, containment, or solution or all of these.

Problems, like risks, as they develop and change over time, often produce a fallout of new and unanticipated problems. These require the problem solvers to be continually vigilant, entrepreneurial, and innovative, either to anticipate and prevent the occurrence of these new inputs or to solve them quickly when they appear. The need for cooperation with other groups can now be an advantage as this, in itself, can lead to innovative ideas. Problem solving always involves uncertainty. There is the possibility of solving or addressing the wrong problem, of missing important issues, factors, or variables, and of introducing new problems because of the strategies and methods that are being used.

Effective problem solving is assisted by an open, creative culture that incorporates a strong concern for the needs and interests of others, particular those in the victim category. Groups that have fluid structures in which rank and status play little part will frequently gain here, but this is not always the case. There is a counterargument that too much fluidity can be dysfunctional. Groups who work on difficult problems in uncertain environments may value the security of a structured and hierarchical group. This will be true of many police problem-solving groups.

Groups responsible for problem solving will normally go through a number of stages. The first will be problem identification. This involves becoming aware of the problem, its nature, extent, and consequences. Next comes the creation of appropriate group structures to tackle it and make a decision on the investigative strategies to be used. Developing appropriate strategies is never an easy task. It requires a search for possible solutions, either new or previously used for a similar challenge. Considerable thought and energy will be required to agree on an approach likely to achieve success, and there can be no certainty that this will be the best, or even a good, approach. Sometimes the principal factor influencing choice will be what a majority of the group will accept. At times a group will disagree, and attempts at solving the problem will be abandoned.

Routinization is another danger. Because a particular kind of problem has always been addressed in a certain way in the past, this comes to be seen as the correct way to continue to address it. But now the environment may have changed, new tools and knowledge may be available, and community and client needs may be quite different. If the problem-solving group is part of a hierarchy, then authorization of the chosen strategy may have to be given by a higher authority. This is likely to be the case in security organizations. The implementation of these strategies will be the most difficult part of the task. It will require continuous monitoring, feedback, and evaluation to check continuing progress. Monitoring is a process that problem-solving groups frequently omit.

Complex problems are often poorly understood and the choice of solution may have to be altered if the problem is framed in different ways. They may be difficult to solve because of the number of different groups that have an interest in the problem and the different values, relationships, and communication problems that arise from this. Poor communication will lead to management and coordination problems. This is true of both the problem solvers and the problem generators, for criminals often have the same control problems as the problem solvers. When communication breaks down the total activity may become so disorganized that goals and objectives can no longer be achieved and the system can no longer function properly. The solution to this is very effective communication across the boundaries between one group and another. There also needs to be a controlling or facilitating individual or group who can see the total picture. In industry this will be the project leader; in the police it will be the senior officer in the group-command structure.

Problem solving requires teamwork, but it also requires leadership of a particular kind. The inspirational leader, one who is able to make leaps in the dark and arrive at conclusions intuitively, in other words the successful entrepreneur, may not be the ideal type. In reality, most solutions come as a result of hard work and effort. The incremental leader who can provide clear guidance and good motivation over a long period of time may be more effective than the one-shot genius whose hunch is a product of good guesswork rather than careful, directed effort. One of the most important characteristics of the effective leader may be the ability to create feelings of "trust" in the groups he or she works with. This is a skill that receives little publicity. Yet being able to trust the judgment of one's leader and colleagues is essential in threatening and risky situations where there is personal danger. It may be equally important in situations where confidence and close cooperation are required. The focus on individualism in today's world has made trust an undervalued attribute in many situations, but it is still an important factor in effective problem solving.

GROUPS WITH PROBLEMS

Groups that have clear objectives, a well-thought-out strategy, an effective leader, and high morale can achieve excellent results. But not all groups function well. Those that have to collaborate over a long period of time may experience particular problems. There are now much greater opportunities for misunderstanding; some international groups may not even speak the same language as another. There may also be conflicts of interest and rivalry as one group seeks to be the primary problem solver and to be recognized as this. There is also the ever-present problem of rumor replacing accurate information. And the transfer of information may be incorrect or insufficient because of relationship difficulties in which emotion replaces fact, or hope and expectation replace reality. Changes in power relations can also cause certain groups to become more or less able to influence others. Questions such as "who do we listen to?" then have to be answered. All these lead to greater uncertainty. The problem-solving process becomes highly unpredictable.

Tight-knit groups sometimes become overintegrated and committed. Powerfully held norms that hold the group members together can result in a loss of objectivity. The group, and its own relationships, then becomes more important than the problem that is being solved. Long-held beliefs and theories can have a great influence on subsequent action. This can lead to prejudice and prejudgment.[7] Groups that work together regularly can get their job satisfaction from a sense of comradeship and from being part of a group that becomes a "family." Teamwork is all important and from this the group develops its own powerful norms on how to behave. In situations where judgments have to be made, this can lead to a partisan form of decision making. The approaches to regularly occurring problems then become part of the group's culture, irrespective of whether they are appropriate.

In industry, where teams are now very popular, it is not always recognized that their members may not be committed to the interests of management. I have worked in coal mining, on the Liverpool docks, and in the car industry. In all these situations a major source of job interest and satisfaction was the "war game" that management and workers continually waged against each other. This could displace the often boring routine of getting coal, loading cargo, and producing cars. Industrial relations may be less volatile today, but most teams settle for targets and norms that they are comfortable with. These are not always the targets that those in authority want to achieve. Helping groups to develop commitment and enthusiasm must be a continuing management responsibility. Having an open, flexible team that provides encouragement, praise, support, and friendship is the best way of doing this.

This chapter has tried to describe some of the problems that managers who are faced with complex problems in uncertain environments are likely to experience. Some may be difficult, even impossible, to handle, but an awareness that these problems do exist can help prevent the problem-solving process from taking routes that will not produce good results and may even worsen an existing situation.

This chapter stresses that many of today's and tomorrow's problems will be very complex, have far-reaching effects for society, and may be continuous and insoluble. That many problems are not very different from risks and can easily become risks if they are allowed to continue without intervention, although some can have a reverse effect and provide opportunities for new thinking and creative improvement. And that complex problems cannot be solved with simple solutions. They are likely to require complex responses and to be addressed from many different directions.

We have also seen that the process of trying to solve problems may produce new and unanticipated problems because of the nature of the intervention. Most important, effective problem solving requires good collaborative relationships in the problem-solving group, with teamwork, commitment, and excellent leadership. This cannot always be achieved. Not all groups work well together. Some may want sole ownership of the problem and resent having to cooperate with other groups. Others can be too tightly knit and create their own dysfunctional norms of behavior.

CHAPTER 2

Choosing Problem-Solving Methods

The preceding chapter described the difficulties and dilemmas of problem solving. Some of these can be avoided or minimized by choosing suitable analysis and design methods to assist understanding and action. A method is a set of principles and procedures to guide the problem-solving process. It also incorporates values that can be identified by examining what it includes and what it leaves out. Some methods are described as having an engineering orientation because they focus on the structure and relationships of machines. Other are called sociotechnical because they give equal weight both to technical structures and to people.

Problems can be solved in many different ways. Experienced investigators may prefer to decide on an approach after they have become familiar with the problem and will derive this from their own knowledge and experience. Others will have a well-tried method, often developed by experts and publicized through training courses and books, that they always adopt. A third group will mix and match ideas and procedures from a number of methods until they develop an approach that seems to fit their immediate problem. By method we mean a logical, sometimes sequential, way of analyzing and solving a particular kind of problem. Methods are ways of structuring thinking and action. They tell the problem solver what steps to take, how to take these steps, and, most important, why these steps should be taken.[1]

Although formal methods may be regarded as unnecessary, even constraining, by the experienced investigator, they do have a number of advantages especially for the person who is new to problem solving or who has had few problems to investigate. First, they can act as an aide-memoire, providing a reminder of the different tasks that have to be completed as the investigation proceeds through the stages from problem identification to problem solution. Second, they can indicate what is important. For example, it is unlikely that a good solution will be achieved unless an accurate diagnosis has been made. Third, if a group has responsibility for handling the problem, then a method can provide a clear, agreed upon approach that all will follow.

The difficulty here is how to design or choose an appropriate method, one that is likely to provide a quick, accurate diagnosis and a feasible, easy-to-apply solution. There is always a danger that a method can act as a straitjacket, focusing attention on certain things while not addressing others that are equally important, but not covered by the selected approach. The complexity of many modern problems makes method selection particularly challenging and uncertain. For example, tackling today's computer-assisted fraud will require a knowledge of how fraud can be carried out electronically as well as a knowledge of how data are captured and held in computer files. In addition, the investigator will need to take account of more traditional factors such as motivation, relationships, security systems and available markets, and if the product of the fraud can be sold to others. The problem-solving process will now more resemble a complicated jigsaw puzzle than a neat sequential set of inquiries.

There are many different tools for solving problems, some mathematical others logical. The choice of which to use depends on the problem solver's knowledge and interests, on how the problem is being defined, and on its simplicity or complexity. Tools often form part of methods but can be used on their own. Examples include decision trees, which are attempts to identify how decisions might be made and their consequences. A criminal decision tree would work out the various options available to a burglar when trying to sell his stolen goods. These structures are useful because they provide a visual network showing how early decisions lead to subsequent decisions, but they are time consuming to make and may not assist the identification of significant variables.

Attempts can also be made to measure the value of information. Mike Wilmer, an expert in operational research, has a method for doing this that takes account of the degree of uncertainty (entropy) in available pieces of information.[2] This is a statistical exercise and Wilmer suggests that it can provide a more accurate estimate of police detective performance than the more usual "clear up rate." If a very difficult problem with a high degree of uncertainty is tackled efficiently, but not solved, this should rate as highly as a simple problem that is solved. A variety of other statistical techniques are also available. These include probability theory and Baysian decision theory. Probability theory was first developed by the Greeks to assist their skill at gambling. Thomas Bayes, a minister born in 1701, developed it further by asking the question How do we know when an event will occur when we know nothing about it except that it has occurred a number of times and failed to occur a number of times? He suggested that as new information was obtained, so the degree of probability could be revised.[3]

Many early methods for problem solving were derived from work study. They are simple, linear, and focus on the tasks that have to be carried out if information is to be rationally collected and used to create a decision tree. The Kepner–Tregoe approach is an example here. This was first developed in the 1960s but is still in use today.[4] This kind of approach can be valuable if a simple, closed problem is being addressed and the objective is smoothing and expediting the route of a set of tasks leading to the solution of the problem. Unfortunately, few of today's problems are like this. Stafford Beer tells us that handling complexity is one of the major problems of our age. He also argues that good decision making is not a linear process but relies heavily on a great deal of feedback. And he suggests that, given this uncertain environment, the best decision processes will be similar to conversations. There will be many contributors to these and each will challenge the others.[5]

A great deal of group problem solving will go through the following stages, although this will not usually be a linear process but one that operates in loops, each loop affected by feedback from one or more of the others. These stages will be:

- Agreement that there is a problem that needs to be solved (with the police this will be agreement that a crime has been committed).
- Agreement on the nature of the problem.
- Discussion of strategies for solution.
- Discussion of consequences of each strategy.
- Choice of first and second approaches.
- Plans for action.
- Implementation of agreed action.
- Evaluation and feedback.

The choice of strategy will be influenced by a number of factors. These include the strengths and weaknesses of the problem-solving group—its numbers, knowledge, and so forth; opportunities and difficulties in the problem-solving environment; and desired results—the elimination or containment of the problem. Lastly, action plans will be made and assigned to each subgroup or individual. There will be estimates of time and costs, and procedures for monitoring and evaluating the performance will be put in place.

Although this approach has a considerable degree of fluidity, it will not be totally open-ended. Some rules of procedure will help systematize performance and documentation and give guidance on how things should be carried out.

An approach I have often used is described here as an example of a method. It is a modification of an approach developed by sociotechnical consultants and researchers at the London Tavistock Institute of Human Relations. Here is a brief description and critique. Although set out as a series of steps, some may be carried out simultaneously and the order may vary according to the requirements of the problem situation.[6]

STEP 1. Decide what kind of problem you are concerned with. Is it reported or discovered, simple or complex, major or minor?

Is it one that has been reported to the police or management and requires their attention in someone else's interest? Or is it one that is on their list of antisocial activities and must be sought out and prevented from happening? Theft of company goods would come into the first category, illicit drugs into the second.

Finding out the nature of the presenting problem can prove very difficult. Its true nature may only emerge some time after the investigation gets under way. A problem-solving group must be constantly checking that they are tackling the right problem.

STEP 2. What resources will be required to solve it?

If it is a simple problem, few resources will be required. If it is complex, following Ashby's law of requisite variety, the knowledge of the problem solvers must be as comprehensive as the complexity of the problem. Does the problem solution require any specialist knowledge? If yes, where can this be obtained?

A common feature of most problem-solving processes today is a shortage of resources. Available resources will have to be deployed in the most effective way.

STEP 3. Make a broad description of the problem.

The problem solvers must obtain a good understanding of the problem by making a detailed description of its nature, the environment in which it has occurred, and the individuals or groups who have caused it or been on the receiving end. What are its most serious aspects, what form have these taken and how have they shown up? Where should the emphasis of the investigation be placed? How much time is available to arrive at a solution? Who are the most probable perpetrators? What are the motives behind the behavior that led to the problem or crime and to what extent did the problem generators achieve their objectives?

But a major feature of many of today's problems is that little is known about them and accurate information depends on research that has not yet been carried out. This has been true of the transfer of mad cow disease to humans and to the spread of e-coli.

STEP 4. Identify the stages from problem identification to final outcome that require investigation.

The problem solvers should identify the main stages or route of the problem's progression. What was the cause of the problem? What form did it take? How did it show up? What activities occurred from the time it showed up to the time that the police or management was informed? What will be its consequences if unchecked? If the problem is a theft of goods that can be sold, what will be the route taken to the final customer and who will be involved? For example, the transfer of stolen goods can move from the burglar to one or more middlemen and then on through a purchasing network until they reach the final customer.

Again this is excellent advice that may be impossible to follow because of missing information or the fact that the problem is too complex for simple descriptions.

STEP 5. What information is required but missing?

The problem solver should now look in some detail at the knowledge difficulties of solving the problem. Where are there gaps in information, or information of doubtful validity? A detailed analysis of missing information would include:

- What information is missing.
- Where it can be obtained.
- What information is most important.
- Who is likely to have this.
- Where it can be accessed.
- How accurate is it likely to be.

It may take a very long time to collect the most important and relevant information. Some may be impossible to find.

STEP 6. Make an analysis of likely direct and indirect personal relationships.

Relationships should be examined and documented next. This process would cover the relationships of those directly involved in creating the problem or perpetrating the criminal activity and the relationships of those indirectly involved. The latter might include associates providing information that assisted in the crime or helped the transport or sale of the stolen or prohibited goods. With very complex problems such as drug smuggling there are likely to be complicated networks of relationships. The identification of these will require the cooperation of other groups such as customs officials, airlines, or border officials. If the problem has been caused by a single individual, working alone, what are his or her likely characteristics?

This is very important as many problem-solving techniques concentrate on the system but take little account of the human actors. Again difficulties may be encountered because the major actors have taken great care to conceal themselves.

It can be valuable to hypothesize the nature and kinds of relationships required between collaborators for the optimal prosecution of the crime. Where are the weak links? What is the payoff for each individual or group? What risks does each individual or group take?

This is important but difficult to carry out.

STEP 7. How does each member of the problem-solving group see his or her role?

Are the different parts of the problem-solving task being logically allocated so that knowledge and experience are being effectively used?

This is also important but it must be recognized that roles may not stay the same.

STEP 8. What additional resources are required?

What extra resources will the problem-solving group require in order to carry out their problem-solving task? Will these be available? How can they most easily be acquired?

Again a useful step, although the resources may not be available.

STEP 9. What is the nature of the problem-solving environment?

What priority should be given to the solution of this particular problem? What is the likelihood of it being solved? Who has an interest in its solution?

This is a very useful exercise.

STEP 10. What will be an effective strategy?

The problem solver or problem-solving group should now examine and evaluate all this information and, after discussions, should arrive at a strategy for action. Proposals for action must contribute both to the solution of the problem and to the prevention of its recurrence. The latter requires actions directed at problem or crime prevention.

This sociotechnical approach is useful in that it identifies important variables that are likely to be relevant to most problem-solving situations. It does, however, have a number of limitations. First, it is not a dynamic model. It does not provide a guide on the relationships between variables. How, for example, does the situation in which the problem is occurring affect the behavior of the different participants, and if this situation changes, as it certainly will, how does this affect subsequent behavior? Complex problems are rarely static. They are dynamic, constantly changing because different factors operating in the problem situation are also changing. It is this dynamism that influences the degree of complexity that has to be understood and responded to. Ideally, effective strategies will be based on sound theories concerning the steps listed above. The wrong theory will inevitably lead to the wrong strategy.

CREATIVE THINKING

Problem solving also requires creativity. Tudor Rickards of the Manchester Business School has a well-developed method for increasing this through training. This method aims to:

- raise awareness of the nature of creativity.
- show how creative performance can be enhanced.
- provide basic skills in creative problem solving.

Rickards sees creativity as a process that produces new and valuable responses to organizational and environmental challenges. These, in turn, enable problems to be managed and solved more effectively. It also facilitates learning, change, and innovation.[7]

The Rickards method takes learning groups through the following processes:

1. *Preparation.* The team first discusses what it already knows about the problem. This can be visually mapped through charts and diagrams.
2. *Searching.* The team now searches for new perspectives and reframes the complex set of issues identified in the preparation stage. It next produces a comprehensive list of goals and perspectives. This can take the form of a set of action statements, each indicating a specific action, labeled as a how-to-statement (for example, how to prevent theft from occurring in the future). The team should contain an experienced problem-owner with responsibility for action. He or she will be looking for new perspectives on the problem that will bring about creative breakthroughs.
3. *New ideas.* The team now focuses on new ideas for each of the goals that have been listed. It searches for these, explores their value, and lists and ranks the relevant ideas for each of the goals. A short list will be made of the most promising ideas.
4. *The action plan.* Finally, an action plan is agreed on. A useful technique for doing this to visualize the idea being implemented. This assists the team in becoming imaginatively involved in the problem-solving processes.

The application of this creativity learning approach will, of course, depend on the opportunities and constraints in the problem-solving situation. Creativity may be restricted through bureaucratic procedures, restricted goals, or rigid ideas in cooperating groups. It is interesting to note that both the police and industry have been patrons of creativity learning.

FAST RESPONSE METHODS

Sometimes problems arise as crises that have to be tackled immediately. There may be no time to proceed through the sequence of problem-solving steps and stages; immediate action will need to be taken. The techniques of "pattern recognition" used by physicians and surgeons may then be the best way forward. When a patient first arrives in the consulting room the doctor asks questions but also looks for presenting physical signs and symptoms. These are then compared mentally with similar cases the doctor has previously encountered. This approach can often provide a quick route to a diagnosis. The same technique can be used with nonmedical problems in situations where immediate action is required. The problem solver will ask the question Have I experienced a similar problem before or do I know of anyone who has? If the answer is yes, he or she will proceed by taking the actions that produced a solution in that situation. This approach is now being used by emergency teams such as the fire department. To be successful it requires problem solvers with considerable experience of crisis situations.[8]

CAN METHODS BE EVALUATED?

It is not easy to select an appropriate method, as the nature of the problem may not become clear until the problem-solving process is under way. Nevertheless, it is useful to make some attempt to compare different methods on the basis of how useful they are likely to be. Judging available methods on the following, or similar, criteria may be of some help.

- How appropriate is the method for the problem that is being addressed?
- Have others used it with success for similar problems?
- Can it cope with the complexity of the problem?
- Does the problem-solving individual or group have the knowledge and resources that this approach requires?
- Will its use require cooperation from others?
- Will its use extend the length of time required for investigation?

- How will the method need to be modified in order to get the best results?
- Is it likely to solve the problem completely or only partially?
- What are likely to be the consequences of using this approach?

The investigator is here trying to get a match between the problem that has to be solved and the method that is used to solve it. Many other questions will be relevant depending on what methods are viable and available and the nature of the problem.

DEVELOPING THEORIES

As diagnosis proceeds the problem-solving group is likely to develop one or more theories on how and why the problem or crime has occurred and how it can be removed, reduced, or prevented. They will have ideas that can be described as theories, models, or hypotheses. Before concluding this chapter let us briefly consider the difficult question of how we think about problems. Most problem solvers use theories because they are ideas that provide explanations. For example, these boys are stealing cars because ... A football riot is likely when Nottingham plays Milan on Saturday because ... Theories usually start with hypotheses—possibilities that need testing before they become a theory.

Theories, if they are to have any validity, have to be built from experience and knowledge. Building a theory is like traveling on a journey, often a long one where the route is not known. Having a theory is arriving at ones destination. The philosopher Gilbert Ryle has described Sherlock Holmes as an excellent theorist.[9] Holmes uses his theories to apprehend and convict criminals, to thwart planned crimes, and to prove the innocence of wrongfully accused suspects. These theories are also used to teach his friend, Watson, effective problem-solving techniques.

Another example of the value of theories is that they can be passed on to others. A good theory will assist the recipient to act or react in new and improved ways. Building valid and helpful theories cannot be done overnight. They require experience, thought, and judgment. Theories will not come from reading a detective's or manager's reports. But they may come from talking to the detective or manager at length, and through watching what he or she does and benefiting from his or her years of experience. This is why mature nurses may be much better at solving problems than junior doctors. Or why an experienced police officer on the beat who is close to retirement can handle a volatile situation better than many of his or her superiors.

Complex problems will require a number of theories, all of which will have to be used. The psychologist Edward de Bono calls this lateral thinking. But Gilbert Ryle suggests that when presented with a specific problem or situation, most of us have one dominant theory; he calls the ideas and propositions that lead to this subtheories. Unfortunately, a great deal of problem solving in the complex situations of today is more like groping in the dark than using a clear theory as an explanation. Too often we have an overload of information in some areas and missing information in others. Theory generation and problem solving then become risky activities because incorrect explanations and conclusions may be drawn.

Once we have a theory that seems to provide a plausible explanation for the problem we are concerned with we tend to pass it on to our colleagues and to other interested groups. This is how ideas spread and become current wisdom. Richard Dawkins argues that ideas behave like genes. They are capable of replicating themselves in order to maintain their own survival. He argues that theories and ideas propagate themselves by leaping from brain to brain via a process of copying or imitation.[10] If police officers or managers learn of a good theory, they will pass it on to their colleagues. The survival of the idea is then related to its psychological appeal and its perceived usefulness. These will depend on the goals and interests of the reception group.

Once a theory is accepted a course of action can be decided. The danger now is that if the theory is wrong, the course of action may be of little value. A recent theory that attracted international attention was business-process reengineering with its claim that business success came from radical reorganization. Only after large numbers of companies had tried this "clean sheet" approach and found it did not work was the theory abandoned. There are many theories at present about the beneficial effects for society of imprisoning offenders and of retaining the illegality of drugs to reduce their use. These are influencing strategies of government but they too may turn out to be wrong.

The lesson here is that theories are useful provided they are developed with care as a result of experience and evidence. Difficult problems, where information is limited, will require a number of theories that need to be carefully tested before one is selected and a decision on action is taken. With groups that have a problem-solving responsibility there is always a danger that a theory will be arrived at too quickly, on the basis of too little knowledge or even on the basis of prejudgment or prejudice. When developing theories and deciding on courses of action it is important to predict their consequences or to try them and discover what their consequences are. Did the government officials who permitted pyramid selling in Albania in 1997 appreciate that they were starting an internal revolution? Should we decriminalize drugs as the head of Interpol has suggested? We do not know what the consequences will be but we could test them by legalizing cannabis and seeing what happens.

Changing situations will require new explanatory theories and new strategies for action. If the problem is how to combat drug dealers, then both the police and the criminals will be trying to anticipate each other's behavior and take appropriate responsive action. Similarly, if management takes successful precautions to reduce large-scale theft or computer-related fraud, then those with an interest in breaking into the system for gain will respond with new approaches and new methods.

LEARNING FROM EXPERIENCE

All problem-solving provides knowledge, and this knowledge is often gained as a result of difficult and challenging experiences. I have acted as a facilitator to many problem-solving groups in industry and have found that most move through stages similar to the following on their journey toward a solution.

- *Awareness* of the difficulty of the problem-solving task they are about to undertake. This, in turn, leads to
- *Uncertainty* on how to proceed and on the likelihood of success. Then
- *Knowledge acquisition* leads to a clearer definition of the problem and a reduction of insecurity. This is replaced by
- *Information overload* as increasing amounts of information are collected. Together with
- *Frustration* as important parts of the jigsaw puzzle prove hard to obtain. Then
- *Depression or elation* as the problem proves hard to solve or insolvable or progress is made. Finally,
- *Review of experience*. We did this very well, we did it adequately, or it proved too difficult.

The prevalence of this behavior pattern highlights the importance of a project leader who is understanding, sympathetic, and able to raise and maintain morale when difficulties are being encountered.

A critical but frequently omitted stage of problem solution is an after-the-event discussion of the analysis, procedures, and theories that have been used and the success of these. This will lead to new learning and improved problem solving in the future. All who participated in the problem-solving activities should participate in the subsequent evaluation. Criticism should be welcomed and regarded as helpful and acceptable. If the problem can later be written up as a case study, this will provide learning materials for new problem-solving groups in the future.

SKILLS AND COMPETENCIES

A problem solver can make a choice of whether or not to use a structured method for the solution of a particular problem. But he or she is certain to need some skills and competencies, and the nature of these will vary with the nature of the problem. Some of the most important were listed in the preface. These were:

- *Knowledge competence.* The ability of an individual to learn from the experience of problem solving and to use this knowledge effectively.
- *Psychological competence.* An ability to work with others, to maintain personal morale, to persevere with difficult problems.
- *Organizational competence.* An ability to think strategically and plan effectively.
- *Innovative competence.* An ability to think creatively, to approach problems from different angles.

Another attribute the good problem solver often requires is an ability to withstand stress. This is more of a strength than a skill, but it may be particularly important in complex, time-consuming investigations where there is pressure for quick results.

Geoffrey Vickers also described some of the skills that would seem to be essential for an effective problem solver. First, *expressive* skills, in particular the ability to use language to question, persuade, and elicit the reasons for attitudes and behavior. These will be very important to the lawyer, detective, or manager. Second, *deductive* skills, an ability to reason logically without the distortions of bias or prejudice. Third, *appreciative* skills, which Vickers describes as an ability to make clear judgments in a variety of contexts and situations. It is these that contribute most to the formulation of hypotheses and mental models. One of the challenges for the problem solver is to identify and eliminate wrong ideas at an early stage in the problem-solving process. This is particularly important when criminal activities are being investigated as they can so easily lead to miscarriages of justice. And lastly, there are *creative* skills that are not easy to define but that assist the development of new ideas and new ways of thinking.[11]

Poor problem solving occurs when constraints are introduced into the problem-solving process. These may include "one man rule"—with a dominant and autocratic senior figure restricting discussion; a lack of necessary skills through inexperience or poor training; and a focus on certain measures—with the police this is often the number of arrests or crimes solved. Further constraints are competition with other groups who are also contributing to the solution of the problem (this can cause a reluctance to pass on relevant information); poor motivation to solve the problem; and, perhaps most important of all, the degree of complexity of the problem situation. Psychologists tell us that we tend to act conservatively. When new evidence is presented we do not change our views as much as the evidence warrants. We are also greatly influenced by who presents the new data and how the data are presented.

Donald Schon points out that it is through solving our problems that we achieve social progress. But a difficulty today is that things are changing so rapidly. This applies to the kinds of problems that have to be solved, the body of knowledge that assists this, and the expectations of society on what the results should be. Schon calls today's problems "messes" because they are not single activities that require correction but dynamic situations that consist of complex systems of changing problems. Problems are interconnected and environments are turbulent.[12]

Problem solving is not always straightforward and problem solvers can get embroiled in conflicts of values, purposes, and interests. A police example of this was the Yorkshire miner's strike of 1985 in which the police had to take aggressive action against a community of local men, some of whom were friends and relatives. Problem solvers always have to use judgment and intuition. Schon calls this "reflection-in-action." And their success is constantly evaluated. Schon suggests that their credibility behaves like a stock on the stock market. It goes up or down with the perception of its success.[13]

Edward de Bono has criticized much of today's problem solving for dealing with what he calls closed systems. He claims that a line is drawn round what is considered relevant to the problem and the chosen areas are then regarded as discrete parts.[14] He argues that with complex systems, once they are reduced to parts, the whole may be lost. He also claims that a great deal of problem solving concentrates too heavily on analysis, on identifying the causes of the problem. This means that not enough attention is paid to what he calls "design." Design is similar to what Chris Argyris has called "double loop learning." It is not sufficient to solve a problem, the causes of the problem must also be identified and rectified. Argyris focuses on the values that underlie much of conventional problem solving, describing many of these as defensive reactions that inhibit success.[15]

De Bono criticizes scientists for believing that the analysis of data will produce ideas. He claims that this usually produces only a limited set of hypotheses. What is required is more creativity, more imagination, and a wide variety of hypotheses, that, in turn, lead to experimental design. He argues that what is regarded as proof is often no more than a lack of imagination and an inability to provide alternative explanations. He makes the challenging criticism that science measures only what is can measure and ignores what it cannot.[16]

This chapter has stressed the importance of researching and critically examining available tools and methods when starting to solve a problem. These can be useful aids to systematic thinking and action, but only if they are appropriate for the problem that is being tackled. The fact that problem solving is a difficult and imprecise process has been emphasized. It may be impossible to do it in an efficient manner, and we may not even know what an efficient manner requires. Nevertheless, many people, especially managers, have to be problem solvers.

CHAPTER 3

Problem Solving by Specialist Groups

Scientists, Lawyers, and Doctors

We have now considered the problems of problem solving and examined some of the problem-solving methods currently available. These may assist problem solvers who value systematic approaches. The next step is to see if we can learn anything from groups who spend a great deal of time solving problems. Three of these are scientists, lawyers, and doctors.

THEORIES OF PROBLEM SOLVING

In the past there have been two principal approaches to problem solving. One is traditional logic, the method most used by scientists and lawyers, in which there is a search for truth and facts are either true or false. The second is what is known as a theory of association. Associationism was a school of philosophy that flourished during the eighteenth and nineteenth centuries and was greatly influenced by the ideas of John Locke. This sees thinking and problem solving as the creation of a chain of ideas in which the relationships between ideas are derived from experience. The approach looks for connections, "trains of feelings," or "streams of consciousness." Learning is a product of confirmation of success, so we know that if A occurs, it is probable that B will always follow. For example, if a pickpocket steals a wallet he or she will then run away to escape being caught.

Both of these approaches have their critics. Traditional logic is viewed as rigorous but unproductive. It can identify what is true but is unlikely to lead to any creative thinking on why particular patterns of behavior have occurred. Association theory, because it is based on relationships derived from past experience, may also be short on creativity. It does not explain the reason for the relationships. These deficiencies have led philosophers to seek theories that are more comprehensive and that take a holistic approach for situations. These should take account of structures—how and why things fit together; of gaps, problems, and disturbances—what the cyberneticians call oscillations. They should also be able to separate peripheral aspects of the problem from core features. And, most important, they should recognize that problems are dynamic—changing over time, rather than static.

Gestalt theory is such a theory. It was developed by Max Wertheimer and others in the 1940s. The group was greatly influenced by the work of the American philosopher John Dewey, who, in turn, had been influenced by Darwinism. The Gestalt school focuses on structures (gestalten) and emphasizes the importance of looking at problems as "wholes." These should not be broken down into elements or the possibility of intelligent inquiry will be lost.[1]

The Gestalt approach assumes that change is a naturally occurring phenomena that we cannot control.[2] Gestalt theory also assumes that change is unpredictable and difficult to plan for, but that human beings and organizations have an ability to adjust to their environments. This attribute is known as self-regulation. These environments can be internal (for example, the family or the workplace), or external (such as the social and physical pressures that affect families and work). The main purpose of a Gestalt approach to problem solving is to increase awareness of the complexity of the change situation and of the processes and interactions it contains. In Gestalt the whole is always greater than the parts, and any part refers to the whole.[3]

More recently David Deutsch has made a major contribution to scientific problem solving by criticizing inductive approaches, which are similar to association theory in that theories are derived from repeated observations.[4] Inferences are then made from the particular to the general. He argues that this approach leads to predictions that are often incorrect. He gives, as an example, the case of the chicken whose owner feeds him corn every morning. This leads the chicken to believe that the farmer is a continuing provider of food. Unfortunately, one morning the farmer arrives and wrings the chicken's neck. Deutsch maintains that observations should only lead to predictions if they can be explained—that the farmer will always feed the chicken because it is a good friend, for example. This is similar to Argyris's concept of double-loop learning in which the first loop is solving the problem and the second, solving the causes of the problem.[5]

Deutsch accepts that inductive problem solving can lead to the growth of knowledge, but he points out that it can also lead to false conclusions. He believes that good problem solving requires good explanations, together with the justifications for these. He supports Karl Popper in believing that all science is a problem-solving process with acceptable theories, or explanations, being replaced by better ones as knowledge increases. Popper maintained that it was impossible to verify or confirm scientific theories with any degree of probability.[6] What was possible was to disprove them. The test of good science was its ability to make testable predictions, which were then given up when they failed the validity test.

Deutsch's view is that problems are best solved by finding new or improved theories that contain explanations that are better than existing ones, and that problem solving should pass through the following stages:

- *Identification*. The problem is identified.
- *Conjecture*. Attempts are made to solve it by modifying or reinterpreting old theories, or proposing new ones.
- *Criticism*. These are then criticized by examining and comparing them to see which offers the best explanation of the problem. Any that offer worse explanations are abandoned.
- *Replacement of erroneous theories*. The old theory is then replaced by the new one.
- *New problem*. This new theory then becomes the next problem to be addressed in the interests of continuous improvement.

Problem solving is also influenced by convergent and divergent thinking.[7] Convergent thinking is when philosophers or scientists try to find one right answer. Divergent thinking is when members of a group seek out different answers. This encourages creativity and can lead to the discovery of a new theory.

Most of today's problems, like the ones to be addressed in this book, are of considerable complexity. Subproblems will have to be taken account of while the problem solver will be bombarded with large heterogeneous sets of competing ideas. When we succeed in solving a problem we end up with a set of theories that, although not problem-free, are better than the theories we started with. Theories that provide more detailed explanations of the reasons for problems are always preferred because they leave less unexplained. Our knowledge grows through solving problems and finding better explanations.

This book examines how today's society approaches the two complex problems of illegal drugs and computer-related fraud. One of its frameworks of analysis is an assessment of the individual competencies and the organizational capabilities required of and by specialist problem solvers. Problems are likely to be tackled in very different ways and by groups with different kinds of expertise. These differences will encompass the "what" of problem solving—what information is needed to address the problem, and the "how" of problem solving—what strategies are used to collect and use this information. These are the competencies or skills that those practicing in these professions must acquire.

HOW DO OTHER GROUPS SOLVE PROBLEMS?

We can always learn from other groups and so, before examining the problem-solving approaches currently used to address illegal drugs and cyber crime, we will briefly examine the methods of three other specialist groups—scientists, lawyers, and doctors. All of these require excellent problem-solving skills if they are to meet the needs of their colleagues, clients, and patients.

Scientists

Problem solving by scientists has always been based on scientific method. This is guided by the objective of establishing truth and has its origins in what Francis Bacon called a process of induction. Hypotheses are proposed that are then judged against experience. If these withstand the test of time, then knowledge advances. Also, as all scientific claims can be proven wrong, there is always the need to replace an early hypothesis with a more powerful one, and this too increases understanding. Scientific method is very different from the day-to-day problem solving of the ordinary person. First, it is more than the solution of a practical problem; it strives to find better instruments to help in the solution or to find better solutions.[8] Second, the scientific method involves controlled experimentation. This requires a precise definition of the problem, its measurement, and the control of its variables. Third, a scientific solution looks for an advancement of knowledge.

Scientists look for uniformities and underlying principles; they are not focused on one problem but on a route to expanding a science. Their hope is that experiments will produce logical results that assist the development of accurate forecasts about the future. Scientific method is, or should be, supported by scientific values, most notably the search for truth and knowledge. Scientists also claim that they are creative as well as logical. They choose problems to study because little is known about them. Creativity is required to suggest answers that can form hypotheses. Yet scientists must also value complete objectivity. They must willingly accept that the brilliant idea behind a hypothesis can be, and sometimes is, totally wrong.[9]

Competencies

The competency scientists require is the urge to increase knowledge, and to do this using methods that are precise and accurate and can establish if a hypothesis is true or false. They must also have dedication and perseverance and the willingness to accept difficulties and disillusionment as experiments fail to produce results. And they must have the ability to communicate proven results to colleagues and, in today's climate, to the world in general. The scientist is always on the side of the future and the viability of the future depends on scientific work.

But it can also be argued that many problems are not solved through logic but through random thinking. W. B. Pillsbury, a philosopher who uses a "naturalist" theory of reasoning, describes how thinking often starts. He says "the animal solves a problem through a number of chance trials ... a scientific problem is solved in much the same way by a number of chance thoughts. One can never predict when a fruitful suggestion is to be made."[10] This fits with Stafford Beer's suggestion that complex problem solving requires something similar to conversation.[11] Many ideas are put forward to throw light on the problem. The step-by-step process of classical logic is systematic and neat, but if a problem is complex it may not be helpful in producing understanding.

Organizational Capabilities

If scientists are to use their competencies to the full, the organization they work for must have certain support capabilities. It must be able to provide time, space, and encouragement together with necessary resources and intellectual freedom. If it is a commercial company it must also be able to turn scientific discoveries into profitable investments. Sir Alan Wilson, past chairman of Glaxo, has described the philosophy of his company. In his view an industry without innovation will inevitably decline. He sees innovation in its broadest sense as providing an opportunity to reduce costs, to produce improved products, and to launch entirely new ones. Research projects grow and then die, either because they have been unsuccessful or because they have achieved their objective and resulted in a product being made and sold. They, therefore, go through a number of stages, and research departments must be organized and managed so as to provide the optimal situation for each development stage. Industry requires a continual flow of bright ideas, and, to be successful, these must be challenging and attractive to the researcher and have potentially valuable commercial results. Wilson argues that good organization is not a substitute for inventiveness and requires the recruitment of the right kind of staff and their deployment over the whole of their working life.[12]

Not all scientists solve problems the same way. Some follow scientific method exactly, stating the problem they are studying clearly and using the orthodox scientific methods to study it. This group usually has a strong need for achievement and is not put off by research disappointment. Another group will have the same clarity of problem definition but be prepared to use original or unorthodox methods to study it. This group is likely to be swift and flexible thinkers and to have good problem-solving abilities. A third group will be prepared to study unclear and poorly formulated problems and to use unorthodox methods, which may include a number of sciences and technologies. This group is very creative and may resemble the classic hero—the inventor.[13]

Coordination and Collaboration

We have argued that the third essential component in complex problem solving is coordination. Today's difficult problems are unlikely to be solved by a single scientist working in a university laboratory or industrial company. Collaboration will be required with different expert groups and with producers, consumers, and policy makers in the outside world. A recent example of this is the e-coli food poisoning outbreak in Scotland.

Hugh Pennington, the scientist who led the inquiry, has described the different groups he had to work with. On November 22, 1996, three cases of e-coli were reported to the Lanarkshire Department of Health. By that evening the number had risen to fifteen. The outbreak grew rapidly and became one of the world's worst, with 20 deaths, 500 cases, and 151 patients admitted to the hospital. Pennington recognized that this was a problem of high complexity. There would be a need to bring together subjects as varied as science, medicine, sociology, politics, philosophy, and the law. In order to address the problem the Scottish office had to establish an expert group in food safety, public health, and microbiology.

This group had a number of very difficult questions to answer. For example, did e-coli originate in the United States where the first case of the disease was documented in 1982? Why was e-coli so common in Scotland but not in Ireland, and in Canada but not in Scandinavia? Why did e-coli not cause disease in its natural home, the intestines of cattle and sheep? Given its limited resources and the complexity of the problem the group now had to decide what to focus its attention on. It chose, as a matter of urgency, the food safety system. It was clear that, despite a century and a half of sanitary reform the existing system was not providing sufficient protection. This meant that it had to consider government policy in this area. Had existing policy been developed on the basis of inadequate scientific information? Had the possibility of poisoning risk been greatly underestimated? The answers to these questions were unclear.

The research team agreed that any policy making in a medical or related area would be characterized by incompleteness and error. A strategy for handling this was to incorporate substantial degrees of overdesign and redundancy into any plans for solving the problem. The research team knew that overdesign and redundancy were often used by engineers when faced with uncertainty. They decided that a group dealing with a difficult medical problem with considerable dangers for the community could use the same approach. This would be greatly preferable to postponing a solution until more information could be obtained.

But there were other difficult considerations that had to be taken account of. There had to be a trade-off between food safety costs and commercial considerations. There was still not enough scientific evidence to make safety have complete priority. The cause of the disease was still not well understood and many hypotheses could not be confirmed. The team now leaned toward a method of proof used in Victorian times in which even if there was not "confirmation" in the strict scientific sense, there could be strong support for the probability of a hypothesis. This was achieved by generating evidence to support a hypothesis through the use of two very different methods. With food poisoning the first could be the demonstration that patients had eaten the same food, the second, that they had also been infected by an identical microbe.[14]

An interesting feature of coordination when complex problems such as food poisoning occur is that this has to be carried out with enemies as well as friends, with opposers as well as collaborators. Farmers and abattoir owners had to be consulted and influenced even though their interests and attitudes were not the same as those of the scientists trying to prevent a similar food poisoning problem from occurring in the future.

Lawyers

The description of how lawyers solve problems is a product of knowledge derived from my personal relationships with lawyers and from two excellent books—*Problem Solving for Lawyers* by Margot Costanzo and *Legal Skills* by Simon Lee and Marie Fox.[15] Lawyers, like scientists, are interested in separating what is true and what is false, but they rely a great deal on precedent for guidance. Case law provides them with a set of legal judgments that have been applied to earlier, but similar, situations. These will indicate the kind of evidence that has been accepted or rejected in the past.

Competencies and Skills

Problem solving is an important legal skill. It is essentially a preliminary search for the truth to provide an expert viewpoint on a contentious issue or make a case for or against a petitioner or defendant in a court of justice. Legal problem solving is different from other kinds because it involves the law. The end product is likely to be a legal judgment that will have important consequences for the lawyer's clients. These may be governments, institutions, interest groups, members of the law-abiding public or members of the criminal classes. Because of the complexity of many of today's problems, lawyers may require expert help from nonlegal advisers. These may include accountants, doctors, engineers, or other specialists. In Britain a further complication arises due to the split in the legal process between solicitors and barristers. This can mean that part of the problem-solving process is undertaken by one group and part by another.

Simon Lee and Marie Fox provide a list of what they consider to be required legal skills. These include:

- To make, apply, and criticize precise distinctions.
- To separate rapidly the relevant from the irrelevant.
- To think logically and critically.
- To research and plan.
- To communicate.
- To work independently with initiative and self-confidence.
- To work cooperatively, to lead, and to support.

Effective problem solving requires productive thinking. Relevant facts must be identified and marshaled, theories must be developed and tested, conclusions must be drawn and action taken. Legal thought follows traditional logic in that it is a search for the truth. It seeks exactness, validity, and consistency. It values exact formulations and judgments, rigor of thought and proof. It demands the gathering of facts, the studying of the connections between these, and the drawing of conclusions from them. Unfortunately many modern problems are of a kind that make this clarity of thinking very difficult. There are usually gaps in knowledge, attempts to misinform, and different interpretations of events. These are constraints that a lawyer has to take into account. Costanzo points out that the lawyer has to achieve an outcome that is professionally responsible and satisfies the client in terms of suitability, time, and cost.[16]

Lawyers, while seeking truth, have to constantly deal with the question What is truth? Costanzo quotes David Kahneman et al.'s experiments on common causes of distortion. These suggest: (1) that vividness of recall affects judgment. Events that are vividly remembered will displace other events seen as of less importance. (2) If important data are not present, they risk being overlooked. (3) Risk assessment is affected by the way the risk is described. (4) Problem solvers are often overconfident; they fail to learn from past mistakes.[17]

Distortions of this kind are likely to affect witnesses; they may also affect lawyers, particularly if cases are prepared in haste. There are also differences in the way in which people treat data. Some people are "variety amplifiers," once presented with a problem they will go into it in great detail, collecting more and more information. Others are "variety reducers." They simplify problems, focusing on the elements they perceive as most important. Both of these tendencies have disadvantages. The variety amplifiers may lose sight of what is most important in their mass of data, while the variety reducers may miss important items of information because these are not seen as significant. Argyris argues for what he calls "double loop" learning. He states that it is not sufficient to understand the content of the problem. Any solution requires that the underlying causes and the values behind these are also understood.[18]

Costanzo provides a professional model of problem solving. This identifies ten skills and four values that legal practice requires. The ten skills are: problem solving, legal analysis and reasoning, legal research, factual investigation, communication, counseling, negotiation, litigation and other dispute resolution procedures, organization and management of legal work, and recognizing and resolving ethical dilemmas. The four required values are: provision of competent representation, striving to promote justice, fairness and morality, and striving to improve the profession and professional self-development. She describes problem solving as covering the following:

- Identifying and diagnosing the problem, including noting the client's situation and problem, the client's goals, supposed and preferred courses of action, and financial resources. Missing information must be identified and account taken of the cost of discovering more. The time available for problem resolution must also be noted.
- Generating alternative solutions and strategies that are independent, systematic, and creative, noting possible limitations to this analysis by identifying assumptions, gaps, and assertions of doubtful value.
- Developing a plan of action including listing possibilities, ranking them, and choosing one.
- implementing the plan including assessing whether the given lawyer is the appropriate person to do so.
- Keeping the planning process open to new information and ideas.
- Continually consulting with the client and ensuring he or she has realistic expectations of the outcome.[19]

These skills, or competencies, are very comprehensive. They could readily be transformed into a strategy or action plan to fit a particular situation. They could also form the basis of an excellent problem-solving approach for other professions besides lawyers. In some, for example medicine, identifying and diagnosing the problem would be the most difficult task and might require the testing of different hypotheses before a satisfactory diagnosis is obtained. This may be less complex with the law or with crime as the fact that a prosecution is being brought implies that there is a degree of clarity about the problem. The difficulty will not be with the nature of the problem but with who has been responsible for causing it.

This kind of problem-solving approach is comprehensive and ethical but can be criticized as not being very creative and not leading to a holistic approach in which the complexity of the problem and its relationship to the environment in which it occurred are thoroughly understood. Learning in the law is greatly influenced by precedent and case law. This means it is focused on the past rather than the future. Costanzo points out that legal problem solving is often constrained by the beliefs and customs of the profession. For example, what lawyers call research, other groups would call search. Research for a lawyer is not testing hypotheses, it is looking up the law in reference books. Lawyers also have some generally accepted notions of professional privilege and confidentiality that may constrain open behavior.

Capabilities

Lawyers generally work in small units and may be less dependent on the organizations that service them, their chambers and practices, than other groups. Nevertheless, they will work better with excellent backup services. Barristers need clerks who will ensure that they get briefs suitable for their knowledge and experience, and that these briefs are well set out and contain all the essential information for a particular case. They will also require a degree of time management so that cases are spread out, giving them space to read and understand briefs before they have to appear in court.

Coordination

All problem solving requires a degree of coordination when it reaches the implementation phase. Carefully thought-out diagnoses and strategies now have to be translated into meaningful action that affects others. Conflicts of interest can now arise between the wishes of the client, or crime victim, and the resources of the lawyer and the organization that supports him or her. The lawyer's client may think that the case has been inadequately presented so that he or she was compensated insufficiently or has not received a fair trial. This is often not a question of poor skills or competencies but of inadequate resources in the wider environment.

The last twenty years has seen a growth in law centers. These are community services set up to provide legal services to groups who might otherwise not have access to them. Their services are usually free and a variety of experts are available to provide advice.

Medical Specialists

It seems that scientists and lawyers place their problem-solving emphasis on seeking truth by separating what is true from what is false. Frequently, but not always, the problems they study are limited in size and have clear boundaries. The scientists aim to work with precise, stated hypotheses; the lawyers also have hypotheses, although these might not be made explicit. Lawyers are interested in making or defending a case, not in making a contribution to knowledge.

Our next group, hospital doctors, is looking for the causes of ill health. They are less interested in what is true or false than the scientists and lawyers and more focused on clinical relationships. Sometimes they can immediately identify cause and effect but they frequently use problem-solving approaches based on association, in which certain patterns of symptoms suggest certain diseases. They then build a broad picture so that they can identify the reasons an individual is suffering from an illness that is difficult to identify. Correct diagnosis is often a result of reviewing past knowledge and experience. Like lawyers, doctors examine the past to help understand the present and the future.

Competencies and Skills

Observation. Doctors use two approaches when arriving at a diagnosis. These are observation and interpretation. Observation is very precise and based on well-tried clinical methods. These include taking a medical history, making a physical examination, and carrying out other investigations, which may include laboratory tests. Interpreting these results requires an assessment of whether anything outside the range of normal physiology is present and if this deviation indicates the presence of disease.[20] The objective of medical history is to obtain an accurate account of the patient's complaint and to relate this to the patient's life experience as a whole. It will include family history and social and occupational history as well as illness. In doing this the doctor is trying to make associations and also to look at disease from a holistic point of view. Medical students today are encouraged to allow their patients to tell their own story in their own way. Good doctors do not rely solely on verbal clues, they also pay great attention to nonverbal factors, such as the patient's appearance—the ways he or she looks, walks, and answers questions.

Histories. Doctors are also given instruction in how to interview. They are told that taking histories is a special form of the art of communication and must be a two-way process. Doctors should know the patient's name, greet him or her with this, and use words that are easily understood. They should appreciate the importance of interpersonal relationships and they should strive to inspire confidence and recognize that many patients are wary of doctors. When the patient is examined, touching should be gentle rather than aggressive.

As with many nonmedical problems, the complaint that brought the patient to the doctor may only be a symptom of a more serious underlying problem. The doctor discovers this by asking the patient to tell the story of his or her illness from the beginning. When the story has been completed the doctor will take each main symptom in turn and examine it in detail. Leading questions should be avoided and care taken that the patient and the doctor understand each other. Terms used by the patient may be unclear to the doctor and vice versa. If the patient arrives with a severe pain, the following questions will be relevant: Where is it located, does it stay in one place or move about, when does it come and when does it go, what is it like—stabbing, burning, pricking, gnawing, what brings it on, what makes it better?

Medical students are also given the wise advice that something that is not present may be as important as something that is, and that the history-building process does not end after the patient is first seen. It must continue until a cure is secured. They are also encouraged to write clear, simple case notes with summaries of the main findings.

Interpretation. The objective of the history-taking, physical examination, and any tests is to make a sound diagnosis. Here the advice is to start with some broad questions such as: What is this person's problem? and Does he have a disability? If the doctor believes the patient does have a disability, then the next logical questions might be:

- How far can this person's disability be explained by his environment—his lifestyle, where he lives, where he works? That is, in geographical, socioeconomic, and cultural terms.
- How far can this person's disability be explained by his own attitude and mental makeup—in psychological terms?
- How far can this person's disability be explained by a disease process or processes—in pathological terms?

The doctor is aware that arriving at a one-disease diagnosis may be misleading as the patient may have a variety of diseases at the same time. In the medical problem-solving process, as with many other problem-solving processes, simple solutions are being replaced by more complex ones.

It can be seen that medical diagnosis is based on a detailed and logical collection of different kinds of information, all relating to the needs and circumstances of the patient. This information will be collected by listening, looking, examining, and carrying out scientific tests in a pleasant and sympathetic manner. The eventual diagnosis will be a result of a careful evaluation of all these factors, an assessment of how they interact with each other, and their comparison with what the doctor already knows through encountering similar cases in the past. The doctor is using intelligence information, association, and experience and bringing these together in a diagnosis that represents a medical hypothesis. The correctness of this hypothesis will be tested by the ability of selected treatments to cure or reduce the disability.

Organizational Capabilities

In order to apply these skills effectively the doctor requires the hospital or practice that employs him or her to provide a high quality of backup resources. In a hospital these include the appropriate environment to assess patients—wards, operating theaters, outpatient clinics and other facilities, nursing care, and specialist services. Another requirement is sound administration and good secretarial support, so that services of all kinds are efficiently managed and sufficient financial and other resources are available to provide these. The doctor also requires time to carry out his healing work effectively and to carry out relevant research. Doctors also require the appropriate tools for their specialism. If they are neurologists these will include tendon hammers, tuning forks, opthalmoscopes, and otoscopes. They will also require the means to record information—such as computers, tape recorders, or dictaphones.

There must be an effective clinical resource that covers how patients are referred to the hospital, the time they have to wait for appointments, and the time before treatments or surgery are supplied. There must also be an appropriate environment for the doctor to assess the patients. This will include well-equipped outpatient clinics and wards and the support workers to service these—receptionists, clerical workers, and nurses. The doctor will also require good personal secretarial support.

Coordination

The doctor has more groups to coordinate than scientists or lawyers. He or she is working in the center of a complex and demanding network of relationships. If any of these break down or cease to be available, there will be adverse consequences for the patient. The most important relationship will be that between doctor and patient, as this can affect the patient's recovery time. Next come relationships with the nursing staff, who are directly responsible for the care of the patient. And there will be relationships with groups who assist investigation and diagnosis. These will include radiologists and radiographers and specialist departments such as pathology. Transport from the hospital will also have to be arranged through the ambulance service. Excellent coordination is also required with the management of the hospital and with local general practitioners. The doctor's efficiency and commitment can be reduced if necessary services are missing or of poor quality. Research carried out by Reg Revans in the 1960s showed how good communications and relationships between hospital staff greatly facilitated the recovery of patients.[21]

The efficient provision of all these services in times when budgets are tight requires considerable thought to be given to the overall organization and structure of the health service. Should many of these services be provided in very large hospitals with plenty of medical resources, or should some functions be decentralized to local hospitals that can provide nursing care but not much else? The British government is still trying to answer these questions.

CONCLUSIONS

What can be learned about problem solving from scientists, lawyers, and doctors? It can be seen that problem solving can take different forms depending upon the objectives of the problem solver, the nature of the problem, and the environment in which it occurs. But, although they approach their tasks from different directions, all three groups have a common objective. This is the search for truth.

The traditional scientist strives to find truth by asking questions that are structured as hypotheses or statements. He or she may start with a hypothesis such as "only hens can lay eggs." The scientist then tries to establish the truthfulness or falsity of this statement. As his or her knowledge increases and he or she becomes certain that other birds besides hens lay eggs, the scientist will formulate more hypotheses to aid the search for new truths.

The lawyer, also seeking truth, finds it not through careful experiments but by searching for facts and evidence. Much of this is obtained by cross-exmaining witnesses and accused persons. The end product is a verdict of guilty or not guilty. This verdict will provide a precedent for similar legal cases.

Both scientists and lawyers require proof that something is either true or false, but this evidence may not be easy to obtain. It is more demanding of the scientist who has to continue his or her experiments until he or she is confident that this proof has been obtained. The lawyer can be satisfied with a lesser state of accuracy, for example, that a piece of evidence is beyond reasonable doubt.

For both the scientist and the lawyer personal competence is the principal requirement, although their achievements can be hindered or helped by the capabilities of the organization that provides them with support facilities.

The hospital doctor, in contrast, has to initiate a much wider and more comprehensive search for truth, probing the patient's physical history and mental state. The aim is to build a total picture of the patient, including work, family, and leisure activities. All of these can provide clues to the nature of the patient's illness. The doctor works through association, looking for information that will lead to a diagnosis of why the patient is experiencing a medical problem. This first diagnosis may be uncertain, even wrong, and the information-gathering process will continue, assisted by scientific tests and technical aids such as X-rays, until a firm diagnosis can be made.

Doctors, like the scientist and the lawyer, are interested in accuracy and truth but they will arrive at this via a different route. Doctors also differ from most scientists and lawyers in that their effectiveness is more directly related to the support capabilities of their employing organizations. If the necessary resources are not provided, medical care will deteriorate.

Doctors, more than scientists and lawyers, also work as members of extensive social networks that contain specialists with many different kinds of expertise. They have to be able to establish successful cooperative relationships with these groups. But perhaps the most important difference is the focus of their attention. This is not a problem that may be technical rather than human, or a specific dispute. It is a human being whose future happiness and comfort, even life, may depend on the doctor's ability to solve a range of connected problems that together are affecting the patient's medical, psychological, and social well-being.

It is apparent that although scientists, lawyers, and doctors are all striving for truth, they take very different routes to establishing this. The scientist uses methods that have as their aim precision and certainty; the lawyer requires methods that will assist the evaluation of different kinds of evidence; the doctor needs methods that are able to bring together and integrate very different kinds of information so that this can become a related set of knowledge. Some of this knowledge will be fact, some hypothesis. For all three groups perhaps the most important information will be that which is missing.

Another major difference between the groups is the extent to which obtaining knowledge requires interaction with other people. The scientist's experiments may require little or no contact with people, the lawyer will have a close but restricted set of relationships on matters related to a particular dispute. The modern doctor who practices holistic medicine will be interested in every aspect of the patient's lifestyle in order to arrive at a correct diagnosis and viable treatment plan.

These differences have implications for problem-solving aids in the future. In the 1980s it was suggested that offshoots of artificial intelligence called expert systems, or knowledge-based systems, would become important problem-solving accessories and might even taken over the problem-solving process altogether.[22] The early examples of these systems were rule-based, and they provided a set of logical steps to assist decision making. These developments now seem less attractive. Scientists do not want the straitjacket of a set formula for making decisions, they need to let their minds roam freely so that different possibilities can be explored and tested. Lawyers could benefit from computer systems that provide comprehensive examples of case law (these already exist), but they do not want machines making decisions for them. Doctors have tried to use expert systems and have encountered problems. They may not agree with the logical processes used by the developer of the expert system and in consequence do not accept the computer's diagnosis. Also, they soon learn what the expert system has to offer and then cease to use it. The area in which technical aids such as expert systems have proven most successful is training. New scientists, lawyers, and doctors can all benefit from contact with a system containing considerable amounts of knowledge about their particular subjects.

The differences we have identified suggest that problem solving has a strong contingency element. Methods, relationships, and problem-solving tools all have to be carefully evaluated to ensure that they are the most effective means for collecting and using necessary information.

CHAPTER 4

Problem Solving and the Police

In the previous chapter we looked at the competencies, capabilities, and coordination needs of three groups renowned for their problem-solving abilities—scientists, lawyers, and doctors. Although all of these will be concerned with our principal areas of interest—illegal drugs and cyber crime—there are other groups that are more directly involved. With drugs, these include the police, drug dealers themselves, and many community groups. With cyber crime there are the companies who wish to protect themselves and the experts who have the difficult task of tracing and catching the hackers and information stealers engaged in criminal activity. In this chapter we will describe how the police approach problem solving.

POLICE PROBLEM SOLVING

The police have a number of distinctive features that separate them from other professional groups. They have considerable powers, including the right to use legitimate force and even the most junior officers can use this when necessary. The law gives each officer a considerable degree of individual discretion, irrespective of rank or length of service. All officers are expected to deal with difficult and dangerous situations, such as public order incidents and national emergencies. These can expose them to considerable risk. Lastly, they are required to have a high degree of personal integrity.[1]

David Bayley suggests that the police have two major functions that he calls "authoritative intervention" and "symbolic justice." Authoritative intervention is reactive and is concerned with maintaining and restoring order. Symbolic justice is more fundamental and long term. It is directed at establishing a climate of respect for the law. This is achieved principally by responding to requests from the public for action when criminal activity is interfering with social stability. Most of the police's time is spent on crimes that have already taken place, although today there is an increasing emphasis on prevention. For example, at present one of the British government catch phrases is "being tough on crime and tough on the causes of crime."[2]

The police have always been problem solvers. Today, they are faced with a great variety of very testing problems, many of which require different approaches and solutions. Despite this complexity their principal problem-solving objective is, and always has been, to assist the stability of society by providing a relatively secure environment in which the population can live and work. Over the years their problem-solving ability has waxed and waned and at certain times the police have themselves been a problem rather than a solution, but they have consistently set themselves the goal of making life safer for their fellow citizens.[3]

The police at present seem to be required to be all things to all men. They are frequently the only twenty-four-hour service agency available to respond to those in need. The result is that they handle everything from unexpected childbirths to alcoholics, drug addicts, family fights, traffic violations, and crime. These require a wide variety of competencies and skills from police officers on the beat. Crime, the activity we are most interested in here, perhaps surprisingly, represents only a third of incidents and many of these may be false alarms.[4]

Crime requires criminal investigation and this is carried out by detectives. Some of these work as generalists, handling all and every crime as it occurs. Others are assigned to specialist units such as the drug and fraud squads. All are responsible for the collection of information about current or likely future crime. This process is known as intelligence. Intelligence covers a variety of activities including using informants, "staking out" areas where offenses are likely to occur, and watching the activities of known criminals. The latter two are called surveillance, which is the use of observation, monitoring, and recording techniques to gather information about persons or activities that can produce intelligence. It may include both visual and electronic means for collecting information.

When large numbers of people are likely to be involved in a major operation it is essential to set up a dedicated intelligence unit. All relevant information will be channeled into this so that the intelligence officer in charge can provide effective assistance to groups responsible for planning strategies and tactics. Intelligence activities can take two forms—slow intelligence and fast intelligence. Slow intelligence relates to the analysis of existing material and local knowledge. Fast intelligence is immediate information concerning the outcome of events that are currently taking place. Both intelligence and surveillance are regarded by the police as effective but expensive in manpower.

Occasionally there may be undercover penetration of criminal conspiracies. For example, the police can set up a drug marketing activity or offer money laundering facilities. Individual officers then act as dealers or money launderer advisers. This kind of undercover activity is also carried out by customs officers, although their responsibility will focus on illegal goods entering or leaving the country.

Competencies and Skills

Police officers require a variety of personnel skills. One of the most important required of investigating officers is the *ability to talk* to people irrespective of whether they are victims, witnesses, or suspects. The purpose of this is to gather evidence and establish whether there is enough information to arrest suspects with a reasonable chance of a successful prosecution. The police talk to people to find out what has happened. Is an investigation necessary? How serious is the crime? Who is likely to have committed it, and what evidence is available to support a prosecution? In Britain, in the past, a decision to prosecute was made by the police. Since 1985 it has been made by the Crown Prosecution Service.

Detectives also talk to people to get them to confess. Many police interviews have this as their objective. This can be done either through demonstrating or suggesting that the police have reliable evidence, or by persuading the offender that "coming clean" will have benefits, such as a reduced sentence. One New York officer describes how he handles an interview situation. "To get people to confess you sit and talk to them. You try to make them relax and gain their confidence. Many positively want to tell you what they've done. They want to get it off their chest."[5]

Personal control is another desirable social attribute of a police officer. The ability to remain calm and responsible no matter how traumatic and difficult the circumstances, particularly when confronting criminals or restoring order in groups of individuals who may be both drunk and violent. To this should be added the ability to show concern and sympathy when relating with the victims of crime.

An important knowledge competence required of detectives is *expertise in the legal requirements* for collecting, recording, and reporting evidence. This can be one of the most demanding aspects of a detective's role. It is a necessary skill as the detective must be able to understand what is taking place in court. Completing paperwork for the prosecution file can present a heavy administrative load. It requires the police authorities to have efficient procedures in place to assist this process.

Detectives are constantly on the lookout for new skills that will help them with their investigation task. *Criminal personality profiling* is one of these. This was developed by the FBI in the 1970s and became an important part of the training of detectives in the United States. John Douglas, an FBI investigator who assisted the West Yorkshire police with the identification of the Ripper murderer, has described the psychological skills required to solve difficult murder cases. First and most important are what he calls "transference skills." He tries to put himself in the role of the criminal and to take on his or her thought processes. He may also do the same with the victim.[6]

Douglas calls this "profiling," and it is based on a fast, comprehensive but careful analysis of all nonverbal clues that are available. He sees this process as similar to a doctor evaluating particular symptoms in order to diagnose a specific disease. Profiling is based on psychiatry, but whereas a psychiatrist normally examines an individual and tries to make some reasonable predictions about how that individual might react to a specific situation, the investigator reverses this process, trying to predict the characteristics of the criminal from the evidence of his or her deeds. Douglas justifies this approach by stressing the complexity of today's criminal problem solving. He argues that in the past most crimes were relatively easy for law enforcement officers to comprehend. The police generally knew whom they were looking for. Today this is no longer the case as a new, more sophisticated criminal has surfaced. This is a law breaker who learns from experience and who tends to get better and better at what he or she does, improving his or her skills over time.

Profiling attracted the attention of British police officers and criminologists, and a unit to develop offender profiling was set up in the psychology department of a British university. But police reaction to this technique has been mixed. The success of profiling is very dependent on careful training. If this is not available errors can and do occur. Yet, although it has to be treated with caution, profiling can provide additional information and a greater understanding of criminal behavior. It is sometimes described as scientific, but in no sense does it meet this claim given the usual definition of the term as proof derived from measurable data. However, by providing information on behavior patterns it can help the police to identify and target likely offender groups.

The *holistic* or *big picture approach,* supported by Gestalt theory, has also been adopted by many police forces. Douglas and Olshaker tell us that the FBI instructs officers investigating crimes to focus on three questions: "What took place?" and this must include everything that might be significant about the crime; "Why did it happen the way it did?" What were all the possible reasons for the criminal's actions? and, finally, "Who would have committed the crime for these reasons?" They emphasize that detectives have to take disparate and seemingly unrelated clues and turn them into a coherent narrative. This makes storytelling an important talent.[7]

Organizational Capabilities

In order for police officers to be effective problem solvers they have to be provided with a work environment that has the capability to give them the right kind of support. This will be a product both of organizational structures implemented nationally and of local force culture and efficiency. In recent years the police have experienced, sometimes suffered, many structural changes. These have all been introduced with the desirable objective of enabling officers to make a positive contribution to the problems and needs of today's social environment. This contribution has been defined as incorporating flexibility and concern for the community.

Competent problem solving by individuals and organizations requires administrative structures that assist the use of personal skills. Institutions must have the capability to change their structures as the environment in which they operate changes and creates new pressures and needs. Over the years the police have carried out many reorganizations to make themselves more effective in an increasingly demanding society. This is an ongoing goal.

To illustrate some of the capabilities an efficient force requires to support its officers we will use the West Yorkshire police as an example.

West Yorkshire is the fourth largest force in England and Wales. It has always prided itself on using the latest management ideas and tools to assist its service to the community. In order to ensure that the most relevant and effective management skills are identified and implemented successfully, it encourages organizational improvement and innovation throughout the force.

Like most major businesses the West Yorkshire police department believes that its first essential task is to decide what it should be doing, both in the present and future, to achieve its goal of service. This has led to the development of a mission statement underpinned by a balanced set of strategic objectives and a performance management framework to align all its services to the achievement of its strategy. The West Yorkshire objectives had to mesh easily with a set of crime reduction objectives produced by Michael Howard, the Home Secretary in the last British conservative government. These were:

- to maintain and if possible increase the number of detections of violent crime.
- to increase the number of detections for burglaries of people's homes.
- to target and prevent crimes that are a particular local problem, including drug related criminality, in partnership with the public and local agencies.
- to provide high visibility policing so as to reassure the public.
- to respond promptly to emergency calls from the public.[8]

These objectives had performance indicators attached to them to check how well they were being achieved.

West Yorkshire police recognized that to be successful in this chosen profession it was important for a continual review of all organizational systems and processes with an emphasis on their contribution to the force strategy. In order to do this it introduced what is called a Process Improvement Program to initiate improvement of the force's core processes. In order to develop this program the West Yorkshire police had to

- identify those factors that had the greatest influence on the force's results.
- identify the highest challenges and opportunities facing the force.
- identify those processes most central to the implementation of its selected strategy.

- develop an action plan for improvement of its most important processes.
- develop an action plan for ongoing process management across the force.

These would be achieved using a number of approaches and principles that could aid new thinking. For example:

- A whole system's view of organization as responsive and able to adapt to its environment.
- Viewing the force as a series of cross-functional processes, not as independent functions.
- Producing a measurement framework that facilitates effective management at all levels.
- Encouraging participation by everyone.
- Improving information experience and expertise leading to better decisions.
- An understanding, acceptance, and ownership of shared responsibility for change.
- A learning approach to work-process design and the application of change tools.

These again incorporated the latest thinking on work design and the management of major change. The approaches used have been developed through experience. The use of techniques to engage large groups of stakeholders in the change process has been invaluable.

An entire book would be needed to document all the projects and approaches included in the Process Improvement Program and but one project will provide an example. This focused on intelligence analysis and development and was seen as vital to the success of the police service. The police cannot do their job without being able to collect and use accurate intelligence.

Intelligence Capability

Intelligence is information that has been subject to development and analysis with that analysis leading to a judgment that it will be useful for certain police objectives. Intelligence has to be up to date and accurate or it is of little use. It is required for planning purposes and for on-the-scene information to assist police operations. It is often a product of surveillance.

The West Yorkshire police's analysis of needs and problems showed that information was not shared between different units and with outside groups, such as the prison service and the courts. Frequently the police did not know whether individuals were in custody or not. The importance of informants was not sufficiently recognized and many uniformed officers did not know how to recruit these. Intelligence activities were not well coordinated and responsibilities needed to be more clearly defined. Most important was the fact that all staff needed more awareness of the importance of intelligence.

The internal report of the police project team made thirty-six recommendations for improvement and provided detailed plans for their implementation. These included:

- An active program to improve the free exchange of information.
- The appointment of extra prison liaison officers to assist the prison service and police to develop better systems for the collection, analysis, and sharing of information.
- The provision of a more coordinated approach to the use of informants. Here it was believed that payment should reflect the quality of information provided.
- It was decided that a new role of intelligence coordinator should be created at each division to stress the importance of intelligence, to motivate officers to give it higher priority, and to direct the program of research. These intelligence coordinators should attend a tailored training course to ensure they knew the new force policy on intelligence. They should, whenever possible, be trained controllers of informants.[9]

The objective of these improvements was to raise the profile of intelligence throughout the force. Quality information must be valued in its own right and a culture of sharing it developed. All police employees must be made aware of how they could individually contribute to the intelligence process. The success of this program would be evaluated through a system of performance measurement, wherever these could usefully and logically be applied.

LESSONS LEARNED BY THE WEST YORKSHIRE POLICE

The West Yorkshire police have learned a number of important lessons on how to improve organizational capability from their Process Improvement Program. The first of these is the importance of participation. They found that experts alone are not usually the best people to make changes, staff who will use the new system must also be involved. The second is that methods to assist problem solving and facilitate change are useful, but these methods must be simple, straightforward, and easily understood by those using them. The third is that new organizational designs need to be flexible to accommodate local conditions. There is no "one best way." The fourth, of vital importance, is that designing a new process is much easier than implementing it. Successful implementation requires establishing and maintaining over time the enthusiastic cooperation of all those affected by the change until the new system is working effectively. Finally, once implemented any new structures or procedures need to be carefully monitored to ensure their continued success.

COMPETENCIES AND CAPABILITIES REQUIRED BY DRUG SQUADS

As this book is treating illegal drugs and cyber crime as examples of complex problems, it is useful to examine how personal competencies and organizational capabilities are developed in and for these specialist groups. Drugs and the drug squad are of particular interest as so much of police time is spent on this activity. In Britain regional crime squads handle the most serious cases of drug dealing, but a great deal of detection work is handled at the local force level.

Competencies and Skills

Drug squads require their officers to have training in a number of essential skills—investigative skills, search and seizure skills, skills in how to run an informant, skills in how to plan and execute a raid, surveillance skills, and evidence-gathering skills. Officers are taught what each of these skills requires in terms of knowledge, but also how to apply them in their day-to-day activities. The focus is on What do we, the police, want to achieve and how do we get there? Training is never rote learning but always through discussion, case studies, and exercises. The aim is to make the drug squad officer an excellent problem solver in his or her area of responsibility through enhancing the officer's ability to think holistically and laterally. Problems must be seen and understood in terms of the total situation rather than a part of the situation. Routine approaches now become creative ones with a variety of options and strategies carefully reviewed before an action choice is made.

Police instructors responsible for training the drug squad believe that the most important skill for an officer is the ability to grow and achieve personal development. Without this, knowledge quickly becomes out of date. Self-development is the ability to find out, and understand, new aspects of any problem the officer may be handling and new approaches for dealing with it. This knowledge would cover how to establish contacts and relationships, how to network, how to achieve targets to ensure prosecution, and many other skills. Most important is the ability to learn so that operational experience leads to greater understanding and competence and vice versa.

Members of drug squads often have to work undercover and this can place them in serious danger. A member of a U.S. drug squad comments:

> Undercover work is very dangerous. You have got to be able to play a very unique role, in that you have to watch what you say all the time, so that you don't talk like a cop.... When you're in the role you are thinking as a criminal not as a police officer.[10]

Members of drug squads also require other qualities. These include the ability to work as a member of a team and to have good relationships with other groups who can be of help. They must also have an excellent memory for detail so that apparently insignificant items of information can be recalled when required and they become relevant. And they must be willing and able to constantly learn from experience, perhaps the most important skill of all.

Specialist Capabilities

The support capabilities required by a drug squad are primarily resources. These could be specialist advice that is available from a variety of sources, for example, forensic science laboratories, or material resources such as vehicles, or technical aids such as sophisticated communication equipment. Officers also welcome help that is not bureaucratic but flexible and responsive, and a top-management understanding of what their role involves.

Securing results is not easy for a drug squad as it is in a no-win situation. Drugs are not going to go away, and the arrest of some local dealers will not alter this fact. Planning is difficult as a drug squad will never know how long a case will take. It may take a few days, a month, or a year. Also, before a case can be started a number of approvals have to be obtained. Surveillance needs higher-level approval, as do taking undercover photographs. Approval has to come from the correct level, and, in Britain, this might be a superintendent or even the chief constable. More approvals are required when the case being investigated moves away from one area and into another and a different force becomes involved. In Britain, if these procedures are not followed, the Crown Prosecution Service will not accept the case.

The drug squad also has to be very aware of the consequences of its activities. If it is successful in prosecuting dealers, there will be fewer drugs on the market, the price will go up, and crime can increase as users try to acquire the extra money needed for a more expensive purchase. The local community will then put pressure on the police to do something about the increase in crime. The drug squad always has the difficult problem of trying to maintain a degree of stability in a very volatile situation. They have to show that they have some control over the movement of drugs into the local market and that, because of their efforts, fewer drugs are becoming available. At the same time their actions must not cause additional problems for ordinary citizens through increased numbers of robberies, or dealers fighting each other for customers.

Coordination with the Local Community

Police forces today strongly believe in the importance of good community relations. This is achieved in many police forces through what is called community policing or neighborhood policing. This is both a philosophy as well as a program because it is an attempt to change the nature of relationships with the public and the way police services are delivered. The aim is to achieve a partnership, with police and community groups actively cooperating with each other. Although the targets for improvement may vary from place to place, broadly they are likely to cover the following:

- Tackling the causes of crime through a variety of initiatives such as family support services and alcohol and drug misuse programs.
- Reducing the opportunities for crime to be committed by, for example, improved home security and street lighting.
- Tackling specific crime problems such as domestic burglary and violence.
- Helping the victims of crime and reducing fear of crime.[11]

Community policing often works hand in hand with problem-oriented policing, an approach developed in the United States in the 1970s.[12] Community policing tends to lead to problem-oriented policing, as a police force that tries to establish close contact will soon become aware of the particular problems that the community is faced with. Similarly, the fact of trying to help communities to solve their problems invariably creates close relationships. The advantages of bringing these two approaches together are:

- A better served public whose concerns are attended to at the source.
- Officers with enhanced job satisfaction from bringing the public real benefits.
- More manageable demands on the police because many underlying problems are solved, reducing repeat calls.[13]

The Brighton Police Department in Colorado provides an excellent example of community policing. Its goal is focused on providing a high quality police service. The Brighton police responded to community needs for quality and productivity improvement by rethinking and restructuring their role as public servants. They defined their mission as providing a total quality service where each police–citizen contact resulted in a satisfactory conclusion. In order to achieve this they agreed that officers should "provide non-criminal services to the community by direction, counsel, and in other ways that do not interfere with the discharge of police responsibilities. They shall perform their services with empathy, honesty, zeal, courage, direction, fidelity and sound judgment." In addition, officers would seek to maintain the respect and approval of the public by "constantly demonstrating absolutely impartial service to law, by offering individual service and friendship to all members of the community regardless of their wealth or social standing, and by offering individual sacrifice in protecting and preserving life, and property."[14]

The Brighton police checked their success in achieving desired community relationships through community surveys. After each contact with an officer the member of the public contacted was sent a small questionnaire asking if he or she was satisfied with the service received.

Britain was not far behind the United States in adopting similar customer-friendly strategies. A major catalyst to police thinking on this subject was the 1982 report of Lord Scarman. He was greatly influenced by the riots in London and Liverpool in 1981 and argued that the police should consult the communities they policed and be accountable to them for their actions. In his report, he restated the earlier ideas of John Alderson, once chief constable of Devon and Cornwall, who also supported changes in police attitudes and behavior. Scarman's belief in community policing was to dominate the national debate on law and order for many years to come and to greatly influence the way the police approached their problem-solving responsibilities.[15]

The two main principles of the Scarman report were "consent" and "accountability," and its aim was to provide a democratic answer to two fundamental ongoing questions: What is the service for? and Whom is it supposed to serve? Although the Scarman reforms were difficult to implement, were interpreted in different ways, and had mixed results, the goal of community policing has remained and become stronger over the years. Most police forces today have a network of relationships with local community organizations that they greatly value and use to good effect. Quality of service has become an important police objective, and, following a 1993 Home Office initiative and White Paper, each force was asked to critically examine and challenge all existing practices and procedures and to set new standards of excellence.

Problem-oriented policing has also been used by the British police to improve community cooperation and relationships. An important part of this philosophy is that problem solving should take place as low down the force as possible. Those officers who deal with the problem in the first instance must take responsibility for handling it. This reverses the normal hierarchy in most police forces where the beat officer is at the bottom and the senior detectives at the top. It means that senior officers must empower and encourage their subordinates to take responsibility for solving the problems they encounter when policing their community areas.

Putting this system in place requires knowledge and resources. Both officers and their subordinates have to be trained so that problems are analyzed and dealt with in a structured manner. Those lower down the hierarchy must be able to show creativity and imagination while dealing with a number of problems simultaneously. A high degree of knowledge and skill are required. At the same time senior officers are asked to change their normal patterns of behavior and provide help and advice rather than orders.

The U.S. and the British police forces are convinced that community policing is the way into the future. The "service" aspect has now been brought back into policing, and much improved relationships between police and community has resulted, while efficiency and effectiveness have been increased.

Lessons that Can Be Learned

What can mangers learn from the groups we have examined in this and the previous chapter? It is clear that all four have a number of things in common. The scientists, lawyers, doctors, and the police are all seeking accurate information, although they use different methods for obtaining this. The scientists have precise questions for which they want answers, and they phrase these as hypotheses. They then use well-tested methods to identify what is true and what is false. The lawyers arrive at the truth through the collection of evidence and the cross-examination of witnesses and defendants. The doctors build up a careful diagnostic picture of a patient's illness through questioning, observing, and testing. The police follow the medical pattern of trying to collect relevant information through the observation and questioning of a variety of informants. Both the doctors and the police have an interest in problem prevention as well as problem solution. This is less true of the scientists and lawyers, although they are interested in improving the methods they use to collect and analyze information.

Each group differs from the others in the extent to which it requires social interaction to obtain information. The scientists require little interaction, except perhaps with other scientists, and this can be competitive. The lawyers have to relate to specific groups and individuals. Many of their communications are in courts of law and have an adversarial content. The doctors have to interact extensively and in many different ways with the patients they are treating. Their communications are restricted to the consulting room or the hospital unless the patient is very sick, when they will visit the home.

The police have a wider network to manage. Both the Brighton and the West Yorkshire police, like many other of today's forces, are trying to solve problems in partnership with members of the communities in which they are located. More than the other specialists they have to develop relationships with a wide variety of groups, both criminal and law abiding, and they have to contribute to the solution of a wide variety of problems. They are doing this in their role as community public servants.

One important lesson from these groups is that problem solving can take many different forms. In the police the officer on the beat is a general problem solver, never knowing when or for what he or she might be called to help. Few of these situations will involve serious crime, but all will require the competencies of fast thinking, quick reactions, and considerable tact. Units with specific responsibility, such as the drug squad, will require excellent planning skills, the ability to use a range of information collecting techniques, and the knowledge of how to take forceful but restrained action when necessary. Drug officers also have to be very aware of the consequences of their actions. The successful arrest of local dealers could lead to an increase in other kinds of crime.

The goal of developing and maintaining good community relationships required both the U.S. and the British police to make major changes in their traditional patterns of behavior. Instead of being guardians of order and nothing else, they now have to become servants of the community, able to help, advise, and guide when problems arise that are of public concern. The achievement of this necessitates new ways of thinking and a more friendly and concerned style of interaction with the public. This requires leadership from the top, training in new kinds of community relationships, and a willingness to assume a new kind of role. To some extent it requires the recruitment and development of a new kind of police officer, one who is good at relating with members of the public in a friendly way, understanding their problems, and responding to their needs.

It also requires excellent officer support from the police administration. There has to be enough officers to provide a physical presence in the community, ideally on foot. Senior officers have to accept that their role is to help and guide more junior officers, not just to instruct them what to do. In both the United States and Britain a program of this kind has to be an ongoing process.

Change of this kind also has to be enthusiastically supported by top management. Senior officers have to be people of considerable insight and vision who see their role as both encouraging change and ensuring its successful implementation. In order to achieve this they have to develop appropriate strategies for their local communities and ensure that these are acceptable and helpful to these communities. This is not an easy task. It can be argued that problem solving for the police is more complex and demanding than for any of the other groups discussed in the previous chapter, even doctors. In order to solve today's and tomorrow's problems the police in both the United States and Britain are being required to make a culture change, to rethink what they should do and how they should do it. This is a challenging and difficult task.

CHAPTER 5

Drug Dealers and Drug Barons as Problem Solvers

The problem solvers we have considered so far have operated in challenging environments, but they have usually had clear objectives and precise methodologies to enable them to develop knowledge in an ordered way. Because of this they may not provide good models for the future. Management gurus predict that this is not going to be an easy ride. There is likely to be an increasing amount of what Robert Gross calls "entropy," defined as the amount of energy unavailable for useful work.[1] An alternative term is "disorder." Gross argues that change is happening fast and everything is becoming more chaotic. Things that used to be stable are now unstable. As a result of these new challenging internal and external environments managers have to develop a capacity to make rapid tactical decisions. They must do this effectively if they are to avoid disorder that turns into unmanageable chaos.

THE DRUG DEALER AS ENTREPRENEUR

A more appropriate role model than those discussed so far may be that of the drug dealer. Dealers operate in volatile situations, with many different activities to manage and with a degree of unpredictability in the pattern of future events. This unpredictability is accentuated by the fact that other groups are dedicated to preventing them from achieving their dealing objectives, which usually involve transporting illegal drugs from one part of the world to another. The rationale behind these operations is profit and so an important goal is to move a product from where it is produced, usually very cheaply, to where it can be sold for large sums of money. A great many problems have to be solved in this process.

It might be thought that obtaining information on drug dealing strategies and tactics might be difficult, in fact this is not the case. One of Britain's most active cannabis dealers, Howard Marks, has spent his time in prison writing a most interesting and detailed account of how he managed his business activities.[2] Cannabis (or marijuana) is a plant, grown commercially in many parts of the world and usually smoked as a joint mixed with tobacco. Cannabis resin is usually sold in brown or green-colored blocks for about $60 to $80 per ounce. In the 1960s it was the most popular drug used by groups such as hippies to enhance enjoyment at social events.

Like any entrepreneur the drug dealer has to find a source for his or her product, has to arrange transport to a selected market, and has then to sell it, either direct to the public or to dealers who act as intermediaries. Well-established drug dealers are likely to have permanent or semipermanent arrangements for doing these things. Their arrangements will be well organized and well protected. Howard Marks, a Welshman who was clever enough to be awarded a place at Oxford University and who received a master's degree in physics there, has always regarded cannabis as a harmless drug that should be legalized. Because it was not, he recognized it as a relatively easy way of making substantial sums of money. Marks, when he first moved into drug dealing, created transient organizations and relied largely on friends to help him with the logistics. He apparently found many students, and even staff, in the Oxford community who were willing to take a risk and act as drug couriers, providing the financial gain made this risk worthwhile.

As his knowledge of the trade and his business activities increased, so his management organization became increasingly complex. He now needed willing contacts in a variety of countries who would share and coordinate a set of increasingly difficult and risky activities. His collaborators were no longer casual friends but people who wanted a long-term relationship and the possibility of continuing profits. There was usually a bent airport or customs official available to progress the product along its journey, provided the price was right.

As Marks became more experienced he learned to import his drugs using circuitous routes. He never brought drugs directly from a cannabis-producing country, moving them first to a noncannabis producer. Also, he would never travel directly to where he was going. He changed planes or moved from plane to train. He knew the customs officials were always watching his movements. There were also informal rules that had to be kept. If a load was lost because it was intercepted by the authorities, the shareholders in the deal lost their investment and accepted liability for any costs. No one else was held responsible for the loss. If there was any kind of rip-off or double dealing then the shareholders did not lose their investment. They got paid the agreed price and the person who was ripped off was held responsible for the loss. A member of the Mafia could escape responsibility if he killed the person who did the rip-off, and this person was usually not hard to identify.

A problem for Marks was that as the business grew and was more and more successful it became increasingly complex and also of greater interest to government authorities such as European customs and the U.S. Drug Enforcement Agency (DEA). He tells us

> cash tumbled in and out of my arms in cities throughout Europe and Asia. Wire transfers of several hundreds of dollars apiece maintained temporary residence in accounts at Credit Suisse, Hong Kong. We all kept moving. We met and discussed plans in strange places. The DEA was always watching and checking.[3]

A challenge for most drug smugglers is how to manage the large amounts of cash that they need to pay their associates and that they accumulate as profits. Marks handled this by opening a number of businesses that could absorb money. One was Annabelinda, a dress shop in Oxford, another was a travel agency in Hong Kong. He also opened accounts and safe boxes in banks all over the world and distributed his profits among these.

Competencies

In order to achieve the successful movement of drugs onto the market, Marks required a number of personal competencies. These included the ability to get people to work for and with him and to inspire a degree of trust in an area where this attribute was in short supply. He also required the ability to think creatively, particularly on how to conceal the illegal drug he was importing so that it would not be found by customs. Sniffer dogs trained to spot drugs needed to be fooled through impregnating goods with powerful alternative smells and perfumes. Methods for concealing drugs in transport had to be identified and tried. One consignment of cannabis traveled concealed in bananas. A regular trade was sustained for a while with engineering machinery being sent to drug-providing countries and then returned to the sender as faulty; cannabis was included in the package on the return journey. Both sides had to think creatively about this transport problem: Marks on how to conceal the goods; customs and drug-enforcement agencies on where they might be concealed. Marks also had to be able to assume and maintain a large number of different personal disguises. This required a selection of names and passports and the ability to persuade others that he was the person he was claiming to be.

To carry out all these things successfully required a number of personal attributes that might be of value to any entrepreneur or manager in the future. These include:

- Super-confidence.
- Ability to generate trust, and willingness to trust others.
- Ability to manage complex situations.
- Tremendous creativity, particularly in finding new routes, and collaborators.
- Ability to talk ones way out of trouble.
- Reputation for being successful.
- Acting ability—can assume different roles and masks.
- Abundance of friends and contacts throughout the world.
- Opportunism—ability to spot new opportunities.
- Energy—many things to coordinate.
- Intelligence—the ability to think ahead and to respond quickly to fast moving events.

Capabilities and Coordination

The principal capability required by Marks from his business associates was effective coordination and good collaboration. His organizational arrangements seem quite close to the kinds of structure that many firms may find appropriate and necessary in the future. Most were transitory, with groups of temporary partners being set up to handle specific business deals. Marks had long-standing relationships with many of his associates, and they seemed to regard him with goodwill. Nevertheless, the logistics of a successful project were extremely complex. People of different nationalities and with different interests had to be able to liaise with each other and link up successfully at key points in an often complex journey across the world. They had to be continually on the watch for drug-enforcement officials and ready to take fast, corrective action if and when mishaps occurred. Moving drugs successfully relied heavily on other people's honesty, cooperation, and ability to deliver. At the height of his career Marks was smuggling consignments of up to thirty tons, a relatively small amount in terms of international trade. Yet the reality was that most of the deals worked. He was rarely confronted by the law.

Entropy Moving to Chaos

Despite a number of terms of imprisonment Marks continued with the trade because it was the quickest and easiest way of making money. But it became increasingly complex as the size of the deals and the profits increased. It also became more vulnerable to interference by professional criminals and their gangs. The U.S. Drug Enforcement Agency was always on the watch as were the customs officials. Gradually disorder increased and moved closer to chaos. Marks, who lived in Palma, describes the situation at the completion of one of his projects.

> There was a ton of messages waiting for me when I returned to Palma. John Denbigh was accumulating substantial funds in Vancouver. He wanted someone to give them to in a weeks time. McCann was in the Sofia hotel, Barcelona. If I didn't get there immediately, he'd come directly to my house in Palma. It was urgent. Moynihan was in the Orient Hotel, Barcelona. He had my Philippine passport. Could I pick it up? Malik was in London. He wanted to discuss some business proposals. Tom Sunde was in Dusseldorf. He needed some more money. Frederick was still at sea but due to unload his cargo of hashish in Canada.[4]

He also provides a vivid description of his home situation.

> One square mile of this island (Palma) was well out of control. A Philippine-brothel-owning member of the House of Lords (Moynihan) was staying at the house of a Spanish Chief Inspector of police. The Lord was being watched by an American CIA operative who was staying at the house of an English convicted sex offender. The CIA operative was sharing accommodation with an IRA terrorist. The IRA terrorist was discussing a Moroccan hashish deal with a Georgian pilot of Colombia's Medellin Cartel. Organizing these scenarios was an ex-MI6 agent [Marks himself] currently supervising the sale of thirty tons of Thai weed in Canada and at whose house could be found Pakistan's major supplier of hashish. Attempting to understanding the scenario was a solitary DEA agent.[5]

Marks finally came to a decision.

> I was not enjoying myself any more. Most of my close partners were in prison. Some were understandably blaming me for their fate. Others were correctly accusing me of endangering scams by doing too many. I was criticized and ridiculed for not being prepared to deal in cocaine. I was not making money. I was under surveillance. I decided to retire.[6]

Marks takes the logical solution to a situation that has become over-complex and overstressing. He decides to get out. Managers in more conventional business who may not be able to do this might have a nervous breakdown or a heart attack. Unfortunately, Marks was not able to make a fast, clean break with the consequences of his drug-dealing activities. The American authorities prosecuted, and he served a sentence of seven years in U.S. jails.

THE DRUG BARON AS INTERNATIONAL CRIMINAL

Drugs today are controlled by large-scale criminal organizations that cross national boundaries. Their development has been assisted by the increased mobility of people as a result of legal or illegal immigration, by loose border controls, assisted in Europe by European Community legislation, and by greatly increased global economic activity, which makes criminal transactions easier to hide.[7] They are as effectively managed as many large industrial companies, although their structures are different. Some, like the Mafia, rely on family relationships to control crime, others rely on networks of temporary relationships that bring criminals together to carry out a particular project.

Like any commercial company they have a need for specialized roles. At the top will be the all-powerful financier who provides money for the operation. He or she will need a "planner" to organize strategies and logistics and a money launderer to disperse and conceal the profits. Below these will be a collection of ancillary criminal roles, including "crooked" lawyers, politicians, and accountants. Then come the groups who physically move the drugs and have access to air, shipping, and road transport stretching from drug source to final market. Lastly, there are the sellers and debt collectors who confront the final customer.[8] Because drug addicts have to find regular sums of money to pay for their addiction, they might be involved in secondary industries. Women may turn to prostitution while thieves require "fences" who can sell stolen goods.

Unfortunately, because the drug industry is so wealthy, its activities can spread from illegal to legal organizations. There is evidence that in many countries drug money is now being used to fund legitimate economic activities, with the danger that these eventually become controlled by criminal groups. Russia and other eastern European countries provide many examples of this trend.

DRUG TRAFFICKING IN COLOMBIA

Colombia provides an example of how international drug trading is organized on a large scale. The Colombian approach to running this major illegal industry has been excellently documented by Manuel Castells in a major work entitled *End of Millennium*, and by Gabriel Garcia Marquez in his classic *Noticia de un Secuestro*, translated into English as *News of a Kidnapping*.[9] There are also many interesting and important articles in the journal of International Security, *Intersec*. Castells tells us that drug traffic started in Colombia in the late 1960s and was initially based on the production and sale of marijuana. Marijuana proved bulky to transport and other parts of the world could produce it more cheaply and so, following the advice of the American Mafia, the Colombian dealers changed to cocaine where profits were higher and competition less.

One of the dealers moving into this new area was a former student leader from Medellin called Pablo Escobar who was already organizing a variety of criminal activities and had considerable experience in avoiding the law. He created the Medellin group of drug dealers. Pablo Escobar was interested in politics and improving the conditions of the poor and had some of the characteristics of a Colombian Robin Hood.

A second group, called the Cali cartel, which came from a higher social background, set up competition and was both more ruthless and more skilled in maintaining good relations with the Colombian oligarchy, which controlled both business and government. This group practiced "social cleansing" and killed hundreds, even thousands of the Colombian underclass homeless and beggars. The Medellin and Cali groups waged continual war against each other, although Pablo Escobar was eventually killed by the Colombian army. The generals, coerced by the United States who wanted his extradition, decided he must be eliminated. Both the Medellin and the Cali groups, although sworn enemies, organized their drug-dealing activities in similar ways and used their management skills as major assets in winning the war against law enforcement agencies.

The management capabilities that these drug barons needed and used were, first, a recognition that the drug industry has to be *demand driven* and *export oriented*. The United States is still the most important market for drugs, although demand from Europe and Asia is increasing fast, and drugs have to be efficiently transported to American users with the certainty of considerable profits. The ability to earn and receive this *profit* was the major motivating factor for the drug barons. In 1991 the cost of producing one kilogram of cocaine in Colombia was estimated to be US$750. The price for transport to the states was around US$2,000. The wholesale price in Miami was US$15 per gram and, in the streets of the United States, it was US$135 per gram.

The industry is global in that it is fully internationalized, but it also has a strict *division of labor* between different locations. The transformation of coca into coca paste takes place where it is cultivated, although at some distance from the coca plant fields. It is then changed into a base from which the cocaine is made, with the product moving north as it is manufactured. Small civilian airstrips cut into the jungle play important roles in the processing and distribution networks as there are few roads. Although Colombia produces only 11% of the coca leaf, with Peru and Bolivia producing the rest, it is the main center for producing cocaine from the leaf. Colombia also has a number of management and commercial centers that organize transportation. There are estimated to be over one thousand cocaine and heroin flights per year.

There is considerable variety in the kinds of transport used, with small planes the most common method of moving large amounts of drugs to the United States. Commercial airlines are also used together with small boats and cargo ships. The Colombian security forces have also captured a minisubmarine carrying three tons of cocaine. Small amounts of drugs are often carried by personal couriers who use imaginative methods of concealment, for example, briefcases made of pressed cocaine, wheelchair frames and hollow surf boards filled with drugs, jeans and skirts soaked in cocaine. Cocaine is also hidden in legitimate merchandise, in the walls of cargo containers and in bulk cargo such as coffee or even bananas. In 1997 the largest discovered shipment was 1,500 kilograms of cocaine, concealed in sixty-three cardboard boxes said to contain microwave ovens.[10] The drug traffickers constantly change their methods of transport, with sea and land transport the most difficult to detect and prevent.

The *facilitation strategy* to enable illicit goods to move across frontiers and boundaries is bribery, especially of custom officials. To make arrival more certain the cocaine is never transported directly to its destination, but takes long, circuitous routes through territories where customs officials are less aware, or less concerned about drugs. Each area will have its network of trusted Colombian nationals to help the goods on their way. Transit across national boundaries is assisted by fake check-ins, claim tag changes, and conspiracies between check-in agencies and ramp handlers. Drugs such as cocaine also require chemicals, called precursors, in their preparation, and these have to be imported. These used to come from Europe and the United States, but they are increasingly supplied by the Latin American chemical industry in Argentina and Brazil.

Successful business activities are made possible and stable through good coordination with other groups. Mexico, because of its proximity to the United States, acts as an important center for drug smuggling into the United States. The National Intelligence Consumer's Committee reports that almost 6,600 tractor-trailer trucks and 211,000 passenger vehicles cross the U.S.-Mexico border each day. Customs estimate that two-thirds of all cocaine entering the United States crosses the U.S.-Mexico land border and is concealed in trucks and goods vehicles. The Colombian cartels also have strategic alliances with criminal organizations around the world, including the Sicilian Mafia, American Mafia, and Russian criminal networks.

These relationships are greatly assisted by the widespread use of new communications technology such as mobile phones and portable computers. These technical aids enable the drug smugglers to keep track of transactions and to change routes and procedures when this is necessary to avoid detection. They greatly increase the flexibility of the drug cartels and their ability to manage the network of complex relationships required to move the cocaine from Colombia to its final destination. In 1995 the Colombian police seized a computer belonging to the Cali cartel and found that it had enabled cartel members to tap every telephone call made into or out of Bogotá, the capital, including calls to and from the Ministry of Defense.

Critical Success Factors

An essential requirement for a successful drug baron is to maintain easy access to the profits that have been accumulated. This requires money laundering that is controlled by the Colombian drug barons but carried out by specialized agents located in the banks and financial institutions of Venezuela, Panama, and Florida. Today, the Colombian drug cartels are estimated to launder $2 billion a year in profits through the companies they own or can influence.

All of this complexity has to be controlled and made to work as an efficient, responsive unit. The control mechanism can be money but is more usually violence. Each cartel has a network of killers together with groups of armed personnel who police and terrorize the territories and areas of interest to the drug barons. They also have a responsibility to prevent competition and to act as protectors. If stability is to be maintained the drug barons also require control over the political and institutional environment. This has to be corrupt at all points including local and national authorities, judges, police, and customs officials. Those in positions of power are often given a choice of receiving substantial sums of money or seeing their families terrorized. In Colombia the Cali cartel developed good relationships with authority through buying its cooperation, while the Medellin cartel and its leader Pablo Escobar went to war with local politicians over a drugs agreement that had been made with the United States.

U.S.–COLOMBIAN RELATIONS

The United States has spent around $20 billion during the past ten years on international drug control programs and on efforts to reduce the flow of illegal narcotics, yet illegal drug cultivation and drug-related activities have continued to increase throughout South America, Mexico, the Caribbean, and Southeast Asia.[11] Part of the U.S. program in the 1980s was the persuasion of the Colombian government to participate in a joint counternarcotic program. This arrangement included an agreement that Colombia would extradite drug traffickers to the United States for prosecution and imprisonment.

The Medellin cartel, very threatened by this, launched an attack on the Colombian government directed at securing the reversal of this law. In order to place intolerable pressure on government officials the Medellin querrillas, known as the "extraditables," kidnapped a number of their relatives, often middle-aged and elderly women. Gabriel Garcia Marquez describes their horrific experiences and their strange relationships with the young men whose duty it was to guard them.[12] Eventually, after years of violent terrorism, the Medellin cartel's leadership was decimated, and Pablo Escobar was shot and killed in 1993. But he had by then won his battle with the Colombian government, as the extradition agreement was rescinded in 1992.

After the death of Pablo Escobar the Cali cartel became the dominant drug dealers in Colombia and are now thought to control 70% of the world's cocaine market. As well as running a major business the cartel has its own military wing. This greatly threatens both the Colombian and the U.S. governments, with the Americans exerting great pressure on the Colombians to reduce the threat. As a result, since the beginning of 1995, the Colombian Drug Enforcement Agency and a Joint Police/Military Commando Unit have been carrying out a major offensive against the Cali cartel. Estates owned by the Cali family have been raided in addition to the companies assisting the money laundering operation. A number of senior members of the cartel have been arrested.

President Ernesto Samper announced his intention of ending all coca production in the country by 1997. But this was an impossible objective given that the production of coca doubled between 1993 and 1995. He also has had to deal with the furious protests of peasants when their crops were destroyed by fire or herbicides.[13] The U.S. government, although continuing to apply pressure on Colombia, has never been certain how sincere the Colombian officials are in their cooperation. This uncertainty was worsened by a suggestion from the Colombian prosecutor general that consideration should be given to the legalization of drugs. He has also suggested very lenient agreements with the leaders of drug cartels, which would mean some of the more infamous serving prison sentences of less than five years.

Relations between the Colombian and U.S. governments continue to be uneasy. The United States regards Colombia as an unreliable ally in the drug war and believes that President Samper accepted drug money to fund his 1994 election. The right to extradite Colombian citizens for trial has now been reinstated, but the U.S. government recognizes that all the blame for illegal drug use cannot be attributed to outside suppliers. It is the United States that provides the market.[14]

Castell points out that both the Medellin and the Cali drug groups, despite their aggressive tactics, always hoped for full integration into Colombian society, perhaps as legitimate businessmen. They offered to pay off the Colombian foreign debt in cash and reinvest their capital in Colombia. This was, of course, completely unacceptable to the U.S. government. Nevertheless, their activities have brought a degree of wealth to a poor country through reviving the economies of Medellin and Cali and providing financial support for national sports such as football. Castell also suggests that the tradition of violence in Colombia throughout its history and particularly in the 1950s has meant that the Colombian government has continual crises of legitimacy and control. The drug barons were, and are, able to take advantage of this by supporting corrupt officials and effectively taking control of the economy.[15]

LESSONS TO BE LEARNED

Can conventional managers learn anything from the entrepreneurial behavior of the drug barons? The three advantages that the cartels have had over the U.S. government is their flexibility, their ability to handle complexity, and their success in establishing collaborative relationships. When President Clinton forced the Bolivian government to introduce stronger responses to the actions of the criminal community, the barons responded by rethinking their organization and activities and implementing counterstrategies with great rapidity. In contrast the actions of the American law enforcement agencies were bureaucratically slow and their attempts at gaining Colombian government cooperation, although frequently offered verbally, had very little real success.

The second capability the cartels had was the ability to manage complexity. New strategies required new behavior in many different groups located in different parts of the world, depending on the transit route and destination of the cocaine cargo. The successful achievement of this depended on positive and negative incentives. The positive one was money; the negative one fear, especially the fear of being murdered.

The third capability, that of successfully managing relationships, may be the most important. John Kay sees the legitimate firm as a set of relationships between different stakeholders.[16] He argues that the successful firm is one that creates a distinctive character in these relationships and that maximizes the value of that distinctiveness. The drug barons require this also. They must have associates who can tolerate a high level of stress, are able to use initiative in difficult situations, yet are reliable and loyal. This is achieved through a combination of severe penalties and rich rewards.

It can be suggested that these abilities of flexibility, effective management of complexity, and development of high quality, collaborative relationships may be important required management attributes in normal industry in the future. Negative and positive incentives will also play their part. Hopefully the positive incentives will be enthusiasm for work, together with high skill, motivation, and job satisfaction. Negative sanctions will not be the draconian and life-threatening penalties of the drug barons, although business failure will always inspire feelings of insecurity and fear of job loss.

The drug market is an easily accessible one, and, so long as it is criminalized, there are very large profits to be made. It runs much like any other business with logistics and coordination being critical success factors. The problem is getting the product to the market in situations that are volatile and unpredictable and in spite of many groups dedicated to prevent its arrival. Success requires quick thinking, fast responses, and the ability to think coherently and systematically when under stress. Are these the attributes that most managers will need in the future? This remains to be seen.

CHAPTER **6**

Understanding the Drug Problem

The first requirement with any complex problem is to understand it as a totality. How has it arisen, and why? Where is it going and what route is it taking? Is it changing its nature or structure as it develops? Will it eventually solve itself or destruct of its own volition or is action required to remove or reduce its effects?

These questions lead us into something very similar to reverse engineering, a process in which engineers take complex devices apart to discover how they work. It is also similar to the diagnostic processes used by doctors who practice holistic medicine. This group is not concerned only with a specific symptom or complaint; the members strive to understand how the whole person, including both the body and the brain, is being affected by a particular disease or dysfunction. The police too follow this "total picture" approach when they try to understand how a particular crime or social problem is affecting the community as a whole.

Reverse engineering only brings understanding if the investigating engineer knows why the machine or device was built. What problem was it designed to address or solve? The parts can only be understood in terms of the whole. Similarly, we can only understand the drug problem in all its complexity if we know who buys drugs and who sells them and the motivations and behavior of each of these groups. We also have to discover the management processes that take these illegal goods from the producers to the consumers and the difficulties likely to be encountered along the route. We have to ask probing questions such as Why are drugs illegal?

and How would the situation change if they were not? Trying to answer these will bring us into the realms and interests of governments, politics, medical science, and the security forces. Finally, and most challenging of all, we have to ask and answer the fundamental question of the problem solver, If we want to change this situation, how do we go about it? It may then turn out that the problem is insolvable and our only recourse is to learn to live with it.

The aim of this chapter is to describe the big picture, given our present limited state of knowledge. What seem to be the different factors that make up the whole and how do these relate to, and influence, each other? A good starting point is an examination of the substances that are being bought and sold.

THE DRUGS

Today's drug trafficking industry is worth a tremendous amount of money, perhaps $500 billion a year, which is more than the global trade in oil. Its consequences affect us all. The average heroin user commits two hundred crimes annually to feed the habit, while gang warfare among dealers threatens the stability of public life. Yet there seems little evidence that governments and the forces of law and order are making any headway in combating this growing major crime.

Illegal drugs can be categorized in terms of their different characteristics. Cannabis, the most commonly used drug, is in a class of its own. It used to be almost the only drug on the market. Cannabis has been known about for a long time. Homer makes reference to cannabis. Herodotus wrote in 5 B.C. that the Sythians cultivated a plant that when thrown on the fire gave off an intoxicating odor and led to much dancing and singing. Cannabis was also known in Europe at a very early date. An urn unearthed in Berlin containing cannabis leaves is believed to date from 500 B.C. It also produces a useful fiber. Cloth made from hemp was common in Europe in the thirteenth century and continues to be used. There has never been a successful effort to suppress cannabis, and in 1969 the United Nations estimated that there were between 200 and 250 million cannabis users in the world.

Cannabis is trafficked and consumed in three forms, "herbal" called marijuana, "resin" known as hashish, and oil. The main sources of herbal cannabis are West Africa, the Caribbean, and South America. This trade is controlled by West African and Colombian criminal networks that associate with Western European criminal groups. Cannabis resin in Europe comes mainly from Morocco and Pakistan. This trade is controlled by Western European criminal networks.[1] Cannabis or "grass" was the popular drug of the 1960s, often grown in people's gardens for personal use. It is still the most-used drug today. Many doctors are frustrated because they cannot take advantage of the pain-relieving properties of cannabis and heroin for their very sick patients.

Opiates are heroin, methadone, cocaine, and crack. They create intense but transient feelings of pleasure. These are tightly controlled drugs that are very addictive. Their use can involve injection with the risks of acquiring serious infections from unclean syringes such as HIV/AIDS and hepatitis. Heroin is a drug obtained from the chemical processing of morphine, a constituent of opium, the resin of the oriental poppy. It often has methadone as its treatment, but this is also addictive. Crack is a derivative of cocaine. Cocaine and crack produce an intense stimulant effect, described as a "rush." This wears off after about fifteen minutes. Withdrawal leads to depression and lethargy followed by increased craving for the drug that can last up to three months.

Asia is the main production center for heroin. The two main locations are the Golden Triangle in Southeast Asia, which includes Laos, Thailand, and China, and the Golden Crescent in Southwest Asia, which includes Pakistan and Afghanistan. Trafficking from the Golden Triangle targets the United States and is principally controlled by the Chinese. Trafficking from the Golden Crescent targets Europe and is dominated by Turkish criminal groups. Street heroin is bought either in small paper envelopes or in packets. It is usually adulterated, frequently with glucose, although more harmful additions can be used and it can vary in its strength. Bought from a street dealer the strength may be between 5 to 20% pure heroin. The dealers uncut heroin may have a strength of 20 to 40%, and the heroin of suppliers can be 40% or more pure.[2]

Cocaine comes from the Andean regions of Peru, Bolivia, and Colombia. Until recently the main market for cocaine has been the United States, but traffickers are now expanding their activities into Europe. Colombian cartels run this trade and are seen by customs as both highly organized and flexible in their business dealings. Drugs are transported to other countries using intermediate stops such as the Caribbean Islands. From there it is not difficult to ship goods to Miami or Mexico and onward to different parts of the United States. Similar tactics are used to move cocaine into Europe. The island of Curacao has ten flights a week to Amsterdam. Shipments are helped on their way by "arrangements" with check-in agents and baggage handlers tempted by the considerable financial rewards. Despite tight security and the imposition of stiff penalties on airlines caught with smuggled goods, drugs continue to flow along these routes without difficulty. This trade is known as the Cocaine Express.

Stimulants and hallucinogens include amphetamine, magic mushrooms, LSD, and Ecstasy. They are sometimes known as "dance drugs" because of their association with the "rave" culture and are swallowed, not injected. They lead to euphoria and increased energy. Amphetamines are the most widely used, although there is evidence that the use of Ecstasy by teenagers has greatly increased in recent years. These are man-made chemically based drugs that find a large market in Western Europe. Most come into the United Kingdom from the Netherlands, although some are supplied by Germany, Poland, the Czech Republic, and by factories within the United Kingdom. The chemicals required for these drugs are readily available.

Other drugs include glues, solvents, aerosols, and anabolic steroids. The effects of these are similar to alcohol. They produce intoxication and euphoria, followed by disorientation, dizziness, and drowsiness.[3] It has been suggested that there are more deaths from glue sniffing by children than adult deaths from more addictive drugs.

Any drug can produce hallucinations, delusions and behavioral disturbance although patterns of effect vary greatly. Early adverse effects can be similar to schizophrenia or psychotic depression. Later effects can include flashbacks, personality changes, and mental deterioration. One solution to the drug problem would be to develop a drug that produced the desired mental state without creating addiction. Unfortunately, this does not seem possible. Susan Greenfield, until recently professor of pharmacology at the University of Oxford, says that drugs work at target sites that become more or less sensitive. It is this change in sensitivity that is the basis of addiction.[4]

Many of these drugs have harmless therapeutic histories. In the nineteenth century cocaine was found to have value as a local anesthetic. This medical use was identified by Carl Koller, a friend of Sigmund Freud. Freud took the drug regularly as a stimulant, describing it as "this magical substance" and declaring that it was not addictive. This conclusion was greeted with some skepticism because although at this time, 1886, little was known about the drug, some cases fo cocaine addiction were already being reported from different parts of the world.[5]

MDMA (methylenedioxymethylamphetamine), later called Ecstasy, was first developed in 1912 by the Merck pharmaceutical company in Darmstadt, Germany.[6] It was intended as an intermediate chemical for the preparation of pharmaceuticals. It was then forgotten but surfaced again after World War II in the chemical warfare records of the United States army, who was testing it for use in the Cold War. It was not heard of again until the mid-1960s when it began to be used in the United States by health care professionals. It was then called Adam or Empathy and was used as a chemical aid in psychotherapy to encourage the inarticulate to talk.

Gordon Alles, an American researcher, worked on the commercial production of the drug and was followed by a chemist, Alexander Selgin, who set up a laboratory of his own. During the next thirty years, Selgin went on to develop 179 mind-altering drugs for the counterculture. Descriptions of these can be found on the Internet under the heading "Phenethylamines I have known and loved." A recent press notice suggests that the developer is proposing to release them on the market.[7] MDMA affects the chemistry of the brain in ways that are not yet understood, but it produces intense feelings of excitement and pleasure. Recent research in the United States has shown it can have adverse long-term effects that injure the brain.

The *European* newspaper in March 1997 published a report from the International Narcotics Control Broad warning that Ecstasy and amphetamines manufactured in Europe were the continent's principal hard-drug problem. The report emphasized that "we cannot now lay all the blame with the South American drug barons, for the producers of synthetic drugs are on our own doorsteps. The Netherlands, reputedly Western Europe's biggest maker and exporter of Ecstasy, has a pivotal role as a producer of synthetic drugs, while factories are also springing up in Eastern Europe.[8] The article produced a strong response from readers. One claimed he had been using a variety of drugs for thirty years. He worked as a physiotherapist, had four children, and had never suffered any ill effects. Other readers supported the legalization of drugs as the only means of removing them from the black market. One letter claimed that by allowing drugs to remain illegal and under the control of criminal gangs we are placing them beyond the control of society. Control of drugs would only be achieved by legalization and regulation.

THE DRUG USERS

Drug users are not all the same. They can be described in terms of their reliance on the habit. There are social users who only use drugs very occasionally, users who use drugs quite extensively in social settings but are not chemically dependent, users who are physically but not psychologically dependent, and users who are both physically and psychologically dependent. The lives of the latter group are dominated by drugs.[9] Social users take drugs at social events such as parties when everyone else is doing this. They can always say "no." Users who take drugs extensively but are not chemically dependent tend to be part of the club and rave groups. They too take drugs in social settings and their intention is to get "high." They abuse drugs but they are not addicts, they can drop the habit when they want to.

Users who are physically dependent have a greater need for drugs because their bodies have become adapted to them. When they stop, unpleasant withdrawal symptoms will occur. However, if they want to, they too can walk away from drugs. They do not rely on them to cope with everyday life. Some of this group may only take drugs in certain situations. U.S. military personnel in Vietnam were heavy users of drugs, yet after returning to the states most ceased to need them.

The serious problem group is the physically and psychologically dependent addicts who rely on drugs to cope with life. As life becomes increasingly stressful they take more and more drugs to relieve the pain. This group cannot give up drugs without assistance, and they can become physically sick. They typically do not seek help until their situation has greatly deteriorated, and they can then find that they cannot stop, that the urge for drugs has become too great. If, with the help of others, they do succeed in breaking their habit, they, like alcoholics, must never use drugs again.

The *Big Issue*, the British newspaper by and for people living on the streets, describes a day in the "Life of Dave," aged 33, who has been homeless for eight years. He is addicted to heroin in spite of "innumerable" attempts to stop using. At 10 A.M. he goes to a phone box and starts phoning the dealers. He cannot do this earlier as they do not switch on their mobile phones until 10 A.M. At 11:30 he goes to the arranged meeting place and buys £20 worth of heroin. How much he buys depends on the amount of money he has made the previous day. At noon he goes back to his temporary room to take the fix, keeping some for later on. This makes him feel better, but the feeling does not last. At 1:30 he sees the doctor at a Day Centre and is given treatment for an abscess in his arm. He spends the rest of the day in the Day Centre and gets something to eat there. At 6 P.M. he starts begging for the next day's money and carries on until midnight. On Fridays and Saturdays he will continue until 3 or 4 A.M. when the clubs close. At 4 A.M. he goes to sleep. His ultimate aim is to escape to a different, drug-free life but he does not know how to achieve this.[10]

ATTITUDES TOWARD DRUGS

Here are typical comments from the club/rave group.

> Taking drugs is like having a cup of tea in the morning. (NOEL GALLAGHER, pop star)

> I take drugs weekly—ecstasy and coke at the same time. With the state of E's at the moment, if you get a bad E it's quite flat, and coke can help heighten it. It can slow down or speed up the feeling. My friends take much the same, replacing coke with speed because its cheaper. Then there's grass for afters. Drugs should probably be decriminalised, but not made legal because with E and grass especially, no one would get any work done. (JACOB, age 23)

> Keeping drugs such as cocaine illegal and unregulated doesn't stop their use, it simply increases the health risks from contamination with other substances. And why fill the prisons up even more? Prison is usually the easiest place to get drugs in any case, so they're no place for anyone with a drug problem. (JOHN, age 22)

> You'd take away all the appeal if you legalised drugs. That's half the appeal, going to buy it from some dodgy bloke and feeling naughty. Anyway I'd rather give them the money than pay multinationals. (MARK, age 27)[11]

Another quote from a twenty-two-year-old aspiring singer seems to have an element of boasting. He claims:

> I've been dependent on every drug, really. I've been through them all. I know how I am on heroin. I know how I am on cocaine. I know how I am on E. I know how I am on acid and so on.

Another user describes the pleasurable effects of taking Ecstasy:

> I get a huge rush and the feeling of well being lasts about six hours. I feel more intelligent, more attractive, freer with my emotions. I am eloquent and able to speak on any subject. I can recall information from my subconscious. It is brilliant.[12]

Drugs are equally popular with teenagers as with older age groups. It is suggested that more than half of all United Kingdom fifteen- to sixteen-year-olds have taken an illegal drug and technically committed an offense. A disturbing consequence of this behavior is the number of teenaged deaths from accidental drug poisoning. A report in the *British Medical Journal* states that between 1985 and 1995, 436 teenagers died, 303 of these were boys and 133 girls.[13] An article in the *Times* Higher Education Supplement reported that a recent survey of 5,000 final-year students found a quarter of students had used soft and/or hard drugs recreationally, while *Cherwell*, an Oxford student magazine, had claimed that 34% of the university's undergraduates had sampled hard drugs.[14]

Different substances appeal to different age groups, and, as the quotes above show, there are now many category surfers. These are people who vary their drug use to enhance its effects. The youth view appears to be that "everyone takes drugs." One young person suggested "it has become the equivalent of Harold Wilson's pipe, or the Queen Mum having a gin and tonic, or your bank manager with a whiskey." If this is correct, as seems likely, then drug taking is not just a problem for society and the police, it is also a problem for industry, as its consequences will greatly affect behavior at the workplace. As I write this one of the headlines in today's paper reads "Newspaper Fires Journalist for Taking Heroin on John Major's Election-Campaign Aircraft." A further column is titled "Broking Boss Has Drugs Conviction" and begins "The man running one of the largest bond traders in the City has a drugs conviction." The column concludes by describing an earlier lawsuit in which the same individual pleaded guilty to possession of cocaine. The writer points out "the case was one of the first to prove long-suspected cocaine use on Wall Street."[15] Industries that seem particularly vulnerable to drug abuse are finance, entertainment, and the fashion industry. There have been reports of fashion models whose employers supply them with drugs as a means of securing their loyalty to the agency.

The effects of drugs on more vulnerable members of society are graphically described in the novel *Trainspotting* by Irvine Welsh and by Melvin Burgess in his novel *Junk*.[16] Here is a quote from *Junk*, which won the 1997 Guardian Young Reader Fiction Prize.

> Yeah. There's a lot of drugs around here. Drugs are just part of life—pleasure, business, they bring you up and take you down, they make you feel good. They take you to another planet, sometimes. Sometimes you have to find your own way back.

> I know what you're thinking. You're thinking, O-oh she's a junkie she's only been away from home six months and she's a junkie already.
>
> You poor brat, you've been brain washed. Look drugs are fun. They make you feel good that's all. Sure, they're powerful, that's why they're dangerous. So's life. If you're in control, then it's okay.
>
> They never dare tell you that, of course. It's not because they want to keep you off drugs. Oh no, they like it, they want you to. They just want to make sure you take the one's that they want you to take. It's all part of the big mind control. Tobacco, booze, medicine—good. Hash, acid junk—bad.[17]

We are all very confused about drugs—some we accept, others we ban. Cigarettes and alcohol, both addictive when taken in large quantities and both likely to cause serious physical damage, are seen by most people as quite acceptable. Only very recently have first attempts been made to sue cigarette manufacturers for causing health problems. Tranquilizers, such as Temazepan and Valium, although addictive, are still prescribed by doctors for quite mild complaints such as sleeping difficulties. Yet a whole range of drugs are designated illegal, and users and dealers will receive prison sentences if they are caught with them in their possession.

There are a variety of attitudes toward drugs. Addicts are often defined as "sick" and in need of medical help and so the drug problem becomes "medicalized." In contrast, younger users say that they and their friends do not want to kick the habit because drugs are part of today's social scene. Drugs give pleasure or enable problems to be forgotten, and this reinforces their use. If the after effects are unpleasant then further drug use will remove these. Some drug users see themselves as persecuted.[18] Richard Miller argues that a war is being waged against those who take drugs and this war leads to corruption, intimidation, even murder. Ideas on action seem somewhat mixed and range from total prohibition, to legislating soft drugs such as cannabis, to legalizing all drugs and destroying the illegitimate market. The chief of Interpol has said on British television that drugs should be decriminalized but not legalized.

THE DRUG MARKETS

All drug markets require a great deal of organization with vast networks of growers, distributors, sellers, and purchasers. Money is a very powerful incentive. When the product that is being sold is also associated with fashion, popular music, and young people having a good time, it must be virtually uncontrollable. A considerable number will not want to stop it or to have it stopped. People take Ecstasy because, they claim, it is fun, it makes them less shy, and gives a sense of "togetherness." Even those not directly involved in buying or selling can secure financial benefits. The *Independent* newspaper quotes a retired New York drug enforcement officer as saying "teenagers in Harlem can make a hundred bucks just sitting on the street corner as a look out. What chance do they have of making that kind of money in a legitimate job on an afternoon."[19]

A report in the *Independent* describes how the doorman at Raquels, a Basildon night club, was a member of an Essex gang known as "The Firm," which supplied the Ecstasy pill that killed a schoolgirl named Leah Betts.[20] Bernard O'Mahoney, the club doorman, licensed dealers to work at the club and sell Ecstasy tablets around the dance floor. Tablets were supplied to the dealers by the owner of The Firm. For each tablet of Ecstasy sold in the club the doorman would get £1 (plus free supplies of Ecstasy, cocaine, and speed), the junior dealer would get £1, and the owner of the firm would take the rest, about £3 per tablet. A contributory factor in Leah's death was the fact that stronger, and more expensive Es were on sale in order to bring in more money to pay The Firm's debts. Three weeks after Leah's death, because of these debts, the three principals in The Firm were shot and killed as they sat in their car.

A British Home Office report by the Police Research Group, "Tackling Local Drug Markets" published in 1996, provides a fascinating insight into the world of dealers, buyers, and addicts. It shows that the market is highly differentiated. There is the teenaged market whose members purchase Ecstasy tablets at raves and similar social events. There is the city slicker market of share buying and selling whose purchase is likely to be cocaine and the big town junkie market of heroin users who cannot survive without their "fix."[21] Some of this buying and selling may have few social effects but a great deal is not so harmless. Davis Prior, a British member of Parliament who confesses that in his twenties he was a regular pot smoker, believes that the dangers of cannabis use for young people are threefold. First, buying it brings them into contact with clever, rich, and persuasive dealers. Second, there is no guarantee that drugs are not adulterated with harmful substances. Third, the long-term health effects are still unclear. Cannabis can have psychological consequences similar to schizophrenia in those with a genetic susceptibility. There is some evidence that the use of cannabis can be carcinogenic. It can also cause impotence in men and lower their sperm count.[22]

Many crimes are committed to obtain money for drugs, young girls move into prostitution to pay for their daily fix, while gang warfare can break out between rival traders with people getting killed. The British

National Criminal Intelligence Service (NCIS) estimated that at least eight murders in London between 1994 and 1997 were linked to the Turkish-controlled heroin trade. Other, more respectable groups, move willingly into this flourishing market. There are doctors and pharmacies who, for financial gain, are known to be an easy touch for drugs, while in the United States a major source of supply can be the local hospital.

THE DRUG BARONS

In the last chapter we described the management competencies and capabilities of drug barons, using the Colombian Medellin and Cali groups as examples. There are many others equally powerful groups. Today the drug trade is owned and managed by crime syndicates that operate on an international basis. One particularly dominant group, increasingly seen as posing a serious threat to Western capital cities, is the Russian Mafia. It has links with the Italian Mafia, and the South American drug cartels. The *London Times* estimates that in 1998 there are about one thousand Russian crime groups operating internationally, excluding the ten thousand in Russia itself. Each ranges in size from fifty to one thousand members.[23] A disturbing problem is the fact that the Russian Mafia groups have now corrupted Russian industry, the Russian state, and the law enforcement agencies. Criminal groups control 40% of private industry, 50% of banks, and 60% of state-owned companies. Two-thirds of the economy is criminalized. John Lloyd, a onetime Moscow newspaper correspondent and author of *Rebirth of a Nation: An Anatomy of Russia*, suggests that if the international groups combined their activities in an organized way, they could pose a serious threat to Europe and to the United States.[24]

Bulgaria is now the main transit point for drugs from Afghanistan to Russia and then on to European capitals and the United States. It is believed that 70% of opium smuggled into northwest Europe comes from Afghanistan. One kilogram of heroin priced at $600 in Tajikistan increases to $95,000 in Russia and to $100,000 in Western Europe. Other drug-based criminal groups operating in the United States and most European countries come from West Africa, in particular Nigeria.[25] These are well-organized gangs in loose-knit organizations that are good at networking. They are influential in Russia, Poland, and Bangkok.

One of the most vulnerable entrance points for drugs entering the United States is the U.S.–Mexican border. Extending for two thousand miles, this is the only border in the world shared by a highly developed country and a Third World country.[26] It is believed that Mexican drug barons are prepared to offer $50,000 in cash for each truck a customs officer will let pass across the border without hindrance, while many trucking companies are owned by the drug barons. The waiting market is huge. Eight-five million Americans have tried illegal drugs and around $75 billion a year is spent on drugs.

Drug barons in the United States are a clever and highly organized group. The trial of the gang leader Larry Hoover in 1997 showed that drug barons operate with the same level of organization as any major commercial enterprise. According to a spokesman for the federal government, "the gang has operated with the efficiency of a Fortune 500 company.... Hoover is an organizational genius with a drug-retailing acumen equivalent to the hamburger selling might of McDonalds." One witness at the trial said that he earned over $100,000 a month selling bags of crack cocaine through an army of about fifty street-corner retailers. All drug sellers had to pay $45 in weekly dues and $35 for the right to sell in "Gangster Disciple" territory.[27]

However, things do change, although not always for socially acceptable reasons. An article in *USA Today* described how homicide was dropping at an unprecedented rate in the United States.[28] The belief was that the United States had the drug lords to thank for some of this decline. Years of violent drug wars over control of the crack cocaine market had created a huge increase in the homicide rate in the 1980s. Now, despite a continued rise in drug use, the illegal drug market has stabilized. Drug barons had marked their territories and taken control. The need to kill competitors had been reduced. FBI statistics showed an 11% drop in killings in 1996, a reduction from 21,600 in 1995 to 19,224.

Although a drug truce among the barons was a factor behind this considerable drop, there were other influences. The emphasis on community policing and the aging of American youth was one of these, while the maturation of the crack cocaine market accounted for some of the decrease. A police spokesman said "A lot of kids have killed each other off already and many are in jail." He pointed out that the same pattern had emerged through modern history with liquor in the 1920s, heroin in the 1960s and early 1970s, and cocaine in southern Florida in the late 1970s and early 1980s. His view was, "a new illegal substance comes onto the market, a lot of street thugs realize how profitable it is, but they are not businessmen, and they kill each other to eliminate the competition. After a few years strong and cunning people take control. In each of the U.S. cities with populations of more than one million, slayings are fewer than they used to be."[29]

Unfortunately, the general view of the drug situation everywhere is pessimistic. The war is not being won, and there are suggestions that there are political and financial reasons why this is the case. A major difficulty in the United States is the desire of the government to maintain friendly relations with Mexico, which a too aggressive antidrugs policy could jeopardize. Another problem is the ease with which criminals can turn illegitimate gains into legitimate profits through money laundering using offshore banks and tax havens. There is a U.S. government reluctance to interfere with these, as so many legitimate business activities would also be affected.

CONCLUSION

Hopefully, this attempt to identify and describe the total picture has provided some useful information. It is clear that the major players are drug users and drug barons, and the desired rewards are the pleasures or needs that drugs provide or can meet, and the vast profits that suppliers can earn. But the picture presented is extremely complex and provides few clues on what to do next. Almost certainly this will depend on the objectives and philosophies of the interested and involved governments. Some, like the Americans, will see the drug problem as a war that has to be won. A war that will require the help of the armed forces and the security services and will prove extremely expensive and demanding. Others will hope that less extreme approaches will contribute to a reduction of the problem and will try a mixture of legal and therapeutic approaches. Another group, now beginning to declare themselves, may try the more extreme solution of legalizing some or all of the now illegal drugs in the hope that this approach will remove the trade from the control of the criminal fraternity. The philosophical position chosen will influence how the problem-solving process proceeds. In the next chapter we will examine the responses of governments, both national and local, to the need for action on the drug problem.

CHAPTER 7

Tackling the Drug Problem

Governments as Strategic Planners

PROBLEM SOLVING

Major problems, which affect countries as well as groups and individuals, are likely to be addressed by a hierarchy of problem solvers. At the top of this hierarchy will be governments and government-sponsored bodies. This chapter will discuss how the drug problem is being tackled at this level. Governments have the ultimate responsibility for drug prevention strategy, and they must have a clear understanding of the problem and of how it is affecting their citizens. This requires "rational reconstruction," the ability to state with confidence "this happened because ..." It also requires "legitimation." Solutions and the strategies used to achieve these must be accepted and approved by a majority.[1] Solutions will only be implemented if they are socially, psychologically, and culturally acceptable.

This means that solutions must fit in with established attitudes and knowledge. They will be accepted reluctantly, or not at all, if they are seen as a contradiction of well-entrenched views. Solutions and strategies are likely to be viewed as acceptable if they have three characteristics: (1) if they "correspond" with known facts, (2) if they are "coherent" and fit with accepted knowledge, and (3) if they are "pragmatic" and there is evidence that they can achieve practical results. The most important capability required of governments is that of initiating action and getting results. Strategies have to be a combination of the ethical and the acceptable. What some groups may regard as ethically correct may not work well in practice.

The great dilemma is whether to legalize or decriminalize drugs. Few countries support legalization, yet the reality is that the drugs threat is greatly increased through the control of the market by criminal barons. This, as we have argued in the last chapter, has frightening spin-off consequences. The amount of illegal money in circulation from drugs is enormous and growing. It enables drug barons, if they wish to do so, to take control of legitimate industries.

THE UNITED STATES STRATEGY

Over the years there have been many changes in U.S. drugs strategy as new attempts have been made to exercise some control over an ever increasingly intractable problem. The government has often compared illegal drug dealing to a "war," and the kinds of actions taken have frequently been of a warlike kind. Drug crops have been destroyed from the air and law enforcement agencies, which include the military as well as police and customs officials, have been brought in to the antidrug campaigns. In 1994, after being criticized by Congress for its apparent lack of success, new policy guidelines were issued. The Clinton administration decided to change the existing policy of trying to intercept drugs as they traveled from their countries of origin to the United States to a strategy of trying to prevent the processing and production of illegal drugs at their source.

This new approach had five basic elements. The first was to increase support for nations such as Bolivia, Colombia, and Peru by improving their police and military capabilities. This would be done by providing training and operational assistance together with necessary equipment. The second element was to try and diminish the power of the drug cartels by collecting the kind of intelligence that would assist foreign and domestic law enforcement agencies to arrest and prosecute their neighbors. The third element was to improve the detection and monitoring of the road vehicles, planes, and ships used to transport illegal drugs. Drug movements could then be traced from their origin in the supplying countries to their arrival in the United States. The fourth element was to give enhanced support to law enforcement agencies operating along the borders of the United States. The final element was to try and reduce the demand for illegal narcotics through education and therapy.

As part of this program the U.S. Defense Department and the Justice Department identified five capabilities that needed dramatic improvement: fast, comprehensive information systems; sensors to improve night vision; mission kill and less-than-lethal technologies to provide a range of responses from guns to persuasion; the protection of personnel on the ground; and the development of simulation technology to improve training, mission planning, and postmission evaluation.[2] This security strategy was designed to take account of the transnational threats of both terrorism and narcotics trafficking. To meet these threats the United States proposed to maintain both conventional forces and specialized combat units.

Between 1987 and 1997 the United States spent around $20 billion on international drug control problems aimed at reducing the flow of illegal drugs. But, despite these heavy costs, little impact was made on the flourishing drug industry. A 1997 review of the drug scene by the U.S. General Accounting Office reported that between 1988 and 1995 illegal drug cultivation and drug-related activities had increased throughout South America, Mexico, the Caribbean, Southeast Asia, and other countries.[3]

The home front was little different with the General Accounting Office claiming that "U.S. and Mexican interdiction efforts have had little, if any, effect on the overall flow of drugs through Mexico to the United States."[4] Mexico continued to be a major transit point for cocaine, heroin, marijuana, and methamphetamine, while efforts by the Mexican government to reduce the traffic were hampered by corruption and limited law enforcement capabilities. Although pressure from law enforcement agencies had caused the drug cartels to change many of their procedures, there had been no reduction in the drug traffic. The number of Mexican trucks crossing the U.S. border was so great that only about 6% could be checked by customs. Two critical questions now were What strategy could be tried next? and Would any strategy succeed in reducing the drug traffic?

The Federal Bureau of Investigation

The new antidrugs program, created by President Clinton, also covered internal U.S. drug strategy. The intention was to ensure a better integration of domestic and international activities so as to reduce both the demand and the supply of drugs. This would be achieved by trying to decrease the demand for illegal drugs through treatment and prevention programs and consolidating and streamlining intelligence activity. The inner working of the drug gangs, many controlled by the Mafia, would be uncovered through a network of informers, undercover agents, and wiretaps.[5] In order to do this FBI agents would carry out "sting" operations by entering the drug market themselves and buying and selling drugs. When a deal was struck, other police officers would swoop in on the purchasers and arrest them. Particular attention would be paid to reducing the demand of hard-core users, who consumed around two-thirds of the illegal drugs that entered the United States and were responsible for a great deal of criminal activity. In 1996 the cost of dealing with this group was $5.3 billion.

Community policing programs in the United States have also helped as they have in Europe. For example, Dallas has a Volunteers in Patrol program that allows residents to get VIP stickers on their cars, patrol their communities, and radio back any sign of criminal activity. Police were now identifying problems before they exploded into murder. They are also establishing relationships with children before they reached the crime-prone ages of fourteen to twenty-four.

Interpol

Another law agency that plays a major role in attempts to control the illegal drug trade is Interpol. Interpol was the creation of an Austrian chief of police, Johann Schober, who in 1923 recognized the need for a body that could fight international crime. Its headquarters is in Lyons, France, and it now has a membership of 176 countries. Not all were initially enthusiastic about the venture. The United States did not join until 1938, and Britain, proud of its own police force and unsupportive of a European initiative, did not become a member until about the same time.

Fenton Bresler describes its development in his book *Interpol*.[6] The new organization was initially called the International Police Commission. It became Interpol in 1946 when telegraphic communication required a shortened form of International Police. Interpol first addressed the illegal drug issue in 1965 when police at a Swiss conference optimistically recommended the destruction of all opium poppies, coca, and cannabis.

Today Interpol is stronger than at any time in its history and it has international drug traffic as its principal concern. Its role is not to arrest criminals but to ensure that investigation runs smoothly across national borders. It runs a large communication network and its principal function is the collection and analysis of intelligence information. In 1985 it created its first computerized index called the Criminal Information System (CIS). By 1990 this was much used by national police authorities. The Interpol Message Response Branch was dealing with ten thousand requests for information a month and 1.2 million requests a year. By 1991 it had streamlined its archives to contain the records of two hundred thousand international criminals. They had all committed major crimes such as substantial illegal drug transactions. There are now many National Central Bureaus (NCB) linked to Interpol. It has a comprehensive knowledge of local contacts and of the different police and legal structures in all member countries. In the United States the Washington NCB acts as a funnel for twenty thousand police centers, state and federal, spread throughout the United States. Since 1990 there has been an Interpol U.S./Canadian interface linking Washington D.C. to Ottawa.

In Europe its job has become both more necessary and more difficult by the opening of national borders. The removal of border controls has been good news for drug traffickers. The Schengen agreement has meant that France, Germany, Spain, Portugal, Holland, Belgium, and Luxembourg have all removed their internal border controls. By October 1997 Austria, Italy, and Greece will also have removed theirs. The United Kingdom is one of the few countries refusing to take this step. Drugs can now travel across Europe virtually unhindered.

EUROPEAN APPROACHES

All EEC (European Economic Community) member states prohibit drug trafficking and give offenders long jail sentences. In France, Greece, and Ireland large-scale drug trafficking can lead to life imprisonment. The main differences between the countries are the laws on possession and use. The Netherlands and some German states tolerate possession of small quantities of cannabis for personal use. Six member states—Finland, France, Greece, Luxembourg, Portugal, and Sweden—legislate specifically against drug abuse. Other countries achieve this by prohibiting possession. All United Nations conventions permit illegal drugs to be used for medical purposes, but there is no agreed-upon definition of what can be prescribed for addicts.[7] The Netherlands, Germany, Switzerland, and Britain have, in the past, carried out experiments that involved supplying addicts with illegal drugs so that they did not have to purchase them on the black market.

In 1997 surveys coordinated by the European Monitoring Centre for Drugs and Drug Addiction made comparative assessments of the use of cannabis. They showed that in the countries surveyed—Denmark, Finland, France, West Germany, Spain, Sweden, and the United Kingdom—

the largest numbers of users were in the United Kingdom, with Spain coming next, followed by West Germany. Sweden and Finland had the smallest number.[8]

This book has stressed the need for effective coordination and collaboration between individuals and organizations if problems are to be reduced. This is also true of governments. A lack of European cooperation in criminal matters such as illegal drugs has greatly reduced the effectiveness of law enforcement in each individual country. There is an urgent need for progress in unifying international criminal law and for the removal of obstacles to justice that arise from countries placing too much importance on their separate territorial rights. The ideal would be a set of internationally agreed-on offenses against the interests of the EEC, with uniform procedures for handling these and a common code of criminal investigation and judicial procedure. There are now moves to achieve this.

One problem slowing down reform is the different history behind the handling of criminal procedures in each country. For example, the present judicial system in England and Ireland evolved from the medieval jury trial, where each side gave its version of events to a jury of lay people that then decided whom they believed. In contrast, continental criminal procedure descended from the medieval inquisitions, where a judge investigated allegations, made a dossier of proof, and then decided whether the accused was guilty or innocent.[9] These differences in procedure, which still exist, can present difficulties when criminals are prosecuted for drug trafficking and international fraud. Very often witnesses and evidence located in other countries cannot be brought to the place of the trial.

All European Union member countries are now confronted with serious problems arising from the production, smuggling, and use of illegal drugs and their associated money laundering activities. This is posing a threat to the integrity of national financial and commercial institutions in Europe.[10] An Interpol consultant, Ramachanda Sundaralingham, has recently claimed that Europe is facing "the nightmare of the millennium" unless drastic steps are taken to control the growth of organized crime. He says "the highways of Europe are now the freeways of the drug trafficker. There are no checks or controls."[11]

The political changes in eastern Europe have also brought with them a high level of organized crime and corruption. For example, in Poland recorded crime has risen by more than 50% in the last six years. Turkish and Albanian gangs are major players on the drug scene in many European countries. A particularly sinister development is that many drug rings that have been uncovered have also been selling arms. Drug profits have been used by countries such as Bulgaria to sell arms to the Middle East. Criminal groups have infiltrated the banking industry in most of these eastern European countries, while the increasing use and access to the Internet has made preventive solutions harder to develop and implement.

It is difficult to know how many illegal drugs are circulating within the European community, although figures are available for the number of drug seizures. In 1994 Spanish customs seized more than two hundred tons of cannabis and Dutch customs had a similar level of success. Italian customs intercepted 6.6 tons of cocaine and the United Kingdom customs fifty-one tons of drugs, worth $800 million, of which 1.3 tons were amphetamines. Moving drugs around Europe is not difficult. Provided enough palms are greased there, there is a clear route across Europe for trucks traveling to Amsterdam, seen as today's drugs capital of Europe. This traffic is not one way. Drugs such as heroin and cocaine have to be "cleaned" before they can be exported, and many of the chemicals required for this operation come from the West. This means that there is a traffic from Europe to the drug-providing countries before the drugs are returned in a form ready to sell and use.

Europe is making serious efforts to reduce the drug problem through strategies that place great emphasis on cooperation between countries. The 1992 Treaty of European Union, known as the Maastricht Treaty, stated that there should be cooperation in the following areas:

- Combating drug addiction.
- Combating international fraud.
- The administration of justice.
- Preventing and combating drug trafficking, terrorism, and other serious forms of crime.

To achieve these a unionwide system for exchanging information was essential.[12] The treaty emphasized that drug addiction must be prevented by appropriate research and by providing health information and education. A drug addiction program formed part of the program and was aimed at securing an improvement in community knowledge of drugs and their consequences. There were also proposals for the study and implementation of methods for preventing drug use and for reducing the risks when drugs were used.

The Maastricht Treaty introduced an internal security structure based on the notion of a Greek temple. This contained three great "pillars." The first pillar was the European communities; the second, the common foreign and security policy, and the third and newest, cooperation in the field of justice and home affairs. The latter introduced nine new areas of common concern including drugs, judicial cooperation, customs cooperation, and police cooperation. Resources for these would include a unionwide system for exchanging information within a European Police Office (Europol).

There were to be three methods of cooperation: (1) between police forces and customs authorities both directly and through Europol, (2) closer cooperation between judicial and other authorities, and (3) greater harmonization of rules on criminal matters. The treaty was generally seen as an important step forward in increasing the level of European Union cooperation. It was agreed that European leaders needed to keep the fight against organized crime and drug trafficking at the top of the European Union agenda.

The enactment of the British Criminal Justice Act of 1994 focused more attention on the need for cross-border cooperation. Europe now recognized that all countries must work together to combat the drug problem. Although there had always been a high level of security cooperation among the member states, this had been managed by a number of ad hoc groups such as Trevi, a group created in 1975 to assist intergovernmental consultation and collaboration between senior administrative and judicial officers. In Amsterdam on June 16–17, 1997, the heads of state of the European Union (EU) agreed to a new draft treaty for Europe, which they signed on October 2. This was a step toward closer integration. One of the issues of greatest concern was the increase in organized transitional crime, including illegal drugs trafficking. It was clear that Europe's citizens wanted governments to coordinate their efforts more effectively and respond quickly and decisively to the challenges of the millennium.[13]

In November 1997 a conference was organized by the European Parliament, the European Commission, and the Luxembourg Council Presidency to tackle the increasing drugs problem across Europe. The topics discussed included synthetic drugs, street-level experience, prevention and research, and law enforcement with international comparisons being made by the World Health Organization and the United Nations. This meeting brought together EU ministers, experts, and Members of the European Parliament. It accepted that across the world forty-five million people were addicted to illegal drugs and the annual turnover from illicit street sales exceeded $500 billion. It also recognized that such large-scale trafficking and the increasing threat posed by organized crime from eastern Europe meant that EU governments must collaborate closely to fight drugs.

European Police Activity

An essential group in reducing drug-related crime in Europe is the police. Europe has 121 separate police forces in fifteen European Union states. These employ over 1.3 million police officers, and their structures and organization vary greatly. Some countries have twin structures such as state police and gendarmerie. Others, like the United Kingdom and the Netherlands have regionalized systems—the United Kingdom has forty-two independent forces. In contrast, in countries such as Denmark law enforcement is organized nationally. A recent development is that, increasingly, private security forces are being employed and beginning to outnumber the police.

Cooperation between forces was a nonissue until the 1970s and 1980s when many countries experienced terrorist attacks. Trevi, the intergovernmental liaison group, then influenced the creation of Europol, the European Police Force, which was set up to assist the joint gathering and analysis of crime-related information. Trevi had always had as its main focus the combating of terrorism and drug-related crime.[14]

Discussion concerning the need for a structure such as Europol first took place in the 1970s through the International Criminal Police Organization (ICPO) and Interpol. At an Interpol conference in 1981 the German delegation proposed setting up a European bureau and a committee was formed to discuss this. But progress was slow until Chancellor Helmut Kohl exerted pressure on the community in 1988. Drug trafficking, terrorism, and international crime were increasing, and Germany felt vulnerable because of the opening of the borders of its near neighbors in eastern Europe. He made the point again at a meeting in Edinburgh in 1991, and later that year, at a European Council meeting in Luxembourg, he proposed that a central European Criminal Investigation Office should be established and be ready to operate by 1993. This was approved by all countries with the exception of Denmark and the United Kingdom, which were opposed to the introduction of a supranational body.

Europe has a different geographic coverage from Interpol. Situated in The Hague, it operates in close association with the law enforcement agencies of EU member states and has liaison officers in participating countries. In 1993 ministerial agreement was achieved, and it was decided that attention should first focus on drugs. A European Drugs Unit, Europe/EDU, was to be established to organize and facilitate the exchange of information on narcotic drugs. The Maastricht Treaty reinforced this decision, stressing the need for police cooperation and for European-wide exchange of information.

Unresolved questions at this time were Should Europol/EDU have executive and/or operational powers so that its officials could conduct law enforcement investigations in member states, and Who would guard the guards? If a citizen wanted to sue for wrongful arrest whom would they sue and how? Unfortunately, just as agreement was being reached on these issues the United Kingdom beef crisis occurred, and Britain refused to participate in formal European Union decisions. However, despite questions and delays, Europol is generally regarded within the European community as a very successful venture.

The European community has recognized that effective strategies for combating drugs require comprehensive, accurate, and timely information. An acceptance of this fact has led to the creation of a number of Euro-databases to assist cross-border investigations. The customs network that concentrates on drug smuggling and revenue evasion is seen as the most successful of these.

The customs authorities have, for some time, also been organizing cooperative ventures. In 1967 a Mutual Assistance Group (MAG) was set up to facilitate relationships between different customs administrations. An important objective of this was to enable operational experts concerned with drugs to meet on a regular basis. In 1994, after the Treaty on European Union came into force, MAG became the Customs Cooperation Working Party. Those present at the Maastricht meeting had agreed that society needed better protection against drugs and crime, and it was decided to set up a European Monitoring Centre for Drugs and Drug Addiction. This center was to have as its principal objective combating drug trafficking, reducing the demand for drugs and acting against producer and transit third countries. It wanted controls strengthened at external frontiers and drug "tourism" reduced. Drug tourism is when dealers travel around the world looking for the lowest prices.[15] There are now some moves toward a single customs service organization with a cross-national structure and an ability to move across borders unimpeded. This seems a logical long-term goal for the future.

WHAT IS HAPPENING IN THE UNITED KINGDOM?

Over the years the United Kingdom has passed a great deal of legislation regulating the use of drugs. In 1920 there was a Dangerous Drugs Act that prohibited the importation of cocaine, heroin, and morphine. Another act was passed in 1925 that regulated the use of cannabis and a third act in 1964 that made it an offense to use public premises for smoking cannabis. Further acts in 1964 and 1965 extended controls to amphetamines and LSD. The Misuse of Drugs Act in 1971 consolidated this early legislation and introduced controls for the importation, export, possession, use, and manufacture of controlled drugs. Subsequent legislation introduced further controls and increased penalties for drug offenses. The Criminal Justice (International Cooperation) Act of 1990 was part of an international effort to reduce drug offenses worldwide. This act covers substances that can be used to produce illegal drugs, even though they have legitimate commercial purposes. In 1994 a new Drug Trafficking Act consolidated all the English Law on drug trafficking.[16]

There can be approaches other than legislation to control drug trafficking. Tony White, until 1996 head of the drugs branch of the National Criminal Intelligence Service, told a British national newspaper that trafficking could be stopped "virtually altogether" by creating an antiterrorist-style ring of steel. But, he pointed out, instead, people chose to support free-trade zones and few customs controls. This meant that the public had also chosen to accept what it considered to be "tolerable" levels of drug abuse. He said "it is the public that will determine what level of menace from drugs they are prepared to tolerate and what they are prepared to contribute or surrender in order to prevent the situation exceeding that level of toleration."

The British government's position as set out in the 1995 White Paper "Tackling Drugs Together: A Strategy for England 1995–98" was clear. The White Paper said:

> The Government continues to reject legislation or "decriminalization" because of the risks of wider use and the need to send a strong anti-drugs signal to young people in particular.... the Government considers a case for change has not been made. It therefore remains strongly opposed to the legislation of cannabis or any other drug controlled under the Misuse of Drugs Act 1971.

Its preferred strategy was set out in the following statement of purpose:

> To take effective action by vigorous law enforcement, accessible treatment and a new emphasis on education and prevention with the objective of:
>
> - Increasing the safety of communities from drug related crime
> - reducing the acceptability and availability of drugs to young people, and
> - reducing the health risks and other damage related to drug misuse.[17]

This set of worthy objectives was somewhat put in the shade by a 1996 report from the European Monitoring Centre for Drugs and Drug Addiction, which estimated that the illegal drug industry is worth £140 billion to £300 billion worldwide, while a 1996 Home Office report maintained that the London drug market alone was worth £600 million. The British government held on to its antidrugs position and reconfirmed this in a 1998 White Paper, "Tackling Drugs to Build a Better Britain."

THE ROLE OF THE BRITISH POLICE

The 1995 government report "Tackling Drugs Together" maintained that the safety of communities from drug-related crime would always be the responsibility of the police. It stressed the need for effective investigation and prosecution arrangements to deter traffickers and dealers, and emphasized the important role of the customs service in preventing illegal drugs from entering the country. In Britain, more problem drug users pass through the hands of the police and the courts than through any other agency dealing with drug misuse. Research has found that drug markets are highly sensitive to police intervention. Police surveillance, assisted by informal surveillance in which bartenders and others who have contact with the offenders try to discourage use, enables a degree of drug containment. Closed-circuit video systems are also of value. Until recently, criminal gangs using violence were relatively rare. In the 1990s this situation changed, with many violent gangs moving into the profitable drug industry.

Like the United States, Britain sees the need to develop strategies to combat the drug menace. Many will be operationalized by the police who must ensure that they have the capabilities to enforce these. This is not simple and straightforward. For example, the interpretation of strategies can differ between one police force and another. The law states that using drugs is a criminal offense and that all offenders should be prosecuted. Yet, this is impossible to implement as the courts would soon be completely clogged with young people on drug-use charges. Because of this difficulty some police forces have made a decision to concentrate their attention on drug dealers. This too presents problems as many are young people selling drugs to fund their own habit. As in the United States, the groups that need controlling are the large drug entrepreneurs who run the purchasing and selling empires. Unfortunately, these are the hardest to catch and prosecute.

While the police are responsible for enforcing the law on drugs within the United Kingdom, it is the task of customs to ensure that as few drugs as possible enter the country. Customs officials need a variety of competencies and capabilities, many of which they share with the police. These include the capability to support very difficult and complex investigations, some of which will involve penetrating criminal groups by appearing to join them, a dangerous procedure for the individuals involved. Many of these endeavors end in violent confrontations in which people can get seriously hurt. This is especially true when customs officers are apprehending boats trying to land drugs in isolated parts of the coast. Trafficking, or the physical movement of drugs, tends to fall into three categories—containers, couriers, and drugs imported by air and sea. Of these, containers are particularly difficult for customs to handle. They have to be unloaded, inspected, and then repacked.

When dealers are caught, an additional difficulty encountered is the reluctance of witnesses to give evidence because they fear physical retribution. Some police forces are now developing witness-protection programs to ease this problem.[18]

Many of these problems are being addressed by the British National Criminal Intelligence Service (NCIS), which provides an excellent example of effective coordination and cooperation. The NCIS is a joint venture involving the police, the customs, and other enforcement agencies. Its role is to act as an intelligence agency that disseminates information on criminal activity regionally, nationally, and internationally. Its mission is "to assist law enforcement and other agencies by processing intelligence, giving direction and providing services and strategic analysis to combat serious criminal activity. The NCIS strategic objectives are:

- Gathering, collating, developing, analyzing, and supplying relevant intelligence.
- Maintaining relevant intelligence databases.
- Liaising and consulting with other agencies in the United Kingdom and overseas.

The achievement of these will be assisted by:

- Setting standards for users in the process of handling intelligence.
- Establishing nationally agreed upon systems and practices to ensure greater integration and effectiveness of the intelligence services.
- Coordinating and monitoring the effectiveness of criminal intelligence to avoid duplication of effort by law enforcement agencies.

This requires:

- Utilizing the channels of communication between foreign countries to take advantage of the intelligence opportunities.
- Being the lead agency in Britain for Interpol and Europol.
- Processing, assessing, and facilitating applications under the Interception of Communications Act 1985 (phone tapping).
- Providing strategic analysis to Her Majesty's government, law enforcement, and other relevant agencies, so that policy and resource allocations can be matched to changing trends and patterns.
- Providing training and advice.

Two committees provide advice to the director-general of NCIS. The first is a Standing Committee on Resources and is made up of representatives from police authorities, the Home Office, Her Majesty's Customs and Excise, and Her Majesty's Inspectorate. The second is the ACPO (Association of Chief Police Officers) User Group and consists of senior police and customs officers. Its task is to develop operational policy.[19]

A NEW STRATEGY

In May 1997 the British government changed from conservative to labor and Jack Straw became home secretary. He immediately emphasized the growing seriousness of the drug problem, pointing out that there appeared to be a powerful link between addiction and crime with one in five of all arrested heroin users. This led him to the conclusion that, in the United Kingdom, there must be 360,000 people in this group and that £1 billion of property was stolen annually to feed drug habits. One of his first moves was to advertise for an antidrugs coordinator to implement a strategy against drugs throughout the United Kingdom. He declared a war against drug addiction and stated that he would introduce strict measures to control drugs in his proposed new Crime and Disorder Bill. Straw proposed to require convicted users of heroin and cocaine to have treatment as part of their probation period. Random tests would be carried out twice a month and if the offender was found to still be using drugs, he or she would face a mandatory three months of drug treatment. Continued drug use and criminal behavior would lead to a prison sentence. This strategy would replace the policy of the previous home secretary, who believed that prison should be the first option.[20]

Keith Hellawell, ex-chief constable of West Yorkshire and the new anti-drugs coordinator, responded very favorably to this initiative. He pointed out that a similar approach had already been used in West Yorkshire through a scheme known as "caution plus." With this approach, offenders were cautioned rather than charged and not processed through the courts if they agreed to attend drug-treatment programs. He welcomed the new judiciary powers in the proposed new bill.

Toward the end of 1997 the British newspaper *Independent* launched a campaign to decriminalize the use of cannabis and appealed to its readers to support this. The suggestion was that the use of cannabis should be permitted, and criminal penalties should be removed. As evidence of an attitude change, the newspaper reported a survey carried out by the London bureau of the Japanese newspaper *Hokkaido Shimbun*. It had sent a short questionnaire to all British members of Parliament seeking their views. Just over a third from all parties voted in favor of decriminalization. There was also a parallel campaign to permit the medical use of cannabis for the relief of pain. In 1998 the new British government produced its report "Tackling Drugs to Build a Better Britain." The key message of this White Paper was the need for collaboration, and that there must be partnerships between different groups to address the drug problem. These would bring together people from the statutory, voluntary, and private sectors to work closely with local drug teams. At the same time there would be strong links with other European countries to further international strategies for addressing the drug problem.

LESSONS TO BE LEARNED

In chapter 6 we stressed the importance of understanding the "total picture" when faced with a new problem. This chapter has discussed the importance of developing an effective strategy as the next step of the problem-solving process. As problem solvers we are now aware of the size of the drug problem and that its consequences extend over a major part of the world, including the United States and Europe. We appreciate how complex the problem is and the need for both a logical overall strategy and well-thought-out operational strategies to address the many different aspects. Tackling the drug barons will require both political strategies and strategies related to aggressive action. Strategies will also be required to enable affected countries to coordinate and implement measures to prevent, reduce, and control the illegal drug situation. The governments and law enforcement agencies of the different countries will need to cooperate here.

It is clear that strategic planning is an important part of complex problem solving. The American and European governments and their law enforcement agencies are all now paying great attention to assessing carefully the problem situation and agreeing to antidrugs programs that they hope will produce desired results. These decisions are likely to be strongly influenced by national politics and values.

The message for those of us more concerned with local than national problems is that thinking strategically will help clarify our mission and objectives in relation to what we are trying to achieve. Complex problems require clear, structured thinking before they can be addressed. Although most problems can be approached from a number of different angles, coherent strategies that fit logically together and provide operational guidance are essential. In volatile situations, like drugs, where criminal behavior is both sophisticated and flexible, these strategies may have to be continually reviewed and adjusted. But strategic thinking should never be abandoned. Muddling through is not an option. However, it must be recognized that when many different groups are involved in the development of a strategy, the process will not be an easy one and partnerships based on cooperative relationships are an essential requirement.

It is important to point out that some problems may prove insoluble. Drugs could be one of these. Despite strategic thinking and well-thought-out counter-operations the war against the drug barons is being lost rather than won. The really critical question here, which most governments are reluctant to address, is if the drug barons cannot be eliminated using aggressive military tactics, can the problem be solved through normal commercial competition? In other words, Should drugs be legalized? Those in favor of this approach suggest that prices would fall, crime would be reduced, major police, customs, and military costs would be removed, and a new source of government revenue would be created through the taxation of drugs. They argue that the reduction in profits would be so great that drugs would cease to be of interest to criminals, and they would move their activities into other areas. This is a step too far for most Western governments who foresee such a strategy leading to a major increase in drug use and to consequences that are unknown. They maintain that any country offering low-cost drugs legally would attract drug users from all over the world. It would become a drug-users paradise.

Another interesting question is what happens if the present situation continues with the drug barons remaining a powerful force and most drugs continuing to be illegal. The answer is we don't know, although it is a challenge to make some predictions. One possible scenario is that the drug barons will continue to be powerful and will acquire an increasing number of legitimate business interests by taking over established commercial activities. These will be well managed but a lack of conventional business ethics will cause business morality and behavior to dramatically change. A second scenario is that the children of drug barons, as in the film *The Godfather*, will not wish to follow their parents into illegal activities; they will prefer to become respectable and responsible leaders of industry. The source of their wealth will be forgotten. A third scenario is that the combined efforts of governments using military, police, and customs resources will eventually defeat the drug barons and drug usage will reduce in amount. This would be the most desirable scenario. It seems also to be the one most unlikely to happen.

CHAPTER **8**

Operational Guidelines for Problem Solving

Previous chapters have stressed the importance of knowing the total picture and of commencing problem solving with some well-thought-out overall strategy. It is now time to consider how the individual facets of a complex problem can be addressed operationally. Most complex problems are too large and challenging to be addressed as a whole. They need to be broken into subproblems. This chapter will provide some guidance on how to proceed at this level before we examine specific problems in Chapter 9.

Problem solving can always be assisted by systematic thinking. This provides a degree of mental order and control and helps ensure that knowledge is effectively used and important aspects of the problem are not forgotten. In this book we have recommended a simple model as an analytical aid. The model requires problem-solving behavior to be analyzed in terms of competencies, capabilities, and coordination. The rational here is that effective problem solving requires individuals and groups with appropriate knowledge competence, organizations with the capabilities to support, deploy, and enhance this knowledge, and structures that enable excellent coordination to take place among groups that are contributing to the problem-solving process.

Once the totality of the problem is understood and an appropriate overall strategy agreed upon, problem-solving groups are encouraged to start a project with a mission statement. This should provide a clear definition of the task they are about to undertake as well as a set of priority objectives. Next there should be a number of carefully thought-out plans aimed at achieving these objectives. The operational details of planning can be assisted by using Stafford Beer's viable system model. He states that the management task associated with problem solving can be described as a hierarchy of activities. These are:

1. Identifying the basic, often routine, tasks that have to be carried out in addressing the problem.
2. Thinking through and documenting the likely difficulties that may occur and inhibit the successful completion of these tasks.
3. Identifying the critical success factors that provide guidance on what aspects of the problem should be given priority or maximum attention.
4. Understanding the nature of the information that needs to be collected and disseminated as the problem-solving process progresses.
5. Creating methods of evaluation—the monitoring checks and measures that can provide guidance on whether progress is being made and whether goals are being achieved.
6. Finally, there will be a need for a constant review of strategy to ensure that results are in fact being achieved.[1]

A continuing, but extremely important task, will be restating and clarifying the strategy, mission, and goals of the project as it progresses and ensuring that all those involved continue to agree with these. In the next chapter we will examine the problems of how to change the behavior of the different groups involved with, or vulnerable to, illegal drugs.

PROVIDING AND ACQUIRING INFORMATION

Acceptable and relevant judgments and decisions about analysis and action cannot be made unless everyone concerned with, or affected by, the problem has a knowledge of what the problem is and its possible effects. Returning to our example of the drugs problem, young people need this knowledge so they can understand that some of the substances they are offered may not be harmless and can have serious long-term consequences. Parents need this knowledge so they are aware of the pressures, attractions, and dangers of the situations in which their children spend their leisure time. Club owners and staff need this knowledge so they appreciate that drug use by their clientele may present owners and clients with serious legal and medical problems. Educational establishments, both schools and universities, need this information so they can warn their students of possible risks both within and outside the educational environment. Controlling and therapeutic groups such as police, customs, welfare, and medical agencies all need this information, while the community in general must be made aware of the risks many young people are facing in today's society.

At present considerable efforts are being made to provide this knowledge, although it is still patchy. Parents are not always well informed but efforts are being made to remedy this. For example, a British pharmacist, the Boots Drug Company, has recently been providing clear, comprehensive, and very readable leaflets on illegal drugs in its stores. Most schools and universities have drug awareness programs that are targeted at new students. Unfortunately, there are knowledge gaps that can only be filled by research. For example, we do not know the long-term effects of certain drugs such as Ecstasy. Is this a relatively harmless drug or will it have adverse long-term consequences? Recent research suggests the latter is the case.

Perhaps the biggest communication gap is that within the general public. In the United Kingdom the press has carried very little discussion of the drug problem and acceptable strategies for dealing with it, although this is now changing. The new labor government's declared intention of making an impact on the drug scene and the campaign in the *Independent* for the decriminalization of cannabis has stimulated some recent debate. Most European governments, including that of Britain, while declaring forcibly that they will never legalize drugs, appear to have few realistic policies for removing the drug barons and their enormous profits. The British government is proposing to put more resources into the destruction of the plants that form the basis of drugs and into preventing further crops, but this seems a mammoth task. It first requires the cooperation of other governments, and some of these are financially linked to the drug trade. Second, drug production is moving around the world to countries that are struggling economically. These now include many of the old eastern European countries together with impoverished countries such as Albania and Afghanistan.

Removing addictive drugs totally from everyday life can be viewed as virtually impossible in the present world environment. Drugs are not going to go away, and it is probable that we do not wish them to, given their therapeutic and other possible, if as yet undiscovered, beneficial properties. We then have to ask What aspects of the drug scene are so damaging to human beings that we urgently want to eliminate them or reduce their effects? The answer to this question is likely to depend on our age, our interests, and our vision of what is good and bad for the communities in which we live. It brings us immediately to the first step in any problem-solving approach, which is clarifying our strategy, mission, and goals by deciding both what we would, ideally, like to achieve and what is a realistic expectation of what can be achieved. With a problem as complex as drugs this leads us to another important question, Is there any broad consensus of opinion on what aspect of the problem should be addressed first, either because it is of considerable importance or because it is most likely to produce fast results?

Many people who accept that drugs are here to stay might agree that if there is a drug market it should not be controlled by criminals. Therefore, the first task is to get rid of the criminals and substitute normal market relations. Others, who are bitterly opposed to drugs, might disagree and argue that the primary objective is to get rid of the drugs altogether. There must be no compromise. In a democracy, the answer to the need to clarify mission and goals therefore requires public debate so that a consensus view can be sought. This debate will not be easy to manage as different interest groups will have different views. The young will not want their social scene removed or damaged, and, at present, this seems to contain a volatile mix of music, energetic enjoyment, and drugs such as Ecstasy. Parents will take a different view and want their children protected from substances that can be life threatening and whose long-term effects are not known. Community residents will want the crime that results from the need for money to buy drugs reduced or eliminated. They will put pressure on the police and government for policies and legislation to enable this to happen. This then raises the question of whether community policies should be based on punishment or therapy.

These points, and only a few are made here, illustrate the complexity of major problems such as illegal drugs. Effective action depends on good decision making and good decisions should reflect community needs. But, while the community will influence decisions on what is to be done, they should not necessarily make these. Communities affected by crime are unlikely to be detached about it and may favor highly oppressive punitive measures. Governments or mediators will now need to intervene and propose policies that are likely to prove of benefit to the population as a whole, including both the victims and the perpetrators of acts that are viewed as antisocial and against the public interest.

Once agreement on where the problem-solving effort should be directed has been reached, a decision will have to be made on whether to focus on one aspect of the problem initially or to operate on a broad front from the beginning. If resources are scarce there are likely to be competing claims. Parents may want the research to concentrate on how their children can best be protected from dangerous drugs, residential communities may want strategies that reduce drug-related crime, welfare groups may want an emphasis on therapeutic programs, governments may require strategies that do not cost a great deal and produce fast and permanent results.

Strategies chosen will also be greatly influenced by the philosophy and values of governments and other powerful groups. Until now reducing the problem of illegal drugs has been seen by many as a war. This approach was widely approved of until it was realized that holding this view meant that the large percentage of young people taking drugs such as Ecstasy were being classed as criminals and as part of the enemy. Parents, teachers, and youth leaders were reluctant to have their children marginalized in this way.

CREATING PROBLEM-SOLVING STRUCTURES

One of the most important means for achieving some success in reducing the drug problem is the cooperation of interested parties. This requires different groups to be willing to work together in a coordinated way to solve a particular aspect of the drug problem. The individuals that make up these groups will require relevant competencies, and, once established, each group will require its own capabilities so that competencies can be effectively used. These capabilities will include the ability to establish relationships with other interested groups, the ability to generate and sustain a set of shared objectives both within the group and with other groups, the ability to agree on and implement appropriate action, the ability to monitor and evaluate the success or failure of what is being achieved, and the ability to pass on to others the lessons that are being learned as the project progresses.

All groups must create the right structures and relationships if they are to work effectively. This is particularly true of groups that are working in partnership with other groups to solve a major problem such as drug misuse. Cooperation needs to start at the top. A common approach is for each interest group to send one or more representatives to a high-level committee responsible for formulating an overall problem-solving strategy. Today, this is sometimes called a "vision group." Ideally its members should be equal in status and influence. Each representative should have the knowledge, motivation, and competence to make a major contribution to addressing one or more aspects of the drug problem. The British government has recently created such a committee to lead the drug program.

A high-level group of this kind is usually responsible for the difficult task of deciding how its goals can best be achieved, and this aspect of strategic planning will normally have three major objectives: the clarification and interpretation of goals, deciding what can realistically be achieved, and producing guidelines for action. It must also take account of the future and of future needs. This means it must try to foresee the consequences of its plans. Most important, as planning of this kind should serve human purposes, ideally, these purposes should be democratic.[2]

It is not always easy for a group consisting of representatives from different bodies to arrive at an agreement on the task they wish to carry out. Although there will be a common agenda this agenda may be interpreted in different ways and produce different, although related, kinds of goals. Factors facilitating or hindering agreement will be, firstly, the aspirations of each individual member of the group and how these affect the definition of the task, secondly, their personal values, and, thirdly, the values and interests of the group they represent. Even when an agreement on goals and objectives is reached there may still be difficulties in deciding how these can best be achieved. How can strategy be turned into effective action?

The vision group, once it has decided on its operational strategy, will need to create other coalitions to translate its objectives into action. These groups should be seen as partnerships taking responsibility for particular aspects of the project. They may be looking after community needs or focusing on the problems of particular groups such as young people or drug addicts.

Groups formed from coalitions of different interests, even when addressing a common problem, will tend to have multiple goals and will have to rely on negotiation and compromise to reach agreement. They will also need to be able to cope with uncertainty as the problem they are confronting changes its nature over time or public opinion and pressure strengthens or weakens. When uncertainty is high experts and troubleshooters will become more powerful as clearer knowledge is sought and conflicts have to be resolved.

As the project progresses relationships within the group may change and the amount of agreement on objectives and action may vary over time. Political interests and pressures will have an important influence, and there will be a continual need for a review of goals and policies. There may also be a need to cope with rival power groups. For example, a group focused on reducing drug use while maintaining that the use of drugs should be a criminal offense may have to cope with influential voices claiming that certain drugs should be legalized.

Policy-making groups will have to be effective at boundary management. They will not only have to maintain the enthusiasm and dedication of their own members, they will also have to establish and maintain good relationships with other groups who can provide support or assistance. If they are working in the public domain, as drug control initiatives must be, they will have to keep the general public informed of what they are doing, why they are pursuing certain policies and not others, and how their activities are progressing. Maintaining public support is vital to their continuing existence. All of these activities require resources, many of them financial.

Groups of this kind will have a practical and political purpose but they will also have an ethical purpose. Kenneth Schneider suggests that most groups dealing with major problems create their own moral atmosphere.[3] Some groups have primarily moral purposes and goals, for example, those associated with the banning of land mines. Some behave as moral agents, the Red Cross being an example here. Some have moral structures. A member of the Salvation Army will be required to support its values and objectives. And some have a moral tone, which is a product of their purposes, behavior, and structures. Environmental protection groups come into this category.

Ethical goals of any kind require certain kinds of attitudes and behavior. Members of the group must believe that what they are trying to achieve is ethically correct in terms of community goals and needs. They must also be able to communicate this ethical position to other groups who may be responsible for particular tasks and to the local and national community. All of these groups, including the top policy group, will require a facilitator or leader who can communicate and protect the ethical underpinning of the task, ensure that the nature of the total problem is not forgotten, and keep the other partner groups aware of what each group is doing.

LEADERSHIP

Democratically organized problem-solving groups of this kind, although they are coalitions of equals, can still greatly benefit from effective leadership. The role of the leader will be to facilitate effective group working. This will involve keeping the group members interested and motivated in achieving their task, helping them resolve conflicts, and ensuring that important aspects of the problem they are addressing are not forgotten. The democratic leader will help the group arrive at a decision on future action but will not make the decision for the group or press a particular approach on them.

The leader will require flexibility and tact. All groups are different and those made of individuals from different backgrounds may take time to learn each other's perspectives and objectives. There are likely to be many different mixes of interests when aspects of the drug problem are being addressed. Local authority representatives will sit side by side with community residents, with the police, and with welfare organizations. These groups may have to be helped to communicate easily and effectively with each other. New groups often go through four psychological stages before they become mature problem solvers. At the start there may be uncertainty and anxiety as each group wonders if they are going to be able to work with the others. Once this is overcome morale can be high as addressing the problem gets underway, but may slump as the complexity and difficulty of the problem becomes increasingly apparent. This can later improve as decisions are taken to initially focus on those aspects of the problem where the group believes progress can be made. Each of these stages can be helped by a leader who is a good facilitator.

An effective leader will ensure that the group has access to any external information it requires and will ensure that its discussions and decisions are communicated to other groups working on the drug problem and to the community in general. The leader should also help the group to achieve the following:

- Ensure that all relevant issues are raised and discussed.
- Arrive at an agreed upon definition of the aspect of the problem they wish to tackle.

- Understand what is involved in focusing on this issue.
- Agree on short- and long-term objectives.
- Accept disagreement and tolerate conflict.
- Value reasoned debate on all relevant issues.
- Strive for equality of contribution.
- Resist external pressures to conform to particular prejudices or beliefs.

Leaders who are also facilitators require good social skills. They must get along well with people, have easy and pleasant social manners, be able to run a meeting, and work to ensure that relationships within the group stay friendly and constructive. Acting as a facilitator is not easy. It requires patience, control, enthusiasm, and the ability to create and maintain positive attitudes in the problem-solving group. The most difficult task is likely to be helping to resolve conflicts of ideas and perceptions in a group representing different interests. These will have to be reconciled if a consensus on subsequent action is to be agreed upon. Most group processes involve negotiation. Conflicts of interests and ideas need to be recognized, brought out into the open, and discussed. A solution is then arrived at that meets the approval of all the members.

A good leader will ensure that the group works as a team and will help the members to acquire more knowledge about the problem they are addressing. He or she will also assist the group to use its resources efficiently and to address effectively the issues it regards as most important. Information on progress will also need to be disseminated regularly to other interested groups and to the public at large. A choice may have to be made between focusing on short- or long-term objectives or trying to achieve both at the same time. Most important will be the need to keep up to date with changes in how problems are perceived. Attitudes toward drugs seem to swing violently from rejection to tolerance to expediency. Current attitudes will affect both the kinds of problem-solving strategies that are selected and how information is communicated to external groups.

SOME EXAMPLES

An excellent example of how good coordination between different groups can lead to a successful conclusion for a section of the community is the example of Kings Cross in London. Kings Cross, best known for its handsome railway station and the distinguished buildings associated with this, had for many years been a haven and hunting ground for large numbers of drug dealers and prostitutes. By 1992 it had effectively become a no-go area for the people who lived there. Many in the area were afraid to venture out of their houses at night. Even the daytime was threatening as both drug dealing and prostitution were twenty-four-hour activities.

At last the residents had had enough. They decided to take action and they put tremendous pressure on the two local councils, Camden and Islington, which were responsible for the area, to get together, work out a joint strategy, allocate a budget, and do something to reduce the drug problem. The council's first step was to relandscape the area and remove the trees that had provided convenient hiding places for drug dealing. Bus shelters had also been popular places for dealing and these, like the trees, were also removed. Next the Metropolitan police and the London Transport police tackled the drug dealers, and in 1993 there were over one hundred arrests made. This police activity removed existing dealers, and care was taken not to allow any new ones to move into the area. Finally, the residents of blocks of flats adjoining the area, often used by dealers for meeting clients, were given a greater sense of security. Flats were protected by janitors, security cameras, and other measures for restricting entrance. Only residents could now have access and undesirables were kept away.

Effectively, in Kings Cross, through carefully thought-out strategy and community cooperation, drug dealing was designed out. Partnership between residents, the local authorities, and the police, together with a holistic approach to a large and difficult problem, had achieved the desired result. Once the drug dealers had left, the local community found that a similar cooperative approach removed the prostitutes. The notorious Kings Cross area is now a safer and more pleasant place to live and work. A result of this successful project was the establishment, in Britain, of a Central Drugs Coordination Unit in 1993. Its main task was to devise an effective basis for the coordination of local action on the drugs problem.

It is important to point out that cooperation of this kind, while producing excellent results for the local population, can result in adverse consequences for others. The problem group may not be disbanded but rather stay in place and transfer its activities to another area. Zurich provides an excellent example of this. Switzerland, with forty thousand hard-core addicts, has one of the highest per capita rates of drug addiction and HIV in Europe. The city of Zurich contains 25% of the entire Swiss drug problem.[4] The Swiss have taken a liberal approach to drugs with a dual track policy. There are tough police measures against dealers but a "harm reduction" approach toward users. In Zurich a great deal of drug dealing and using activity took place in a large park, known locally as Plazpitz or Needle Park. The local authority accepted this situation and allowed social service organizations to distribute sterile needles and provide drug counseling. Heroin addicts were given regular allocations of the drug so that they did not have to commit crimes to obtain it. The police were discouraged from entering the park.

Eventually protests from local residents forced the police to close the park. Thousands of addicts now moved to an unused railway station where an open air drug market soon became established attracting 1,500 users a day. The policy of welfare without police intervention continued. Again community protests caused the railway station to be closed and drug activity then moved underground. The city authorities now began to review their liberal policy. They found that despite their counseling and health activities, the number of addicts was rising, drug-related crime had increased, and the number of addicts with HIV infection was over 50%. The Swiss government was now pressured by its citizens to carry out a referendum on drugs and drug policy. Many people were unsure that a welfare-oriented strategy had good results or any positive results at all. Both drug use and the associated crime had increased. But, despite these anxieties, the result of the referendum was confirmation that the welfare approach, with its daily donations of free heroin, should continue. Majority public opinion was that the reduction in crime, because addicts no longer had to steal to ensure their drug supplies, made this the better strategy. Drug use in public places would continue to be tolerated, and the police were asked to concentrate their activities on destroying the dealer network. This consisted principally of foreign nationals.

It must be pointed out here that Switzerland, and Zurich in particular, is very vulnerable to the drugs trade. Zurich is an ideal distribution point for traffickers who are moving drugs to other parts of Europe. It has many refugees and asylum-seekers who are in the country illegally and see drugs as a way of earning a living, and Swiss banking confidentiality makes it an ideal place for money laundering. It seems that despite the severe social and political problems that result, many of the citizens of Europe still favor a liberal policy.

The message here is that community initiatives to control drugs should be encouraged and supported financially, but it is very important to be aware of the likely consequences. In London care must be taken that drug dealing and using are not just exported from one area to another so that they become someone else's problem. In Zurich it is a question of which is the lesser of two evils—a liberal policy that reduces crime but may increase drug use, or a tough policy that imposes legal penalties but is likely to increase crime.

LESSONS TO BE LEARNED

This chapter has stressed the importance to effective problem solving of creating group structures with members that can work effectively together and of finding leaders or facilitators these groups will value and respect. These leaders should, ideally, have an ethical position and a vision they can share with the group together with a clear sense of purpose. They also need social and political skills that can help their groups think systematically and realistically about the problems they are addressing and follow this with appropriate action that contributes toward the containment or solution of the targeted problem. They must be able to help the group to work through its conflicts and disagreements and arrive at a degree of consensus. And they must do this without dominating the group or imposing their own opinions. This is not an easy task and such leaders are hard to find. Action to solve problems in difficult and complex areas is best taken in small steps with careful testing of each new initiative. Unless a major crisis is looming that threatens a breakdown of society, the "big bang" approach should be avoided.

CHAPTER 9

Different Groups with Different Problems

One of the difficulties of complex problems is that a variety of sub-problems will have to be addressed, many dealing with different issues and different groups of people. All will require their own operational strategies. This chapter discusses some of the challenges presented by groups affected by drugs.

THE USERS

Younger School Children

The problem here is to prevent children from viewing drugs as an attractive part of growing older and becoming "cool." This is the group that has to be persuaded and helped to say no to drugs. Young people have to be assisted to make responsible choices though a program of drug education that attracts their attention, fits in with their lifestyles, and is seen as in tune with their interests. Programs of this kind can most usefully take place in schools and must be tailored to the interests of different age groups.[1] Such a program has to start early, in primary school, before the opportunity of using drugs is presented to them by older children.

Effective problem solving is always helped by good research, and a considerable amount of research has been carried out in Europe to establish how children can best be positively influenced to resist drugs. To test the effectiveness of different approaches, a Dutch program has provided different kinds of drug education to children in four sections of the city of Rotterdam. One program took a shock–horror approach with the intention of frightening children away from drugs. A second provided children with relevant information but did not try actively to influence them. A third focused on the issues that children themselves thought were important. A fourth was the control group and received no information at all. None of these programs prevented children from taking drugs if they wished to do so, or reduced the numbers already taking them, but it was found that the shock–horror approach was the least effective. The most effective was the approach that addressed the issues the children themselves thought to be important.[2]

This leads us to the question of what capabilities are required by the organizations that provide drug information. Schools need skilled communicators who can gain children's attention and interest and persuade them to consider carefully the pros and cons of what is offered to them in the outside world. Teachers may not have high credibility here; a younger age group may have a more powerful effect. Some schools have invited ex-drug addicts to give talks on their experiences and this certainly frightens many listeners. It may, however, as Dutch research has shown, make drug taking more, rather than less, attractive. Also, most children, when first experimenting, will restrict themselves to cannabis and dance drugs such as Ecstasy and have little contact with the harder drugs.

Some drug abuse resistance programs aim at giving children a knowledge of drugs and their consequences and, at the same time, teaching them resistance techniques so that when offered drugs they have the skills, confidence, and degree of assertiveness to say no. Weekly classes for children in their last year at primary school are provided by the British police over a period of seventeen weeks. This group is targeted because they are most likely to come into contact with drugs when they move up into secondary school. The aim is to motivate and support schools in their efforts to advise young people on the dangers of drugs.

Parents are difficult to contact without some major government-sponsored communication program. Efforts to provide information such as leaflets provided by Boots the Chemist, a British retail pharmacy, are well worthwhile but often of short duration. Television could be a help but it seems to avoid the drug problem except as a vehicle for programs on beating crime. It is interesting that the Australian teenage soap, *Neighbours*, which appears twice a day on British television and addresses most social problems affecting young people in its fictional episodes, has not yet raised the issue of drugs. One British education authority, assisted by the police, has introduced a project called "Parents as Educators." The aim of this program is to bring the parents into the classroom to learn about drugs so they can give accurate advice to their children. This, in turn, provides the parents with the very valuable competence of having accurate knowledge. A much more difficult problem is how to help young children whose parents themselves are drug users.

The message here is that it is equally as important to prevent problems from occurring as to address them when they have occurred. The old adage "prevention is better than cure" still has a great deal of truth. A second message is that prevention, like cure, requires effective coordination between interested groups who must work together closely. A third message is that drug education must be relevant to the targeted group and offer something that is attractive to it. It has to become fashionable. Unfortunately, to make it so is never likely to be an easy task because the role models of the younger generation are unlikely to be parents or police. They are much more likely to be their older brothers or sisters, pop stars, or music groups.

Teenagers and Older Groups

This group presents particular difficulties that may prove impossible to overcome. Research on problem solving has demonstrated that the most successful approach is for those who experience or cause the problems to contribute to their solution. Young people who take recreational drugs have little incentive to do so. They are happy with the present situation. Because of the powerful association of drugs with popular music, efforts to influence the late teen and early twenties age group to avoid or abandon drugs have so far had very little success. Young people explain that participation in today's dance scene is a wonderful experience. The combination of people, music, and drugs such as Ecstasy is a powerful, heady mix that creates friendship, enjoyment, and exhilaration. All of this fills the vacuum of dull, ordinary lives with few or no job prospects for many. These attitudes are reinforced by statements from popular bands and their leaders that it is "cool" to use drugs and that their use has no disadvantages.

Matthew Collin, in his book *Altered States*, shows clearly the major influence of music upon the drugs scene.[3] He points out that when a powerful beat and a mind expanding drug are brought together everything becomes interlinked and each stimulus enhances the other. The feeling of companionship and unity are intensified by the reactions of parents and other adults. These are generally negative and these negative reactions are reinforced by the legal requirement for young drug users to be prosecuted. Young people then have the added pleasure of thumbing their noses at authority.

Given this situation we have to ask what problems are seen as requiring action and by whom. Should we, the older adult community, accept this situation and let music with drugs take its own route to wherever it is going? Should we interfere and try to change it or should we try to persuade young people to do something about it themselves? We also have to be pragmatic and answer the question What is possible? There is no point in wasting energy and resources on a situation that cannot be influenced. And we need to examine carefully and correctly the likely consequences of any strategy we choose. Sometimes unanticipated consequences can be worse than the original situation. We also have to be clear about who the "we" is here. Is it adults generally, parents, teachers, the police, or just a group of elderly busy bodies?

A number of different groups have an interest in solving particular problems. Parents, if they cannot stop their older children from taking drugs, want to be sure that the cannabis or Ecstasy they use is pure and not contaminated by other harmful products. They, and most responsible members of the adult community, want young adults not to move on to addictive hard drugs such as heroin. The police, while trying to uphold the law, may believe that the more important problem is the crime that provides young people with the money for drugs rather than the drug-taking activity itself. Club owners also have a number of interests. They do not want to lose their licenses through the sale of drugs on their premises. They do not want to have to deal with illness or even death through misuse of drugs, even though the drugs were acquired elsewhere. But, given a preference, many club owners would prefer their clients to be using drugs rather than alcohol. Most drug users are not aggressive and do not cause trouble, while alcohol can produce violent behavior.

If concerned adults decide to tackle some of these problems they have to decide what strategy is likely to produce the greatest good and whose "good" they are primarily focusing on. Is it their own or that of their children? They also have to decide what factors they are able to influence. Almost certainly the music industry is not one of these. The contemporary world is a dynamic one, and music, like dress and behavior, has "fashions." Today it is for loud, heavy beat music that requires energy, arouses excitement, and encourages drug taking.

To understand where we are now, it helps to take a look at the past. Matthew Collin describes how the dance–drug scene changed radically from the 1970s to the 1980s and is still changing. First, it greatly expanded in size as the club scene changed into the rave scene and warehouse parties became the favored social activity. The year 1988 was a "summer of love" with Ecstasy widely used to assist the formation of friendship groups cemented by music and dance interests. In the summer of 1989 eleven thousand youngsters descended on an airfield in England for a night of euphoric dance activity inspired by nonstop music with a powerful driving beat.[4] This was to be the popular leisure pattern until well into the 1990s. The fact that both the taking and selling of drugs had draconian legal penalties had little effect on youth behavior. Drug-taking and -selling were now frequently carried out by the same individuals, who sold drugs in order to have the means to buy them for their own use. Ecstasy was becoming a source of income for many young people. Some of it is negative effects were also beginning to show up. There was an occasional death, gang fights were becoming common as rival drug traders competed for customers, and the thrill of using Ecstasy was influencing some young people to move on to other, more addictive, drugs.

Drugs were now becoming big business. Major criminals were moving in and creating countrywide selling networks. Most Ecstasy tablets came from the Netherlands but some were made in Britain, and instructions on how to make them could be found on the Internet. The West Yorkshire police found a workshop in a small town called Osset run by a young man who was not a chemist but was making amphetamines by following instructions in a book. Drugs made in this way introduce a further hazard as they are unlikely to be pure, because profits are increased through the use of baking powder and other foreign substances. Despite a great deal of police activity drug use continued to spread. The organizers of raves used a sophisticated telephone communication network to move these gatherings rapidly to different sites as the police discovered where they were to be held. But, despite the need for complex sound and lighting systems, this led to many raves being held in sordid surroundings. There are reports that one ended up in an abattoir.

As always, fashions change and the rave scene ended in 1990. Clubs became popular again, and this gave the police a greater degree of control.

Many police forces were now focusing their attention on drug dealers and leaving the Ecstasy users alone. There were just too many of them. The music also changed at this time, using more powerful rhythms and stronger drum beats. It was aggressive, noisy, and continuous and attracted the young to drug use so that they could have the energy and motivation to stay with the beat all night. Some users now replaced Ecstasy with more dangerous drugs such as heroin, LSD, speed, and cocaine.

Ecstasy, cannabis, and clubs were now an important part of the youth culture. In 1993 the British dance scene was assessed by the Henley Forecasting Centre as being worth £1.8 billion a year. No one in youth entertainment could afford to ignore it. The unofficial view in many police forces was that drugs should be decriminalized but not legalized. If users no longer suffered penalties there could be a more open debate on solutions to the drug problem. In 1997 the new labor government publicized its intention to pay great attention to the drug problem. It proposed to appoint a drug supremo who would head a high-powered committee with a brief to coordinate more effectively the different programs directed at combating the use or ill effects of drugs. Keith Hellawell, the chief constable of West Yorkshire, was given this post.

The problems that need to be addressed in the United Kingdom have also been tackled in other countries. The association of the music industry with drug use means that clubs must have the capability to control what happens within their walls. In the Netherlands most clubs have the facilities to test the purity of Ecstasy so that clients that buy the drug know that it is not contaminated with other, possibly dangerous, substances. This has not yet happened in the United Kingdom. Clubs also need to control whom they employ as doormen and bouncers because they have been found to play a major part in drug buying and selling. There is also a government threat to remove the licenses of clubs that allow drugs to be sold or used on their premises, although this has not yet become law. But these possible restrictions place clubs in a dilemma. Can they monitor all their clients to check where they are obtaining drugs and if they are using them on club premises? Also, if they do this will it not merely drive young people elsewhere? And, if they were to succeed in eliminating drugs would not the young merely replace these with alcohol? There are many questions to be answered. The situation will certainly change in the future as music changes and youth fashions change, but these changes will not come about on the initiative of club owners. They are much more likely to be the result of cultural and social changes by young people themselves.

One of the most useful recommendations of the 1995 British government report "Tackling Drugs Together" was for a policy of "harm reduction." This suggested simple safety measures such as drinking water always being available in dance halls and clubs. Clubs would also be expected to control the use of drugs on their premises. Health risks would be reduced by the provision of a help line service, through publicity programs to increase public awareness of the risks of drug taking, and through providing care services for drug abusers. The Department of Health would monitor these services.

Problems for the police include how to interpret the law. Should they follow it to the letter and prosecute young people taking drugs, or should they turn a blind eye to the users and concentrate on finding the drug dealers? Here the difficulty is that it is usually only the small-timers who are caught. The controlling drug barons are very clever at keeping their identities secret. Another problem for the police is how to define the limits of their role. Should they just take responsibility for law and order or should they accept some responsibility for problem prevention by setting up, or participating in, drug rehabilitation centers and program? The answers to these questions will be influenced by government policies and by their own motivations, values, and interests.

Problem solvers who wish to address what they regard as undesirable behavior in this age group have to take a very pragmatic approach. The young want to be left alone and so there will be few supporters among them for change. Nevertheless, society wants to protect them from some of the potentially damaging aspects of their behavior. A policy of "proceed with caution is required."

The present campaign to legalize or decriminalize the use of cannabis could solve some of today's problems but it would risk introducing new ones. Legalization would remove the selling process from the black market and ensure that the sale of these kinds of drugs could be controlled. This would also reduce the crime level but might greatly increase the use of cannabis in addition to introducing some safeguards. Today many dealers sell both soft and hard drugs, and there are inducements to young people to try both. The Dutch argue that their brown cafes, which openly sell cannabis but no other drugs, provide a buffer against a movement to more addictive and harmful drugs.

Michael Howard, the British Home Secretary under the Conservative government, argued that both legalization and decriminalization were completely unacceptable. Legalization he saw as removing all existing controls enforced by the Misuse of Drugs legislation. Decriminalization meant not enforcing existing laws in special circumstances. He argued that to maintain criminal laws on the statute book while not enforcing them brought the whole of the criminal law into disrepute. He did not accept that there could be a "pick and choose" attitude to law enforcement.[5] The new Labour government seems also to be taking this position. But attitudes can change.

Addicts and Addiction

This is a problem area where most people would like some remedies, both to reduce the high level of crime that results from the need to buy drugs and to assist the members of society who are experiencing personal problems because of their need to use drugs. Today, there is a great interest in helping addicted users to give up the habit. Unfortunately this is a complex and difficult task that both therapeutic agencies and the police are now trying to address.

We have stressed the importance of starting any problem-solving process by obtaining an accurate picture of the total problem situation. This is particularly the case with the drug scene where there is a great deal of prejudice and misinformation. Paul Lockley, a drug counselor, describes some of its complexities.[6] He suggests that there are two kinds of addiction: psychological addiction, which is the formation of a habit that is difficult or uncomfortable to break, and physical addiction in which the user's body is so altered by the drug that it cannot do without it. Some drugs, with heroin as an example, produce different kinds of behavior depending on who is using them. These can include mental changes such as euphoria and greatly increased activity, or they may lead to the sharing of a certain lifestyle or the breaking of the law in order to obtain the drug.

Illegal drug use tends to start in late adolescence if drugs are readily available. The curiosity of the young leads to an urge to experiment, particularly if friends are also experimenting. It may be easier to say yes to drugs than to say no. There is also the added attraction of taking a risk and of thumbing one's nose at authority. Parental behavior can also be an incentive to use drugs rather than to avoid them. This is often true if one or both parents are drug users, or heavy drinkers, and alcohol is seen as a way of solving or removing problems. In addition there is the powerful incentive to use drugs because their results are enjoyable. Users value the changes in mental state that can occur. They want to experience the "kick" and the "buzz."

The important problem that has to be solved here is how to help users of addictive drugs, who wish to do so, to abandon the habit. Few can do this without help and the role of the drug counselor now becomes very important. People who become counselors require some very particular competencies. They must understand why people use drugs and how they are affected by this use; they must also establish a close relationship with the people they are helping and understand the nature of this relationship; and they must actively want to provide effective assistance that will enable users to live without drugs. This requires them to be sympathetic and nonjudgmental. Paul Lockley describes some of the objectives of a counselor. These might include influencing the user to try to give up his or her habit; acting as a channel of help; providing support; acting as a role model; sharing beliefs and ideas; maintaining and understanding the ongoing relationship.[7]

All of these require competence in establishing and maintaining relationships. Influencing users does not mean telling them what to do but helping them to solve their own difficulties. Acting as a channel of help is recognizing that drug users are not helpless, they are capable of controlling their own lives. By establishing a relationship a counselor can help them feel secure, supported, and accepted. Providing support also means increasing the user's self-esteem and self-confidence. Hopefully, he or she can learn some skills from the counselor such as greater self-control, more objectivity, and a clearer picture of personal needs and objectives. Successful counseling is also greatly assisted by a degree of openness on the nature of the relationship and how this is progressing. The needs, hopes, and fears of both the user and the counselor should be discussed, together with any difficulties in the maturing relationship. This will not always go smoothly. There will be times when both feel and show aggression, and this must be accepted. Both the counselor and the drug user have to learn from each other. The role of counselor can be a formally established community role or it can be provided informally by, for example, family doctors.

The organizations and groups that drug users have contact with will need certain capabilities in order to provide the support that both the user and the counselor require. Support groups can be of great assistance here. These can range from family groups and groups set up by concerned members of the public to professional and medical groups such as drug problem centers, which both assist the drug user and his or her relatives and friends. Families of drug users often experience a great deal of stress and welcome help, but those providing this must have a clear idea of the kind of assistance that is being sought. Paul Lockley suggests that there are five main categories of support—emotional support, material support, self-esteem support, informational support, and companionship. All of these will require different capabilities in the organizations providing help and different competencies in the counselors working there. Many support groups provide a number of these services, for example, information, emotional support, and companionships.[8] Few provide material support, although they may have the information necessary for the client to obtain this.

Good coordination with other groups is an essential part of any rehabilitation policy. Many police forces have excellent drug rehabilitation programs. For example, in West Yorkshire in England there is a Fast Track System for drug addicts who want to break the habit. The police will abstain from prosecution if an offender who is an addict will accept a place on a drug rehabilitation program. Addicts who agree are then given priority places on programs that are in short supply. In West Yorkshire this initiative is jointly funded by a number of organizations including the police, probation service, and the health service. If drug users fail to attend meetings during a twenty-eight-month bail period, they will be returned to the normal police system and face criminal charges. During the first six months of this project a total of 157 drug users were referred for help and treatment instead of receiving a caution or court action. The British government is now extending this program.

Keith Hellawell, the British anti-drugs coordinator, has pointed out that "treatment costs one tenth of the cost of imprisoning someone and has six times the success rate of incarceration." He stressed that this was not being soft on criminals but tackling the root cause of society's problems.[9] With addicts the police were dealing with very different people from the Ecstasy takers of the dance scene. They were involved with a group that had moved on from soft to hard drugs, or which had started its drug history with dangerous and addictive drugs. More than 60% of property crime was directly linked to people who needed to fund a drug habit. Others involved in helping drug addicts have also made the point that while getting people into treatment quickly and effectively gave the best results, particularly for young offenders, rehabilitation alone was not enough. Ex-addicts needed something to fill the vacuum left by the removal of drugs. They need programs that offer a range of social, training, and leisure activities.

The rehabilitation of drug users is an excellent example of effective problem solving in which individual community helpers are given the competencies to provide therapy and organizations, such as community support groups, are assisted to acquire the necessary capabilities. Necessary skills and resources are heavily focused on creating positive and productive relationships between addicts and helpers so that addicts gain the self-respect and self-confidence to enable them to abandon the drug habit. The offer, by the police, of rehabilitation instead of prison is also an incentive to reform. Two further things are required: sufficient programs and help groups to meet the needs of all addicts and the provision of jobs so that ex-addicts can move into gainful employment.

So far we have been talking about the young and often unemployed. But there is another group of drug addicts that badly needs help but is careful to conceal its drug-taking activity. These are members of professional groups such as doctors, dentists, lawyers, and airline pilots.[10] There is also a heavy group of users in financial services, although these are more open, and less concerned, about their habit. Drug-impaired professionals are not an easy group to assist because most will want to continue working in their high-powered and important jobs. Yet, some of these jobs can affect the safety of other members of the community. There is also a tendency for members of this group to believe that their addiction is less than it is and many are cross-addicted. They use one drug to minimize the unwanted effects of another.

Like all addicts their addiction progresses through a number of stages: a quest for euphoria, a desire to feel normal again, and, finally, a struggle to survive. Like our less privileged addicts they can be greatly helped by counselors who are members of the same profession. The same is true of support groups made up of caring professional associates. In an attempt to speed up recovery a technique called intervention has become popular in the United States. A group of friends or relatives surprise the addict in a daily work situation and point out how much they are being adversely affected by his or her addictive behavior. They show distress, but also love, concern, and a desire to help. If the response is positive the addict is immediately transported to a treatment program.

Another, older, form of treatment is detoxification. This involves a gradual reduction of the addictive drug. This can work but frequently has undesirable psychological consequences as well as physical problems.

Addicts will later relapse unless the treatment is followed up with psychological assistance. Some addicts are encouraged to think of themselves as sick, a state that relieves them of responsibility for their actions and improves their self-worth. This approach too is seen as controversial unless it also has a psychological component. The addict has to be assisted to take control of the situation and his or her recovery.

CHANGES IN DRUG USE

The popularity of certain drugs changes over time. In the early 1980s crack cocaine was a much-used drug in the United States, while cannabis use declined. This situation changed in the late 1980s with cannabis once again becoming the preferred drug. In Europe, at this time, Ecstasy was starting to appear on the drug scene. This was a new threat as it was a chemical-based drug and did not need importing from distant countries. It could easily be made in local laboratories. Preventive action was now focused on the class-A drugs—heroin, cocaine, and LSD. In Europe most of the LSD came from Amsterdam. In the 1990s drug use continued to grow, but the pattern of drug use started to change again. Cannabis was still the most popular drug, but there was an increase in the use of heroin, while amphetamine use was decreasing.

A number of powerful influences, such as the fashion industry, were glamorizing drugs. In 1997 President Clinton accused the world fashion industry of portraying "heroin chic" by photographing models who appeared to have taken drugs and who were posing in bathrooms. This was widely reported in the British press but immediately denied by the industry, which maintained it was showing "real" people, not people on drugs. Yet there were signs that the media were glamorizing drugs. A fourteen-year-old girl was quoted in the British press as saying that heroin "was the coolest, chic-est thing you can do."[11]

Other observers suggested that the dominant factors in drug use were price, use, and peer pressure, not fashion. Heroin could now be smoked, there was more on the market, and one smoke could cost as little as $8. The reduction in price was due to Colombia becoming the dominant exporter instead of Asia due to its ability to use the existing cocaine distribution system to market heroin. This heroine was potent, pure, and cheap. It seemed the drug market was changing in response to changes in market forces. New drugs were appearing on the rave scene together with reduced price versions of existing drugs.[12]

LESSONS TO BE LEARNED

What can we learn about problem solving from examining drugs, their use, management, and effects? The first most striking message is that large problems of this kind, while needing to be understood holistically, cannot usually be treated as single entities. They consist of many difficult subproblems, some of which will be easier to address than others. For example, persuading young children not to take drugs may be relatively simple, whereas attempts to influence teenagers and young people in their twenties may be much more difficult. Attempts to prohibit the manufacture and distribution of drugs has not proven to be successful, and the drug industry continues to grow in size.

Understanding the nature of the problem that is being addressed and having clear short- and long-term objectives and strategies is always a useful starting point with any major problem, although it must be recognized that in dynamic environments both the problem and the objectives and strategies may change over time. There must be continual monitoring of their relevance and applicability. The definition of the problem and the strategies selected must also fit with the needs and interests of the groups who are affected by it, and here the victims or potential victims should have a high degree of priority. This means that crime reduction should come first when community needs are considered, harm reduction should be the goal with young adults, while therapy and reestablishment into normal society should be offered all drug addicts. Broadly, these are the remedies that are in place at present, although there are not enough of them and they need more financial resources and better coordination.

One of the most important influences on how problems are defined and the kinds of strategies and objectives that are selected to address them will be the values of powerful interest groups. Drugs present a problem here because there is a clear division of opinion. Governments, including the British government, want drugs to remain illegal even though this stance may make the problem more difficult to solve. They are influenced here by political considerations, one of which is the belief that they will lose votes if they move to decriminalization or legalization. They also do not know what the consequences of such a change of policy would be. There have now been many experiments in which addicts have been provided with drugs, including some in the United Kingdom, but none on a very large scale. The alternative view, which is gathering strength at the present time, is that drugs such as cannabis should be officially decriminalized and no legal action taken against those who use them. This policy is supported by evidence from the Netherlands, particularly Amsterdam, where the brown cafes have been catering effectively for users, and the police have argued that they prevent young people from moving on to harder drugs. Today, reactions are not so positive as cafe behavior has changed and their influence is no longer so benign. This debate urgently needs to be resolved before new problem-addressing programs are introduced.[13]

Once strategies and objectives are agreed on, or while they are being discussed, attention must be given to necessary competencies and capabilities. Are people with the required problem-solving skills and knowledge available in the right numbers? Do the organizations that need to be involved have the resources to support the problem solvers in the field? With issues such as drugs a shortage of money is always likely to be a major constraint.

A particular feature of large, complex problems is the need for good coordination by the different groups who must work together effectively. These range from governments to community and self-help groups. All will need to be clear where their task boundaries are located so that responsibilities do not overlap unduly, and they will need to identify and agree as to their areas of responsibility. Good communication and the sharing of information on a fast and continuing basis will be essential, and the development of networked information systems will be a valuable aid. Electronic information is no substitute for face-to-face contact, however, and meetings to discuss policy and progress should be regular events. It is in this area of coordination that many problems in combating drugs have been experienced in the past. European countries have been reluctant to work with each other and to share information, while problem-addressing groups, such as police and customs, have become rivals instead of collaborators. But increasingly these problems are being solved by the development of cross-European information systems and by joint police and customs activities.

For those interested in theory, Ross Ashby's Law of Requisite Variety can provide some useful guidelines.[14] Ashby argued that only variety can control variety. By this he meant that if a situation were complex, with many variables, then the techniques for dealing with the situation would need to have the same amount and kind of variety. Ashby applied his theory to engineering, but it is equally applicable to other kinds of problems. If Ashby's law is accepted this means that the law enforcement groups trying to eliminate the drug barons must have the same kind and level of knowledge as the drug barons themselves. They must understand their objectives and strategies, their operational management techniques, and the problems they experience in moving drugs from source to customer. It is here that weak links may be found. Similarly, those trying to prevent children from experimenting with drugs must understand the children's world, the power of curiosity, and the urge to be like older role models. They must also have something to offer as an alternative attraction. Drug addicts will, in turn, require facilitators who can sympathize and understand their addiction and help them move on to other ways of solving their problems, if they wish to do this. An important therapeutic need here will be contact with individuals or groups who can provide acceptable employment.

Ashby also points out that with most problems you can go so far and no further, continuing to take action will not lead to better results. This can also be applied to the social problem solver who should always be aware of what can realistically be achieved. Extravagant ideas of future progress should not be encouraged as further effort will be wasted energy. Ashby also provides some suggestions on how to deal with and regulate very complex environments. Here again he is addressing engineering issues, but his ideas can usefully be transferred to the problem areas with which this book is concerned. For example, one way to get control and achieve results is to lower standards, so easier goals are set. Ashby recognizes that this is not a desirable solution, but he argues that it should not be forgotten. Another approach is to increase the power of the regulator until it is able to deal with the complexity. This would mean increasing the size of the law enforcement agencies until they were able to overcome the drug barons. Ashby realizes that this is often impossible to achieve in engineering, and when applied to drugs, it would mean governments spending vast amounts of money on the police, customs, and military.

Another way of dealing with excessive variety is to establish which variables are linked together and can be controlled as a single unit. Ashby calls these constraints, but they could just as easily be called linkages. For example, if the police persuade a club owner to take pains to exclude drugs, they will be controlling the behavior of clients, of doormen who often manage the drug selling activity, and of dealers who will not be able to operate there. Three problems will be solved through a single initiative. The more linkages that are identified, the more a single or a small number of actions can control them. Ashby also assessed control over periods of a year using what he calls an assessment of the "grand disturbance." He argues that what matters is the long-term picture. Translating this into problem-solving success in the drug area means that just counting the number of dealers caught is not enough. What matters is an assessment of the reduction in drug dealing over a twelve-month period.

Ashby defines design as communication. He argues that the act of "designing" or "making" a machine is essentially a communication from "maker to made." Similarly, designing a problem-solving program or strategy is communicating an ethical position, a set of values, and a series of practical operations designed to achieve a desired result. This communication stretches from those implementing the program to those benefiting from its results. He suggests proceeding in stages so that each part of a program can be tested before the next is implemented. It can then be reversed if it has proven to be a mistake. He also believes in "amplification," describing an amplifier as a device that, if given a little of something, will emit a lot of it. It is hoped that this book will act in a small way as an amplifier, enabling problem solvers to solve problems more quickly and more effectively than they have done in the past.

CHAPTER 10

Cyber Crime

A New Kind of Fraud

Our next complex problem area, cyber crime, is different from the drugs challenge and requires different methodological approaches. The competencies and skills required to tackle drugs are not far removed from those of a doctor. They require a holistic approach in which the total situation is understood and a strategy for cure or improvement is developed. There are many subproblems that have to be recognized, understood, and managed with each likely to affect the others. Also, a number of groups have to cooperate and coordinate their activities if progress toward a solution is to be made.

The cyber crime problem, in contrast, is closer to the work of the scientist and lawyer. It requires recognizing that a crime has been committed and finding out exactly what has happened. In most situations protective devices will have been breached and preventive measures will have failed. Somehow an intruder has managed to break in to the system. The investigator needs to discover what has happened, how it has happened, and why it has happened. What was the objective of the break in? All this can often be accomplished by one or a small group of security consultants.

Many companies will respond to attack by merely closing the hole that has occurred in the system and going no further. Others will want to carry out some systematic research to establish how the intruder was able to enter the system, where he was physically located, the nature of his electronic journey, the obstacles he had to overcome, and the nature of the theft. Was it information or money? All this requires the knowledge and application of a scientist.

In this chapter we will describe the nature of the cyber crime problem and provide a case study of how a hacker was traced from his location in Germany to an American university laboratory and then on to U.S. military bases.

A CHALLENGING PROBLEM

A new, complex, and threatening criminal activity has now arrived and is spreading across the globe. It is believed to be costing the European and U.S. economies millions of dollars a year, although no one knows what the exact cost is. It has been called cyber crime because it involves the transfer of money across electronic communication systems such as the Internet. It is likely to affect every aspect of business, although as yet we have few ideas on how to deal with it. It covers a wide variety of criminal activities including data fraud, data spying, and data theft. Prosperity is being put at risk by gangs that are attacking insurance companies, banks, investment firms, and public agencies. These gangs are making as much money as those operating the drug trade.

The newspaper *European* (November 13–19, 1997) has reported that cross-border frauds in Europe are enriching criminals to the tune of $69.3 billion a year.[1] The 1996 United Kingdom National Computer Security Survey estimated that theft had increased 60% and that the average cost of a theft had increased from $7,700 to $25,000 since the previous survey. A 1997 survey of 130 United Kingdom and 95 French company directors, commissioned by the insurance company AIG Europe, found that 70% of them felt that an attack on their information technology (IT) infrastructure was the most likely crisis they could face. Very serious crime is also increasing. The director of the FBI told an international computer crime conference in New York in March 1997 that law enforcement agencies throughout the world must cooperate with each other to fight on-line crime. He provided three recent examples: a Russian citizen with a laptop computer in St. Petersburg who tried to gain access to millions of dollars in Citibank, a convicted terrorist who used a laptop to create plans to blow up a dozen U.S. plants, and a Swedish teenager who hacked his way into a Florida computer system and shut down a 911 emergency response computer network for an hour. The FBI speaker described this last example as "a dress rehearsal for a national disaster."

Companies are not usually organized to deal with these kinds of problems, but governments should be and are, in fact, making some progress. European officials are preparing to bring in new laws to regulate the cyber economy. Brussels is about to press for the harmonization of anticrime legislation throughout the community as discussed at the 1997 Amsterdam Summit. A committee of the Council of Europe is also starting work on a convention to enable the police forces of Europe to fight cyber crime. It is hoped that this convention will be signed by the year 2000 and will form the basis for future EU legislation. It is forecast that by 2000 up to $1,700 billion of financial transactions will be made across computer networks. But there are still many problems. There are no agencies to deal with cross-border crime in Europe. Different countries are bringing in different regulations. Some countries do not even have a legal definition of fraud, and, at present, the European Commission has no direct powers to combat fraud. Lax controls by any one EU member directly affect the others. Luxembourg now acts as an entry point for pirated compact disks, which are then distributed through Germany. Cross-border investigations are very difficult. For example, the Swedish tax authorities are not allowed to give police or prosecutors information they have received from abroad.

Computer crime includes credit card fraud, theft of data, hacking, and virus spreading with the opportunities for the greatest criminal gains occurring through the rapid growth in network facilities, especially in banking and electronic funds transfer. A great deal of this fraud is concealed because banks and other financial institutions are reluctant to make this information public and possibly lose the trust and confidence of their customers. Yet private information must be protected from unauthorized access. Business data can be a valuable commodity to competitors, and its theft could lead a company to disaster.

There are increasing legal requirements to protect data. Professional corporations such as law, medical, and accounting practices could face lawsuits for failing to protect client or patient information. Boards of directors have a fiduciary and due diligence responsibility to protect corporate assets, including valuable business data.[2] Governments are now less likely to excuse management inaction over fraud. The *European* has reported a speech by Helen Liddell, economic secretary to the United Kingdom Treasury, in which she condemned "senior managers who turn a blind eye to inexplicable profits and bank their performance bonuses, and the professional advisers who lend credibility and retain their contracts" as complicit. She suggested that the British government was considering applying a concept of "should have been suspicious" to management in fraud cases.[3] These problems can only increase. More and more money is moving from country to country faster than ever before. More and more business data are becoming electronic, and there is an increasing amount of electronic exchange with suppliers and between companies. For example ICL now trades electronically with over 60% of its suppliers.[4]

Unfortunately there is still widespread ignorance about the possible security threats these developments bring, especially at company board level where there is a considerable amount of what the British Audit Commission has called "computer blindness." Knowledge of security risks, if it exists at all, is restricted to certain security-conscious groups, and these are unlikely to include either senior management or lower-level employees. Outsourcing has also increased the vulnerability of data to theft or improper use. Many companies send data to be processed abroad, and important company functions are subcontracted to other external organizations. The United Kingdom government has now subcontracted much of its IT work to a number of U.S.-based service companies. Management also needs to be aware that although organized criminals are constantly on the lookout for any illegal activity that can make them significant profits, major threats may lie inside the company. Employees who have grudges, low morale, feel they are underpaid, or simply recognize that there are opportunities for fraud, may all try to manipulate the system.

Although prosecutions are still uncommon with many white-collar offenses being handled informally rather than through the courts, computer fraud is as equally capable of being prosecuted as paper fraud was before the advent of computers. The Computer Crime Unit of New Scotland Yard provides a number of specific definitions of computer fraud and of crimes dependent upon computer technology. These are:

- *Computer crime*: Crimes where a computer system or data is the target of a guilty act. These crimes may include offenses of "hacking," computer viruses, or other malicious programs.
- *Computer related crime*: Recognized crimes that are created by computers or information technology. These crimes may include software copyright or computer pornography.
- *Computer-aided crime*: Crimes where a computer, or associated technology, has been used in place of a typewriter, ledger, or telephone. For example, altering data on a computer in order to dishonestly appropriate money or property. A new kind of threat in this category is "cyber extortion" in which a criminal threatens to remove or corrupt data unless he or she receives some recompense. This may

be money but it may also be the restitution for some perceived personal wrong such as loss of job.
- *Computer-based evidence*: This is crime in which the evidence is merely held on a computer. For example, where an individual is dealing with stolen property and the details of the transactions are in the computer.

THE INTERNET

The Internet originated from a network used by the U.S. Department of Defense called ARPANET. This evolved into a network linking super computer sites funded by the U.S. National Science Foundation. Initially the Internet was seen as a communication vehicle for academics and researchers, and it was not subject to any form of monitoring or regulation. It now reaches the vast majority of countries and consists of millions of computers. Each network may have between one and five hundred users. It has been estimated that the Internet now comprises about 876,000 networks.

If the users of the Internet represent a cross section of worldwide society, then it can be assumed that the criminal elements using the networks represent a cross section of the world of crime. In the United Kingdom, computer and Internet use is regulated by the 1990 Computer Misuse Act. The Computer Crime Unit of New Scotland Yard has responsibility for investigating allegations of computer crime, including offenses contrary to this act. Because of its increasing economic importance, the extent of criminal activities within the Internet is expected to grow with accelerating speed. In spite of this the precautions taken by companies connected to the Internet are extremely inadequate and even part-time hackers can gain access easily.[5] There has also been a major increase in deliberate abuse and criminal activities. Companies that move onto the Internet without the right security measures can encounter security risks that should not be underestimated. It is important they are aware of these. If some or all of their computer systems were to crash because of security problems, this would involve enormous financial losses.

The U.S. National Consumers League has set up a number of Web pages to warn all Internet users against cyber crooks and alert them to the ten most-used scams. Among the most common are undelivered Internet and on-line services; damaged, defective, misrepresented, or undelivered merchandise; pyramids and multilevel marketing; and misrepresented business opportunities and franchises. The German government has announced plans to police the Internet in Germany proactively. In a private legislative act known as the Information and Communication Services Bill, it proposes that the Internet be viewed as just another form of media, albeit an electronically published one. The aim of the bill is to stop any neo-Nazi information from being disseminated across the Net.

Examples of minor crimes are the selling of bogus degree certificates on the Internet—a process that greatly alarmed British universities—and the sending of offensive and misleading e-mail messages by an employee of a British financial services company, which were seen by thirty thousand customers as soon as they were sent. Others included the releasing of a virus that made other viruses more difficult to spot and disinfect, and the introduction, by a hotel chain employee, of a system that made it appear that all hotel reservations throughout the world had been made by a particular travel agent, who would then collect a 10% commission. Many similar crimes have been investigated by the Computer Crime Unit of the Metropolitan police in London. The West Yorkshire police secured the first conviction for computer fraud in 1991. A computer user had created fictitious employees and caused their wages to be paid into his bank account.

All police forces have some officers specializing in fraud investigation. London has had a fraud squad since 1946 and this is run jointly by the Metropolitan and the City of London police. Officers from the two forces are also located within the Serious Fraud Office, which was set up under the British Criminal Justice Act of 1987. The police work closely with teams of lawyers, accountants, and other experts in fraud cases, with about seven out of ten of these involving company employees. Unfortunately, computer crime is not often brought to the attention of the police, although there are increasing pressures for this reporting to take place and some U.S. state laws now require this.

SERIOUS CRIMES

A 1997 investigation sponsored by the European commission identified ten of the most serious hi-tech crimes. These included mobile phone cloning, thought to be growing at a rate of 40% a year, credit card and other banking frauds, counterfeiting of brand-name goods and pharmaceuticals, fraudulent investment schemes, smuggling of cigarettes and alcohol to avoid customs duties, and fraudulent bankruptcy and insurance cheating. The research suggested that in many cases the proceeds from these illegal activities were transferred abroad.

The risk of financial fraud has been greatly increased by the complexity of new products such as derivative securities and by the lengthening of the processing flow of many transactions. Derivative fraud takes the form of unauthorized trading, unrecorded transactions, off-market trades, and fictitious counterparts. Because dealing rooms can commit millions of dollars in seconds, risks are very difficult to control. The employees involved have been named "the new breed of rocket scientists." They have been described as young men and women "armed with powerful computers, who occupy the front offices of many financial institutions and risk the capital of the bank each day with complex positions in exotic products." It has also been suggested that the complexity of what is taking place is rarely understood by senior managers.[6]

An early examples of a wild trading disaster is the case of an employee of Merrill Lynch who, in 1987, lost $377 million in a few days. In 1993 traders in the treasury department of Japan's largest oil company, Showa Shell Sekiyo, lost $1.1 billion as a result of unauthorized speculation. A particular difficulty today is that it is not always possible to separate financial recklessness from deliberate fraud. This was true of Nick Leeson and the collapse of Barings Bank. Leeson, while trading with SIMEX (Singapore International Monetary Exchange), manipulated his computer records so that the massive sums he was trading did not show up on the computer. This was done by offsetting false short positions against long positions. Long positions are when the market is expected to rise; short positions are when it is expected to fall. He fixed his computer program so that Barings in London did not receive accurate information concerning what was taking place. Barings Bank crashed with losses of £535 million and investigations are still taking place to discover whether Leeson made any personal gains from this manipulation of the system. Leeson's extreme risk taking was not perceived because the London management were traditional bankers and not experienced in derivative trading. They also did not have a sophisticated control system that would identify possible fraud, although there was one on the market called BRAINS. Barings did eventually decide to install this £10 million system, but by then it was too late, Leeson had destroyed the bank.[7]

Companies face serious risks from their computer systems even if they are not on the Internet. A survey of U.S. companies in 1994 showed that half of those contacted had suffered loss as a result of problems with data security in the last twelve months. More than two-thirds of these were caused by the firm's own staff, half of them accidentally. The causes included lack of backup files, viruses introduced by staff's own disks, and operating errors including the accidental deletion of data. Companies on the Internet are even more vulnerable with 24% suffering from unauthorized access through hacking. Senior executives are often amazed at the ease with which their top secret systems can be accessed. Where fraud is concerned every attempt is made by offenders to avoid or corrupt security procedures and to take advantage of loopholes when security is weak. Differing rules and procedures in different countries greatly assist this process. One important point to remember is that employees are not always the offenders, often the employer is the beneficiary and is engaging in dubious practices to increase his or her profits.

HACKERS AND HACKING

Hacking is electronic burglary.[8] Hackers fall into the following groups: students and teenagers, people from inside the company, competitors, hackers from the computer underworld, criminals from the drugs or Mafia world, and professional hackers or industrial espionage agents. With students hacking is a kind of hobby. It is often carried out for fun by young people who get a kick out of breaking into a supposedly inaccessible system. Like drugs it can become an addiction, the more protected the system the more the hacker wants to test its vulnerability to attack, with every new, important, and well-protected system becoming the next challenge.

In the 1960s and 1970s hacking was a relatively harmless pursuit. Hackers were young, intellectual, and idealistic. Many had a code of conduct that championed the free sharing of information and required that accessed data were not harmed in any way. The challenge was to find it, not to use it. Today hacking may not be so innocent. It can now have a criminal intent, either to steal data for personal gain or to alter, publicize, or destroy it so as to do the owner serious damage. Alvin Toffler believes that industrial espionage is on the increase. Many companies want more information about the plans, products, and profits of their competitors. This is called "competitive intelligence."[9] In Britain hacking is illegal. The

1990 Computer Misuse Act states that it is an offense to secure unauthorized access to a computer and to secure the unauthorized modification of the contents of any computer.

Figures released in the United States show that computers at the Department of Defense were attacked 250,000 times by hackers in 1995. Two-thirds got into the system and less than 1% were detected. A serious problem for many companies is that they do not know they are being attacked and that they are losing sensitive data through unauthorized access to their systems.

A new form of hacking is associated with blackmail. These hackers threaten to put defamatory information about a public figure on a target company's Web site and then let the selected victim know about the publication of the material. If the threat is ignored they make a small change to the company's Web site to force it to take them seriously. In the United Kingdom in 1997, the *Daily Telegraph* reported that hackers had attacked the labor party's Web site. An official picture of Tony Blair had been replaced by his spitting image puppet and the slogan "new labor, new Britain" had been replaced with "new labour, old lies."

In the 1980s, I was working in the Digital Computing Company, in Boston, helping with the development and implementation of XSEL, one of Digital's first expert systems. One day in March all of Digital's networked computers in the San Francisco area began to slow down. In addition they all began producing continuous printouts. Each printout aggressively stated "The phantom, the system cracker, strikes again. Soon I will crash your disks and backups on systems A. I have already crashed your system B. Have fun trying to restore it." The FBI was called in as California had a state law prohibiting unauthorized access to computer systems. But the offender was never caught. This was the start of a growing recognition throughout the world of the vulnerability of computer systems.[10]

Soon many of these attacks changed from the relatively harmless fun of trying to beat a difficult technical system to the more sinister aim of trying to corrupt systems through the introduction of a computer virus. The Computer Crime Unit (CCU) of the United Kingdom Metropolitan police define a virus as "a computer program which makes copies of itself in such a way as to infect parts of the operating system and/or applications programs." The first major virus infection was in 1987 when the IBM Christmas card worm infected large numbers of IBM mainframes worldwide. Once it got into a system it reproduced up to 500,000 times an hour, disabling the whole system. In the 1980s viruses were spread mainly through software copied from one disk to another and installed on the computer manually. The latest viruses, once in a system, are activated by standard commands. Viruses called "trojan horses" are designed to keep out of sight. No one knows that they are there. Worms are viruses that can reproduce across computer networks. One Internet worm infected 6,000 Internet modes within hours of being released.

Members of the British police Computer Crime Unit encourage firms suffering from virus invasion to contact them and report the nature of the attack. This enables the CCU to assess the damage caused by viruses and may assist the identification and prosecution of those responsible for creating and distributing them. The May 1997 issue of the *Journal of Secure Computing* describes a virus Web site operated by a United Kingdom citizen that offered hundreds of viruses in files that could be downloaded by anyone who accessed the site. The *Journal* found this site and notified the Internet service provider who barred access and impounded the contents to be used as evidence. Both the local police and Scotland Yard's Computer Crime Unit were informed and proceeded to prosecute the individual responsible. Viruses are not always introduced simply to cause damage. A virus can be introduced into a system to target specific information without the owner knowing anything about it. For example, a sinister new virus has been developed that can replicate itself, transferring to other computers via e-mail. This was discovered in the United States and could now be corrupting data in many different systems.[11]

A description of the personalities and motivations of hackers is provided by Katie Hafner and John Markoff in their book *Cyberpunk*. They say that many young men are seduced by the thrill of exploring today's international computer networks. Hackers have their own bible, the *Hacker's Handbook*, which was banned under the United Kingdom's 1990 Computer Misuse Act but is freely available in the United States. Like legitimate professional groups they also have meetings and annual conferences and talk to each other on the Internet. But, even if many have no criminal intent, they are increasingly viewed as malicious intruders and also time-wasters. Unfortunately, some do have objectives that are destructive or associated with fraud, and society is becoming increasingly afraid of the damage they can cause.

Businesses must be aware of the risks from hackers, physical theft, and viruses. Poor security standards are often a result of poor company organization. Firms do not have security officers, training in security is not provided for system managers, and there are little in the way of security guidelines.[12] Hackers usually succeed through a failure of access mechanisms, particularly passwords. Companies need to take action before problems occur. They should recognize that factors such as organizational culture, accountability, access control, data encryption, and physical control can all increase or decrease vulnerability. Responsibility for data should be spread throughout the organization with everyone accountable for the data they personally use. The use of data should become transparent with access controlled by the originator or by a central administrator. Although experts maintain that all protective devices and strategies are flawed and none can guarantee complete security, when users are accountable for their own data, security comes a step closer.[13]

CYBER TERRORISM

Cyber terrorism is an extreme form of cyber crime. Its intention is to oppress through fear. It can be described as major and threatening IT based attacks on the integrity of an organization's IT system. It takes many different forms. For example, deliberate attempts from outside to destroy or injure a company, the propagation of "race hate" material on the Internet by subversive groups such as German neo-Nazis, hackers looking for financial gain or personal excitement, and serious criminal fraud from disgruntled current or ex-employers. Banks and financial institutions are particularly vulnerable to cyber terrorism if they do not adequately assess their security weaknesses and take remedial action.[14] In 1996 the *London Times* reported that hackers had been paid £400 million in extortion money to keep quiet after a logic bomb attack had compromised the systems of a number of banks and investment houses. The banks sought to buy silence so that customers would not lose confidence in the integrity of their systems and take their business elsewhere. Many countries now see this kind of threat as a major problem. President Clinton has sponsored relevant research and recommended measures to protect the United States infrastructure in banks, the Stock Exchange, the Pentagon, and the Department of Justice. These measures include the establishment of an information and warning center to collate breaches in computer security throughout government and industry. The U.S. government now believes that cyber terrorism is as great a threat to the United States as nuclear, chemical, or biological proliferation.

SECURITY ASSISTANCE

The data security challenge is now very big business. It is claimed that the market for security advice and equipment is worth $6 billion with the expectation of $13 billion being reached in the year 2000. Because the arrival of ingenious new crimes is a threatening aspect of the increase in electronic communication, a new group has appeared on the scene—computer forensic scientists. Computer forensics is the analysis of computer data with a view to its presentation in a court of law as admissible evidence. Under the British Police and Criminal Evidence Act of 1984 it is the duty of any person proffering evidence to ensure that it is authentic and accurate. Forensic scientists assist this. They are frequently called in by the police to act as expert witnesses, and they may be called in by users to stop undesirable practices such as hacking. They are also skilled in finding data that criminals may think they have wiped out but that is still inside the machine. They know the weak system points that criminals make use of in fraud and data theft. But bringing successful criminal prosecutions is not easy. The FBI claims that the chances of a successful prosecution for fraud are twenty-two thousand to one.

Another less professional group entering the security business are ex-hackers, many of whom spent a misguided youth breaking into other people's systems as a hobby. One, who now works as a security specialist, maintains, "Unless you have actually tried to break into computers, I'm not sure you are in a good position to know what to do to stop others."[15] He also argues that the world of hacking has become much more sinister since the early 1980s. For example, he is now advising companies on the terrorist use of hacking techniques. One of the recent growth areas in computing has been the use of "tiger teams" or groups of hackers by firms anxious to test the security of their systems.

UNDERSTANDING THE PROBLEMS

What can we learn from this brief description of cyber crime? Does this criminal activity have any similarity to the illegal selling of drugs or are there major differences? One large difference would appear to be the means for carrying out the crime. With drugs these are mainly people, and people in considerable numbers. People are required to grow or manufacture the drugs, to transport them to a variety of different markets, and to sell them. Considerable numbers of people are also required to manage the undesirable effects of drugs. Police, customs, and the armed forces must attempt to catch and eliminate the drug barons, communicators and educators must warn the very young of their possible ill effects, doctors and therapists must help those who become addicted and cannot drop the habit of their own accord.

The cyber crime situation is very different and can be successfully carried out by an individual, or small groups of individuals, assisted by electronic technology that facilitates the fraud, receives the virus, or contains the desired information. But there are some similarities and many of the same problem-solving tools can be helpful in both the drug and cyber crime situations. Neither drugs nor cyber crime are unique, clearly defined, and bounded problems. They more nearly resemble clusters of smaller problems, each of which requires its own prevention or solution technique. Although the number of people involved will be much smaller in cyber crime than in the drugs field, nevertheless, people play important roles in both, either as preventers of crime, as solvers of problems arising from criminal activity, or as victims.

Some of the same problem-solving approaches may apply to both of these illegal initiatives. Drug law-enforcement agencies are advised to create realistic strategic plans that prioritize objectives, estimate required resources, and specify necessary action. Companies vulnerable to cyber crime are also advised to have clear corporate strategies that will help them avoid, ward off, or become aware of criminal activity. These are essentially prevention strategies directed at ensuring that any kind of cyber crime is made difficult to achieve and, if it does happen, that company personnel will quickly become aware of this. In the next chapter we will examine the nature of problem solving for cyber crime.

AN EXAMPLE OF CYBER CRIME AND ITS SOLUTION

Finding out how cyber crime is carried out and thwarted is not easy but, as with drug dealing, there is once again an excellent book describing in great detail the methods used to break into systems and how to prevent this from happening. Problem solving in this area is a complex and difficult subject because a great deal of technical knowledge about computers and networks is required. It requires some of the tools of the scientist and lawyer in that the "truth," in the sense of a knowledge of what actually happened, is important. It also requires the careful and systematic surveillance techniques of the detective.

Clifford Stoll, an astronomer and systems manager at the Lawrence Berkeley Laboratory in California, provides an example of how the computers in his laboratory were broken into both in an attempt to obtain information on what the laboratory was doing but also as a means to gain access to other networks and systems, many of which were associated with military activities.[16] Stoll became aware that something was wrong when he noticed a 75 cent discrepancy in the lab's account statement. This made him suspicious because computer-produced accounts do not have this kind of error. He decided to check and establish why the error had occurred. He soon discovered that someone from outside had accessed the lab computer. Stoll, a scientist with a scientist's competencies, was not content to ignore this. He wanted to know why and how it had happened. He quickly discovered that a legitimate user named Sventek had accessed the system, done nothing for thirty minutes, and then disconnected. Sventek had once been a member on staff at the lab, but he was now working in England and had no reason to access the Berkeley computer. It seemed his password had not been erased and someone else was using it.

Stoll's next step was to keep a record of who was using the system. He did this initially by wiring a large number of printers into the system so that each incoming message was recorded. He found that the hacker had spent three hours scanning the system and that one printer had recorded each of his commands and each response from the computer. He also found that the access route was a firm called Tymnet, a communications company that interconnected computers to major cities around the world. Tymnet could be entered through a local telephone call and would then send the message to any part of its network. This meant the hacker could be anywhere in the country.

Pursuing his interest in access Stoll discovered that there were a number of ways outsiders could get into the Berkeley system. There was an account called "guest," intended for visitors, but which anyone could use. There was also a program that had a bug in its software. This allowed files to be moved from person to person electronically without any check on who was receiving the file. The puzzle was why anyone would want to break into the system of a laboratory whose function was astronomical research.

Stoll decided to observe and trace the activities of the hacker. Where was he located, was he a local person or from farther away? Stoll also decided to keep careful records of all his tracing activities and their results. He would not let the hacker know that he was being observed. Because having large numbers of printers attached to the systems was not a viable long-term solution, Stoll decided to sleep in the office with two terminals available. One was to handle normal communications, the other was to watch the system. The latter would beep every time someone logged on. Clifford would then immediately ask the Tymnet management to trace the connection and find out where it had originated. Stoll also decided to tell the FBI about this illegal activity. Their reply was "We are not interested in a 75 cent loss, we'll come in when you've lost a million dollars."

Stoll was now using his scientific training and knowledge to guide his investigation. He was following some of the methods of physics, such as to record all observations, to speculate, but to trust only proven conclusions. He also applied some of the principles of physics. One of these is that if two things happen close together they are probably caused by the same input. His first important finding was that the hacker was not just interested in the Berkeley computer, he was, in fact, using this system to access other computer systems, one of which was owned by an army base. The latter too had a hole in its security system. As time went on, as a result of his perseverance and willingness to sleep in the office, Stoll found that the hacker was targeting a number of military bases and installations and was able to get into most of these. He was not able to enter the very secure systems holding classified information, but less secure systems presented few problems.

Stoll encountered a number of difficulties with his investigation. Identifying the hacker required telephone line tracking and many telephone companies were not willing to do this. He also found that security agencies such as the CIA and military special investigation offices were not very interested. No important classified information had been stolen, and they did not have the resources or the motivation to do detailed monitoring. Despite these setbacks Clifford decided to continue with the research. He was inspired to do this through meeting a famous scientist with a Nobel Laureate who advised him to go on.

> Don't try to be a cop, be a scientist, research the connections, the techniques, the holes. Apply physical principles. Find new methods to solve problems. Compile statistics, publish your results and only trust what you can prove. But don't exclude improbable solutions, keep your mind open. Dead ends are illusory. When did you ever let a "do not enter" sign keep you away from

anything. Go around the brick walls. When you can't go around, climb over or dig under. Just don't give up.[17]

By now the hacker was greatly extending his activities, he could not be closed out of a system he wanted to enter. If one door closed, he found another way in. Stoll decided he must embark on a continuing twenty-four-hour watch but one that did not involve sleeping in the office. His solution was to buy a pocket pager so that his computer could call him whenever the hacker logged on to the system. The hacker was now using computers other than Berkeley's to access military installations, and Stoll warned the system managers of what was taking place. When they did not believe him he suggested that they check their telephone bills and find out how many unregulated calls there had been.

But Stoll still had no idea who the hacker was. He seemed to be active at strange hours, as many of his activities occurred in the middle of the day when the expectation would be that a hacker would work at night. This raised the question that perhaps he was not a resident of the United States. Clifford then had an intellectual flash of light. He thought of echoes and canyons. If you shout messages across a canyon the echoes will tell you how far the sound has traveled. To find the distance to the canyon wall, just multiply the echo delay by half the speed of sound. This was simple physics. He obtained advice from Berkeley electronic technicians and found that they could do this with computers. All that was needed was an oscilloscope. They watched the requests for information coming in from the hacker and timed the echoes of the pulses. They were three seconds apart. If the signals traveled at the speed of light the hacker must be 279,000 miles away. This meant that he was resident on the moon, an unlikely possibility. After considerable thought Stoll realized that the hacker was using networks to move his data and these are constantly rerouted, assembled, and disassembled. Every time they pass through a different node, they are slowed down.

Stoll continued with the echo timing experiments and established the time delays of friends and colleagues in different parts of the United States. New York to Berkeley was about two thousand miles. It had a time delay of a second. So a three-second time delay meant around six thousand miles. Perhaps the hacker lived in Europe. But who in Spain, France, Germany, or Britain would be interested in obtaining U.S. military information?

After consulting network experts and checking the telephone numbers used by the hacker the place of message origin was found to be West

Germany. The hacker then used a complex route to reach his target computer. He first went into a German network, which transferred him to Tymnet. From Tymnet he accessed the Berkeley Laboratories computer and then moved to his target groups. Another interesting question was given that this complex network movement was expensive, who was paying for the phone calls? Further research showed that one of the intermediary networks was picking up the bill without noticing that there was anything unusual about it. Stoll also discovered that there were groups in West Germany who practiced hacking as a hobby. One was called the German Chaos Club. However, this club was unlikely to be the intruder because it was not interested in military information. Another question was the nature of the hacker, was it a person or a computer?

During this period Stoll had to keep the hacker interested and prevent him from becoming bored as information became harder to obtain. Stoll's warnings had now resulted in many military installations closing the holes in their systems. The hacker must also be prevented from finding out that he was being traced. The solution was to provide him with a great deal of detailed but phony military information. Stoll invented a new Star Wars project and a new network, SDINET, to handle this. The FBI, who had now become more interested in hacking, also asked Stoll to provide a psychological profile of the hacker. This was to cover such things as when is he active, what is he expert in, what are his idiosyncrasies. They also stated "don't speculate, but try to identify the man." Given that to Stoll he was only an electronic phenomenon, this was not easy to do.

By now the German police had become interested and had offered to trace the call access procedure in Germany. They traced him to the University of Bremen and then back to Hanover. Finally his home phone number was identified and the German police moved in. An arrest was made. He turned out to be a man named Markus Hess who lived in Hanover and had started hacking as a hobby. He was short of money and so he began selling information to the Russians. They were interested in any information that he could get, it did not need to be classified. They were also interested in learning hacking techniques such as how to break into networks and in information about Western technology. Hess was able to supply all of these.

Hess had broken into at least twenty-four military computers. The police also found that U.S. army bases in Germany were being accessed via the United States. The ease with which this took place was due to inadequate security procedures. Stoll makes the point that any system can be insecure if it is badly managed. Some problems arise from genuine design flaws, but most are due to poor administration. People do not know how to make systems secure. And there are particular difficulties with networks that are similar to securing a small city. He also claims that it does not take brilliance or wizardry to break into computers, all that is needed is patience.

Industrial espionage has now become big business. Spies need never leave their home countries. It is also easy; all that is needed is a few small computers and some network connections. Security is a vital necessity, but security has a cost. Really secure computers and networks are usually expensive to build and difficult to use. There has to be a balance between usability and security.

Stoll was a successful problem solver because he had the necessary *competencies*. His astronomical research background meant that he had the knowledge and techniques of a scientist. His combinations of astronomy, physics, and computer science made him an effective solver of problems. He also had many of the psychological characteristics of a creative problem solver. He was a fluent and flexible thinker. He was able to generate new ideas rapidly and apply them. He was an original thinker who enjoyed handling complexity, and he was highly motivated to solve the hacker problem. He kept going despite experiencing setbacks and disinterest.

The *capability* of his own organization to help him solve the problem was good. He was given the time and tools despite the fact that this meant he must neglect the demands of his official job, which was to provide computer support for the research of the lab astronomers.

Coordination with other groups was essential. He needed help to trace phone lines and connections and to monitor the hacker's activity. At the end of the chase he needed the assistance and cooperation of the German police. Official U.S. crime prevention groups at first showed little interest. The FBI did not understand the nature of the problem and was only prepared to assist if large sums of money were involved. The CIA took a similar stance. The military installations that were being invaded by the hacker were also not too disturbed as classified information was not involved. They closed the holes but did not look for the hacker. It must be remembered here that these events took place seven years ago when the seriousness of the computer security problem was less well known. Clifford Stoll performed a valuable service in drawing the attention of crime prevention organizations to this fact.

What can be learned about computer security problem solving from this case? First, protecting the system from access is of the greatest importance. Some systems, and this seems to have been true of both VAX and UNIX machines, can have design flaws that permit outsiders to break in.

Even today, few systems are safe against the determined hacker, especially if he or she has a criminal intent. An interesting feature of the Berkeley case is that the Berkeley computer was not the hacker's principal target. It was primarily a means of accessing other, more relevant computer systems. The dilemma for most companies is where to draw the line between security and usability. Tight security systems are expensive and often make access difficult for legitimate users. Military installations with classified information and money-rich organizations such as banks may have no option but to install them. An important task for all organizations, especially when they are installing new systems or becoming part of networks, is knowing where the weaknesses are located. Another important requirement is for all staff to understand the importance of security and what each individual needs to do to ensure this.

A second important lesson is for firms to be aware that someone may be breaking into their systems and to be continually on the lookout for such an occurrence. When an intruder is spotted it is essential to discover how and why this is happening. How is entry being achieved and what is the hacker seeking? Is it information, revenge, profit, blackmail, or is it a student breaking in for kicks?

Next a decision has to be made on what to do about the intrusion. Does the firm plug the entry point and do nothing else or does it, like Stoll did, make determined efforts to find out who the hacker is? Is the threat kept secret or are the police informed and other associated companies warned? If it is decided to try to identify the hacker then a tracking process must be initiated. It may be impossible for the company to do this on its own and specialist help may have to be acquired. This may include computer forensic scientists and national and local police bodies. If it is an international company, EEC groups such as Interpol and Europol may have to be involved.

Small companies are particularly vulnerable to viruses that are introduced maliciously. Important data can be corrupted or lost to the extent that the firm can no longer function and has to close down.

CHAPTER **11**

Addressing Cyber Crime Problems

Cyber crime differs from drugs crime in a number of ways. One important difference is those aspects of the problem that need to be given particular emphasis. With drugs a major challenge is catching and eliminating illegal producers and dealers; with cyber crime it is achieving effective protection against intruders who wish to access computer systems illegally. These invasions can have a variety of objectives and take many different forms, some of which were described in the preceding chapter. The perpetrators can be within or outside the company. This means that companies have an urgent need to protect themselves. Important and well-tested first-step capabilities that contribute to increased security are risk assessment and risk management. This can be a major task as, ideally, it should cover all current business activities and strategic plans for the next five years. There must be a recognition by everyone in the company that information is a valuable commodity and that both criminals and competitors can be trying to secure it. Companies are advised to prepare for attacks by ensuring that responsibility for investigating problems is clearly specified and known by all staff, that external legal advisers and police have good relationships with internal management, and that there is a crisis management plan in place that is tested regularly.

RISK MANAGEMENT CAPABILITY

Risk management involves a two-phase approach: an assessment of risks and the management planning and control activities that implement organizational actions to reduce or eliminate risks.[1] The task of risk management is to search for incidents or threats that can prevent the technical and business environment from performing as it should and to modify this environment so that it becomes less vulnerable.[2] This task is best begun by answering a number of questions about the nature of the technology and business environment that has to be protected. First, how important is this protection going to be? Will the country be placed at risk if certain army systems are accessed by enemy agents? Will businesses collapse if their vulnerability is shown through unauthorized entry? This may be the case with major banks. Will a company experience inconvenience but not serious loss if it is invaded by intruders such as hackers? The answers to these questions will demonstrate the seriousness of the security task, how much attention must be given it, and the likely costs that will be involved.

Other relevant questions are How large is the system that needs protection? Is it a system that covers the activities of the whole company or is it a more local information system? What is the nature of the technology that has to be protected? Is it new with the likelihood that some attention has been paid to security in its design, or is it an old legacy system that offers easy opportunities to would-be invaders? Also, how much experience does the company have in handling security matters? Are there some in-house experts or must this expertise be acquired from outside? Does anyone in the firm have the title "risk manager"? Lastly are all members of staff security-conscious or does a new, more security-conscious climate need to be created?

RISK ANALYSIS CAPABILITY

An important part of risk management is risk *analysis*, which attempts to establish and rank the most serious risks that need to be avoided. Steps will then be taken to minimize these while less important risks are given less attention. Here it is important to achieve a balance between the benefits of greater security and the cost of protection. Too high a level of security, while providing maximum protection, can result in a system that is both difficult to use and expensive to operate. The losses may outweigh the gains.

Risk analysis requires identifying the area that is vulnerable and finding the risks. This is not easy because it is not always possible to know what the risks are, and their identification requires a clear vision of what the company is trying to achieve and what it regards as success criteria. Gurpreet Dhillon and James Backhouse have described some of the precautions that firms take to increase computer security.[3] The most common are security checklists that identify every kind of control that can be implemented. These can also act as evaluation checks for an existing system, identifying what controls are there and others that could be added. The limitation is that they focus on "what can be done" rather than on what needs to be done. More sophisticated methods are scenario analysis and simulation studies. The former involves identifying hypothetical events while the latter is expensive, time consuming, and requires special software.

Risk analysis also involves risk *assessment*. This is an analysis of the seriousness of different risks by determining the probability and potential damage of each one. For example, major risks come from a large concentration of data in one place and the fact that data are increasingly accessed through local area networks (LANS). A difficulty here is that not all of these users will be known.[4] Risks are not always separate and distinct, there can be relationships between them. The book *The Cuckoo's Egg* tells how the ability of a hacker to enter a university laboratory computer opened up the possibility of entry into the computers of military bases.[5] Risk analysis identifies risks; risk assessment tries to estimate how likely risks are to happen and how serious the consequences will be. Break-ins depend on a variety of things: the computer and networking systems in use, the existing infrastructure (Internet or not), existing security measures, how attractive the company is as a target, where the company is located, and its size and number of staff.

Risk *prioritization* implies a recognition that all companies cannot be protected from all risks and that the next best thing is to choose a subset of the most serious, or the most likely, that can be managed without too much cost or difficulty. Risk impact is the magnitude of the loss if a break-in or fraud occurs. Risk control involves further actions to reduce the risk and to trigger further defensive actions if a criminal activity occurs.[6] Risk control also covers the monitoring of risk on a regular basis. Is existing protection still effective? Have new risks now appeared? This leads to risk reassessment. Monitoring, together with the detailed documentation of any problems or illegal activities when they occur, is essential to avoid complacency. Too often companies will work out a detailed risk-management program and then forget that they have done so. The program is not used because of a lack of accountability or commitment or because of incompetence or ignorance. Risk-management programs need to be the responsibility of all employees with everyone appreciative of their importance and value.

Finally, companies need to be aware of the costs of breaches of security and that these are likely to greatly outweigh the costs of providing protection. They will include loss of business through loss of customer confidence, a particular risk for banks; the costs of recovering the system; the cost of insurance investigations; and the cost of court action.[7]

SECURITY CAPABILITY

Once risks have been assessed, prioritized, and the need for strategies to reduce them accepted, it is useful to identify security tools and actions that can provide protection. Judith Jeffcoate has emphasized that any effective security system must fulfill two functions: the prevention of attacks and the detection of attacks after they have taken place. She provides a list of security measures. These include *authentication checks* such as digital certificates and signatures, so that the right of users to access a system can be ensured. Next comes *access control* with passwords or smart cards to prevent unauthorized access and *confidentiality* through the use of data encryption. Then there are *integrity checks* to detect the unauthorized creation, alteration, or deletion of data, and *nonrepudiation*, which ensures that a partner to a transaction cannot deny his or her involvement. Measures for the detection of attacks include *audit tools* such as log files so that historical information can be checked and *real-time monitoring* to establish what is happening now.[8] Products that will assist these security measures include servers that will check identity and authorization, firewalls that prevent access to private networks, antivirus scanners, and a new set of devices called trust services. These incorporate protective functions in their design. Computer vendors are now encouraged to produce computer systems that can be trusted. Procedures that are unusual or deviations from a normal pattern are made difficult to conceal. These systems are used extensively by the U.S. Department of Defense.

Viruses, discussed in the previous chapter, are another common problem. They can be aggressive and destroy data, producing what one attacked U.S. air force base has described as "a continual state of information war." The latest viruses corrupt user data and, once in a system, use the standard commands of the application concerned. They also reproduce and try to infect as many systems as possible. Virus prevention tools check all the different ways a virus can get into a system and are able to block access. Unfortunately, many new viruses can beat antivirus software.

In addition to devices that protect against fraud, the computer industry is launching forensic tool kits that can help establish when fraud has taken place. They can search systems and check for illegal or inappropriate use. They can give users advice on the actions they can take when fraud is found. There are also attack simulators that systematically look for security loopholes and list them in reports. They replicate what hackers do when trying to enter a system. All of these devices are welcome developments in a security area where problems are increasing, not decreasing. Unfortunately, new security loopholes and viruses are appearing all the time.

An important guide to good security has been developed by the British Department of Trade and Industry, with the help of major companies such as Shell International, Unilever, Marks and Spencers, and a number of others. The BSi Code of Practice for Information Security Management gives detailed advice on every aspect of computer security. There have also been attempts to harmonize security systems in Europe with France, Germany, the Netherlands, and the United Kingdom trying to coordinate and combine the best features of national initiatives. In May 1990 a first draft of a document called the Information Technology Security Evaluation Criteria, also known as the White Book, was issued.[9] By 1998 there should be a new European Commission Directive on data protection that will aim to harmonize data protection within the EEC and create a Data Fortress Europe. It will also block the transfer of data out of Europe to countries considered to have inadequate data-protection standards.

Other important international initiatives are also taking place. The G8 nations—the United States, Britain, Canada, France, Germany, Italy, Japan, and Russia—met in Washington, D.C. in December 1997 to discuss new threats to the human race. One threat that was given considerable attention was cyber crime, and they looked at digital threats in five main areas: pedophilia and sexual exploitation, drug trafficking, money laundering, electronic fraud, and industrial and state espionage. The ministers present agreed to give much higher priority to training their law enforcement officers to combat cyber crime. This was influenced by an earlier report from President Clinton on critical infrastructure protection, which had concluded that the United States, and other nations, had no effective means of protecting itself from devastating computer attacks on government and industry. The only way of combating this threat was for nations to share information and have common strategies. The G8 meeting agreed to do the following:

- Create contacts available twenty-four hours a day so countries can quickly track computer criminals.
- Train and equip enough law enforcement officers to fight high-tech crime and help agencies abroad.
- Review their legal systems to ensure high-tech crimes are treated properly.
- Build computer crime issues into treaties and aid agreements.
- Improve cross-border searches of data files containing information on criminals.
- Develop quicker ways to identify hackers and trace attacks on computer networks.
- Carry out a criminal prosecution in the country the suspect flees to if extradition is impossible.
- Work with the industry to find new ways to detect and prevent crimes.
- Use new technologies (e.g., video links) to obtain testimonies from witnesses in other countries.[10]

ENCRYPTION CAPABILITY

A valuable security tool is cryptography. This can be used to ensure data's confidentiality and integrity. It can also assist user authentication and nonrepudiation. David Kahn, author of *The Codebreakers*, has described, in an article in the British *Daily Telegraph* newspaper, the history of cryptology.[11] Julius Ceasar used a simple version of this and much later it became an integral part of code-making and code-breaking. During World War I radio messages were always coded, although these codes proved relatively easy to break. Alan Turing, later to become a Reader at Manchester University, became renowned for breaking the German Enigma code. This helped the Allies to win the war. Today, the most common security approach is cryptography. Encryption is putting a readable message known as "plaintext" through a computer program that translates the message into unreadable "ciphertext" using algorithms. Decryption is translating the message back when received by someone who has the "key." Cryptography can be used to protect personal messages over the Internet and for military intelligence. It can ensure data integrity, authenticate users, ensure a message gets to the correct user, and maintain confidentiality. Some organizations use their own proprietary algorithms to protect their data. Others use published or public algorithms such as the American Data Encryption Standard (DES).

The principal difficulty in maintaining the security offered by a strong cipher is protecting the key that translates data into code and back again. This key has to be available to all people sharing the system, and these users could be large in numbers, with a failure in key protection affecting all of them. A common method of protection is to have different keys for encryption and decryption, but here, as in other areas, security is constantly being eroded by technical advances that negate protection, such as through developments in computing speeds and mathematical theory. Both of these enable very strong keys to be broken.

Encryption presents a dilemma between the need of companies for commercial privacy and the need for access to communications by law enforcement and national security agencies. This is particularly the case in the United States where in 1992 the FBI proposed legislation that would enable it to conduct wiretaps of digital communication networks. The bureau wanted to prohibit any technology that hindered its ability to do this and, in consequence, it has restricted the export of some U.S. encryption devices. This problem has not been resolved with the FBI pressing the U.S. government to require telecommunication companies to ensure law enforcement agencies can tap transmission lines.[12]

The U.S National Security Agency (NSA) argues that easing encryption export rules would hurt NSA's ability to analyze foreign communications. The information gathered by the agency is considered vital to countering terrorism and drug trafficking.[13]

INVESTIGATION CAPABILITY

A major difficulty for most managers is recognizing that a security problem exists. Many may never find out that their files are being accessed or that they are losing money through fraud. Fraud presents particular problems because this kind of criminal activity is most frequently carried out by someone inside the company. The first step is always to find out who has committed the crime, how, and why. A logical next step is to consult the police, and this is good practice if it is certain that a criminal activity has taken place. However, the police are unlikely to want to investigate if there is any doubt as to whether a crime has been committed, and the company may not want to notify them in if it is anxious about adverse publicity. The alternative is to carry out the investigation internally or hire a security company or a forensic computer scientist.

If the company decides to investigate the crime itself, it needs to act logically and systematically. The first step will be to create a crisis management team. This should be small, contain relevant expertise, and its members should report directly to the board of directors. Next the seriousness of the threat must be evaluated. How will the business be affected, who within or outside is most vulnerable, can the worst effects of the threat be diminished or avoided, what actions need to be taken to restore the situation to normal and to catch the criminal? Legal advice is now essential as computer evidence may be required for prosecution or for an insurance claim.[14]

At present, fraud is one of the easiest kinds of crime to commit and the least likely to encounter prosecution. There are problems in many countries in defining what fraud is, whether to prosecute, and whether to imprison.[15] Fraud, today, is also extremely complex. It is multilayered and may require different skills to prevent or identify it. It also has wide ramifications and can affect large numbers of the public. This is especially true if the organizations targeted have been governments, banks, or finance houses. One important way of making progress is by learning from past mistakes. This can only be done on a wide scale if frauds and other computer security problems are made public.

When a major fraud turns into cyber terrorism and becomes a disaster, responsible companies will have a business continuity plan in place ready to be implemented. This involves establishing which are the most critical functions of the business, and these will vary according to a company's nature. Maintaining cash flow might be the most important task for a small company, while another might place more importance on getting priority production out. But almost certainly the most important need is to ensure that employees can function adequately after the disaster, for it is they who will have to get the business running again. Many companies are unprepared for a serious incident even though fraud experts suggest that a majority stricken in this way do not survive for more than two years.[16]

ORGANIZATIONAL CAPABILITY

Present security approaches focus on technical aids to protection, yet other factors may be equally or more important. Dhillon and Backhouse have criticized current approaches to security as being oversimplified, too prescriptive, and neglectful of people issues. They point out that most strategies assume that information systems have strict boundaries that can be protected and monitored; that they are discrete processes with input, throughput, output, and feedback; that organizations can be considered secure if identified needs are met, and that overall security can be achieved by analyzing the constituent parts of the system.[17]

An alternative view is that crimes are committed by people and that much more attention should be paid to the organizational and social context in which the crime takes place and to the social processes involved. For example, well-thought-out organizational arrangements can assist the provision of protection. Opportunities for fraud can be avoided through work structures that split responsibilities and have clear lines of inspection and authority. Nick Leeson was able to break Barings because his activities received little or no supervision (see chapter 10). The fact that he was apparently making money for the bank meant that he was given almost total autonomy.

There are companies, and I have worked in some of them, where sloppy or uncaring management leads to a general atmosphere, at every level, of "I'm going to take what I can from this firm, either legally or illegally." This attitude can be particularly strong if the firm has poor personnel policies and treats its workers badly. Research in the United States and the United Kingdom suggests that in many work environments there is a percentage of employees who will never steal or break company rules. There is also a group of employees who are out to test the controls and abuse the system. If this group is unchecked and grows in size, honest employees will leave, enabling the corrupt group to commit misdeeds on an even larger scale.[18] The company is then on a suicide course. It has lost its ethical base.

It is worth stressing again that there is still little understanding of the size of the threat caused by illegal practices such as hacking. The U.S. Department of Defense, the world's largest computer user, has warned that only one in 150 hackers gets detected. The DOD warns that attacks of this kind can be a serious threat to national security. They give as an example an attack on the Rome Laboratory, the U.S. air force's premier command and control system. Here two hackers seized control of laboratory systems and stole tactical and intelligence research data.[19]

HOW INDUSTRY IS TACKLING THE PROBLEM

Cyber crime is investigated by the police, but it is suffered by industry. This makes it important to obtain industry's point of view. I have interviewed senior management and security staff in two major companies, ICI and Shell, in order to learn how they define the problem and the strategies they use to combat it.

In 1988 the *Journal of Management Accounting* reported that computer fraud was rife, and that company finance departments must take responsibility for fraud prevention and detection.[20] It also stressed that a very low priority was being given to risks and that the problem would increase as companies moved to on-line real-time systems. Today, the threat has greatly increased, and rigorous measures are being taken to ward off criminal raids from an international fraud environment. Companies are advised to have expert investigative teams available in case this happens and to build up a relationship with experienced officers in their local police force.

ICI has an ex-assistant chief constable as its security adviser. He believes that the most serious threat is from hacking as a manifestation of industrial espionage. If access is obtained to the company's computer files, data on its products and its financial position could be passed on to competitors. This would greatly weaken its competitive position, reveal its plans for the future, assist other companies contemplating a take-over, and result in insider dealing of shares. ICI now has a department dedicated to computer security that takes responsibility for problems within the system. These would include both hacking and the introduction of computer viruses. An important part of its security plan is the creation of a computer incident response team. This includes a solicitor, an information technology manager, an investigation expert, a hands-on expert, and a forensic computer consultant. It is now a very powerful group that investigates problems as they arise and develops data protection strategies.

But, despite this excellent planning, ICI recognizes that the problem is a very difficult one to control. There is, first, the difficulty of knowing when an unauthorized person is gaining access and, second, the problem of identifying and preserving evidence. The new rules regarding the disclosure of evidence to the defense in criminal trials are also causing great problems and may inhibit taking offenders to court. The fact that the prosecution has to make all evidence available, including evidence not used in the trial, means that the very data the hacker was trying to steal would become public knowledge. It is, of course, this data that the company has a vital interest in keeping confidential.

It is also difficult to ask for police help when hacking is suspected. The police need proof that criminal activity is taking place, they do not have the resources to respond to unsubstantiated suggestions that something is wrong. ICI sees its only defense as making the system as invulnerable to attack as possible. This is not easy as the expert hacker has the ability to invade almost any system and no one can say with confidence that their system is totally secure. Prevention is also expensive. The need for firewalls and other protective devices greatly increases costs, while monitoring systems for security require constant surveillance to check that there is no unauthorized access. In the end the problem becomes a race for knowledge. Each new protective device is only marginally ahead of an expert hacker whose objective is to beat that device.

Another very sensitive area that can relate to computers is corporate liability. Any disasters that are a result of gross negligence or lead to manslaughter can result in criminal prosecution if a criminal intent can be proven. A toughening of this area of the law has put great pressure on management to get things right. In Britain, a parliamentary working party is discussing disasters with liability and the ICI board has prepared a document on security standards, setting out its policy and required standards. These apply to ICI plants throughout the world. At the ICI Runcorn plant, where the security adviser is located, security is taken very seriously. There is a crisis management room that applies practices similar to those used by the police. For example, incidents are managed using a bronze, silver, or gold command structure, indicating their degree of seriousness. This is identical to the approach used by the emergency services.

In recent years ICI security has been made more difficult by the number of companies on the Runcorn site, many no longer owned by ICI. Outsourcing has also created problems, as important computer activities may now be handled by outside firms. ICI security guidelines state:

> The foundation of good security is a proper assessment of the security threat and the establishment of the security risk acceptable to the Company. This

> requires close co-operation with external authorities, e.g., police and other relevant agencies from whom information on the threat may come....
>
> In the case of information systems, which can present particular technical vulnerabilities, IT security and Group Internal Audit must be involved from the outset. The ICI IT security function has published its own Security Policy which is consistent with the overall ICI Group Security Policy and will work in close co-operation with relevant Security Advisers where necessary.

Shell has much the same security policies as ICI does. It has its own guidelines on security that everyone must adhere to. It protects itself through firewalls around the periphery of its systems and around each subsystem, and it carries out a regular audit of its security measures. But, like ICI, it recognizes that protection cannot be total, and that a company is only as secure as its weakest player. Problems may include the fact that the company has to do business with any part of the world and that it is not always easy to define what constitutes fraud. Management recognizes that many people today are in the business of selling information, and information brokering has become a multimillion dollar industry, yet there is no legislation to prevent competitors getting addresses and spreading misinformation. Shell sees the best preventative measures as having good codes of practice and ensuring that these are adhered to, while making fraud as difficult as possible. This means that if a criminal does break in, it is not easy for him or her to progress through the system. Shell also tries to be aware of its own security gaps and weaknesses and to develop relationships of trust and respect with its customers. Everyone in the company is expected to be aware of security risks and ensure that good business practice keeps these to a minimum. If any criminal activity is detected Shell goes straight to the police. There is no attempt to keep it secret.

REQUIRED COMPETENCIES

Most advice on security focuses on what the company must do to protect itself and on the capabilities it requires as an organization in order to do this. But effective security requires intellectual and psychological competencies, and these are skills individuals must supply. Cyber crimes are carried out by people with powerful objectives and motivations, and these need to be understood by those trying to entrap them. At the same time protection requires committed staff who as individuals are constantly vigilant and on the look-out for breaches of security. These staff need to know exactly what to do and whom to tell if they suspect that security breaches are taking place. The following competencies, also called intellectual attributes or skills, would seem to be essential.

Cognitive Competencies

Cognitive competencies include an understanding of the possible threats to the business situation from cyber crime and a recognition of the need for continual vigilance. This needs to be reinforced by an up-to-date knowledge of the available technical, organizational, and human relations measures that can assist security. As both crime and its prevention have increasingly sophisticated tools and methods associated with them, this knowledge will need constant updating.

Communication Competencies

The competencies of communication would include the ability to communicate and explain the need for vigilance to colleagues and subordinates and to arouse and maintain their interest in security. People who have information have an advantage over others. They understand company policy and what is expected of them in an emergency. Communication skill is a particular requirement for top management. Information that comes from the top of the company is much more powerful than that occurring lower down.

Implementation Competencies

Many companies are excellent at developing strategies but very poor at implementing them. Plans are made and published but then forgotten. No one has responsibility for their implementation. Implementation also requires a different set of skills from strategy formulation. Developing strategy is an intellectual exercise, implementation requires action. If a crisis has already occurred then this action will need to be both appropriate and fast. Effective implementation is greatly assisted by a degree of power. If an influential person at the top of the company is pushing for greater attention to be paid to security, then this is likely to happen. But influence alone is not enough. Even the managing director will need to keep repeating the security message if it is to endure. The message has to become internalized and a part of the company culture. There need to be regular meetings to review security measures, and these need to be chaired by a board-level manager.

Problem-Solving Competencies

Problem-solving competencies would include the following:

- The ability to get everyone in the company involved in problem solving for improved security and to do this before problems occur.
- A knowledge of how to organize work so that responsibility for critical business activities is distributed in the most effective manner to secure protection against data theft or corruption.
- A recognition of the weak lines in operational computer systems so that these can be effectively guarded against.
- A knowledge of how to implement planned procedures when a security alert occurs.
- An ability to learn from the experience of handling security risks.

These competencies are important at every level in the organization, but they are particularly important at the top.

COORDINATION

Coordination is always important. At the risk-management and strategy-development stages there has to be internal coordination between departments so that security priorities are accepted and agreed upon and plans are developed that have general agreement. If a criminal activity is discovered then fast implementation becomes a necessity, and coordination will very likely involve external groups such as security investigators, lawyers, and the police. All of these individuals need to understand the nature and importance of the attack, to share information, and to agree on appropriate action. Coordination now needs to be creative. At a later stage steps must be taken to see that the crime cannot occur again.

ATTITUDES

For all of these competencies to be effective, they must be accompanied by positive attitudes. Staff must feel committed to the organization and that its interests are also theirs. This commitment is likely to be strongest when people feel proud of their company and of the contribution that they are making to it. They also need to believe that the company has competent leaders and is both successful and a good employer.

LESSONS LEARNED FROM CYBER CRIME

The lessons that problem solvers can learn from cyber crime are different from those they can learn from the drug scene. Cyber crime, much more than drugs, is about prevention in situations where the possibility of attack ranges from very possible to unlikely. While the drug problem is apparent to most people, although definitions of how much it is a problem vary, the cyber crime problem is hidden and often unheeded. Many managers are quite unaware of it, and this is true at all levels in the company from the board down. Those that do realize that fraud or illegal access to files is possible too frequently have an "it can't happen here" attitude. Nevertheless, when companies are aware and decide to take precautions some useful problem-solving lessons can be learned. One is that there are now available a considerable number of technical aids to protection. These will deter many criminals and especially those that are located within the company. They make fraud more difficult to carry out. Unfortunately, serious professional criminals will usually have the skills to get past these devices and this means they have to be continually upgraded.

A second valuable lesson is the usefulness of risk-management techniques in assisting an accurate diagnosis of vulnerability to attack. Risk analysis and assessment can then lead to effective security strategies and plans to prevent attack, to know when it is happening, and to respond in a way that causes least disturbance to the company. A difficulty, already referred to, is that excellent strategies can be formulated, then forgotten and never implemented. As with all serious problems there needs to be an awareness that cyber crime is a continuing long-term threat, and that a culture of caution and constant surveillance needs to become an important part of company values and attitudes.

One difficulty with cyber crime, which is not part of the drug problem, is that the availability of so many technical solutions can mean that total reliance is placed on these and little attention is paid to the attitudes, fears, and needs of people. Crimes are carried out by people, they have to be investigated by people, and the criminals caught by people. The survival of the company after a successful crime is likely to depend on the people it employs as staff. Nevertheless, the importance and cost of the technical interface that acts as protection can mean that the human factor is given little consideration. Effective security requires continual vigilance and a constant watch for the very small clues that show something is going wrong. This is best carried out by those who produce or use the data, and it requires each member of staff to take responsibility for the security of the data he or she handles.

At a national level, the U.S. Department of Defense is trying to improve problem solving associated with Internet security through scenario-based games. These games are directed at alerting people to the magnitude of the dangers that may confront them in the future. The participants are first presented with a very difficult theoretical situation without having the time to do any meaningful analysis. Two days later they are given a further briefing in which the situation has gotten much worse but it is still impossible to understand what is happening. There is no evidence to show who is the criminal behind the events of what his or her intentions are. The point of the exercise is to demonstrate how difficult problem solving in this area is and to try and improve ways of tackling possible security threats through thinking in unconventional ways. There is little government confidence that technology alone can prevent dangerous break-ins.[21]

Perhaps the most important message for managers is if technology assists protection then make good use of it, but do not put your trust in technology alone. Your best protectors and detectives will be your own staff, provided you and they are knowledgeable and aware of the criminals at your gate. One of the principal differences between the drug problem and cyber crime is that cyber crime technology is constantly evolving. Whereas the popularity of different drugs varies according to fashion and price, little else changes. The next threat for managers is the increasing proliferation of networks and the use of the Internet for all aspects of business, both within the firm and in its relationships with other companies and customers. Many of these problems have yet to be experienced.

CHAPTER 12

Money Laundering

Where Drugs and Cyber Crime Meet

The last stop on our problem-solving journey is an examination of the place where the profits of illegal drugs and cyber crime end up. This is money laundering, a term used for the movement of money obtained through criminal activity. Drugs and cyber crime go their separate ways until both groups of criminals need to conceal their large profits. They then make use of the sophisticated techniques of money laundering in order to spread their money around and deter crime prevention agencies from becoming aware of their existence. Money laundering can be described as a series of transactions that attempt to conceal the true origin and ownership of property obtained by unlawful means in such a way that it appears to have come from legitimate sources. This process has been used since the first private bank came into existence because from that time criminals have had the need to convert the money they made from their illegal activities into cash or possessions that appeared to have been obtained honestly. The term comes from the United States where the Mafia in the 1930s and 1940s hid their illicit profits from bootlegging, gambling and prostitution by buying new laundromats that were becoming popular.[1] Until the mid-1980s the procedure was quite simple. Money was sent to a country where banking activities were kept secret, such as Switzerland, which for many years was considered an excellent hiding place. It was then brought back into circulation as "clean" money, with its origin unknown.

Money laundering is frequently a product of organized crime but is not itself always designated a crime. In 1970 the United States became the first country to declare money laundering illegal. Britain was second in 1986 when the British Parliament passed the Drugs Trafficking Offences Act. Few other countries have antimoney laundering legislation. The British National Criminal Intelligence Service (NCIS) has described organized crime as having four principal characteristics. It is a group activity; its primary purpose is financial gain; it is a criminal activity that is long term and continuing; it is carried out irrespective of national boundaries. Other characteristics are that it is large-scale; it generates proceeds often used for legitimate purposes; and it is carried out by groups with some discipline and structure.

Because money creates power, money laundering brings with it the social danger of consolidating the economic power of criminal organizations, enabling them to penetrate the legitimate economy. There is evidence that when organized crime invests in legitimate business activities it attempts to dominate the market and to engage in predatory pricing, extortion, and corruption.[2]

The term became well known with the explosion of the drugs trade in the early 1980s. Vast sums of money were then passed around the world, stimulated by the flourishing South American cocaine market. The term "narco" dollars had arrived. Every year, in Europe and North America, some several hundred billion dollars are available for laundering. In the United States the amount is estimated to be between $300 billion to $500 billion. A considerable percentage of this comes from the drug traffic. In 1995 it was estimated that at least 60% of the world's money was held offshore. Over $600 billion passed through the banks of the Cayman Islands, the fifth largest banking center in the world. The British Virgin Islands have over 120,000 trust companies registered there, with many nominee shareholders or directors.

Most money laundering schemes uncovered in Europe in the early 1990s were relatively unsophisticated, but some of the very large cases are extremely complex. An example is stated by William Gilmore in his book *Dirty Money*. Eastern European groups were involved in this and the laundering was carried out by two Chechen brothers, who were murdered before the operation was completed. They arrived in England in late 1992 with approximately five million U.S. dollars in cash and the same amount in German marks. Their first step was to place substantial deposits in a major British clearing bank and in American financial institutions in London. Accounts were opened in "shell companies" in the Bahamas and the British Virgin Islands. A shell company is a firm that seems legitimate but has been set up to conceal the movement of money. Other domestic and foreign banks were approached and money was deposited in a large variety of different currencies. A London-based company in Park Lane was then established to manage the movement of the money. Next electronic transfers were made to accounts all over the world—Los Angeles, Vienna, St. Petersburg, Nicosia, Moscow, Warsaw, Paris. The end product was a widespread net with complex methods for establishing hiding places for a very large amount of money.[3]

All laundering seems to have three common factors: The launderers need to conceal the ownership and origins of the assets; they need to maintain control over the assets; and they need to change the form of the assets. It is also a three-stage process. First, the placement stage in which there is a deposit of cash in a legitimate account, for example a branch of a London clearing bank. Here it may be mixed with the fraudster's own money or with money from other victims. Second, the movement of these funds in such a way as to conceal their origin and ownership. This is called layering. Now the money may be electronically transferred from London to New York and then on to other destinations, possibly ending up once again in Europe. And third, the integration stage in which funds are converted into a form the criminal can control. Some may be withdrawn as cash, the rest used to buy a property or set up a shell company. For example, Howard Marks, a public school-educated narcotics dealer, created a boutique in Oxford called Annabelinda to hide his increasing profits from the importation of cannabis. Many female graduates had their wedding dresses made there. As his drugs business and profits grew, Annabelinda was not sufficient concealment and he invested in a Hong Kong travel agency. Brian Charrington, a drug dealer who operated in Teesside, had a car-selling business as a front.

Helen Norman suggests that the phenomenon of money laundering has arisen because of a combination of two factors. First, the advent of offshore havens that were originally seen as offering an opportunity for tax avoidance. Today, they act as "black boxes" shielding the criminal from the glare of investigation. These offshore organizations provide the opportunity to form companies, together with banking confidentiality and a minimum amount of banking regulation.[4] Second, the electronic transfer of funds as a result of the advent of new technology and the "information highway" via satellite and fiber-optic communications. This technology means that cash can be paid into a bank account opened in the name of either an active or a shell company in a country or organization that asks few questions regarding the money's origin. This money can be sent around the world as a "stream of electrons." It can be passed on electronically through a series of accounts held in different names in different countries in an attempt to destroy the audit trail. Or it can be drawn only on the use of a credit card in a cash dispenser in another country, with the credit card settled (with no questions asked) by a bank in an offshore jurisdiction.

The best place to hide money is a corrupt bank and the Bank of Credit and Commerce International (BCCI) in the United States became famous for its three thousand criminal customers. This was a $20 billion rogue empire with operations in sixty-two countries that was shut down in 1991 as a result of the combined efforts of the United States, Britain, France, and Interpol. Its criminal activity was discovered by a team of U.S. customs agents who disguised themselves as money launderers operating on behalf of a group of small firms. They won the confidence of a major laundering broker servicing the Medellin cocaine cartel and they engaged in "smurfing," the term used for spreading money around so as to conceal it. They were instructed to use banks belonging to BCCI, and it soon became clear that BCCI knew that the money it was handling was drug-related. After $31 million had been successfully laundered out of the country by customs itself, the bank was closed down, and eighty-four people arrested. This caused a sensation in the international banking community because BCCI was the largest private bank in the world.[5] In the end BCCI got off lightly. Plea bargaining meant that all charges were dropped against the parent company in Switzerland.

Banks now try to protect themselves by a set of security measures that include requiring customer identification, the introduction of strict record-keeping rules, and the reporting of suspicious transactions. Needless to say, determined criminals have ways of getting around all of these. It is likely that money laundering will become easier rather than more difficult in the future. The growth of electronic commerce means that electronic money will be widely used and dirty money become even more easy to conceal. The lifting of barriers between eastern and western Europe has added to the problem. In Russia control of both drugs and laundering is virtually nonexistent. A further problem is that it is not easy to distinguish money laundering from legal trading activities and many criminals are prosecuted for tax evasion rather than marketing illegal goods. This was true of Al Capone, the famous Chicago gangster, during the U.S. period of alcohol prohibition.

TRACING THE PROCEEDS OF CRIME

Tracing is the weapon used against laundering. It enables cash or other valuable assets held in one form, at one place, at one moment in time, to be located in another form, at another place, at a later date. Successful tracing has been described as "lengthening the victim's reach." It enables lost assets to eventually be recovered.[6] But the longer its reach and the greater its protection against fraud, the more complex it becomes. It requires great skill, perseverance, determination, and a knowledge of how money can be moved around in different ways, including electronically. A further complication is that assets can change their form as they travel. They may undergo a physical change becoming some form of property, or a cosmetic change becoming a different currency. Because tracing is difficult there are pressures for the criminal justice system to develop an efficient and effective method for tracing, freezing, and eventually confiscating the proceeds from criminal activity. Money laundering must also be criminalized.

The word "tracing" implies finding and following something along a difficult, extended, and concealed route. But it is also a term used by lawyers to describe a set of rules for identifying property to which a claim has been made. Tracing tells the victim where the money is hidden. "Restitution," another legal term, answers the question of whether the victim can claim it back or get compensation for it. Misappropriated funds are often laundered through a series of bank accounts. The problem is how do the victims identify what is theirs? The legal concept of tracing evolved in an era when electronic transfer of funds was unknown and when the scale and complexity of transactions was insignificant compared with today's cases.

The mixing of funds makes tracing very difficult, but it can be done. An increasingly popular investigative technique is known as "controlled delivery." This allows the laundering to take place but keeps it under constant and secret surveillance until it arrives at its final destination. The intention is to identify the principals in the activity, not merely lesser players. The method has been used extensively with drugs by the FBI in its fight against the Mafia. It is even more valuable for money laundering.

With drugs it is easy to establish if substances are illegal. It is less easy to know if funds are the proceeds of crime.

Paul Matthews gives examples of tracing. A British businessman was deprived of a large sum of money through a fraud carried out in Amsterdam. The money passed through several bank accounts in several countries before being used to finance a property development venture. It was traced through matching debits with credits along the route taken by the money, but at one point the trail was almost lost. It had become difficult to separate the stolen money from other money in a particular account. In another case one defendant was a foreign bank said to have received a British company's funds via a series of transactions in which it received money in sterling from another bank, in exchange for Turkish lire. The original money had now been replaced by another currency. After a major robbery at London's Heathrow Airport in 1985 tracing enabled the insurer to recover much of the money, but it was a difficult process. A complex web of bank accounts had to be unraveled stretching from the United States to the Caribbean and including London, Europe, and the Far East.[7]

PROBLEM SOLVING THROUGH INTERNATIONAL COOPERATION

An editorial in the *European* in May 1997 claimed that "the 1990s are in danger of becoming the decade when international crime becomes Europe's leading business." European member of Parliament Gijs de Vries is quoted as saying "we have a modern equivalent of the ten biblical plagues: drugs trade, fraud, corruption, trafficking in human beings, counterfeiting, piracy, illegal cigarette trade, car theft, environmental crime and terrorism."[8] All of these can end in money laundering. There have been a number of attempts to control this at the intergovernmental level through increased cooperation between judicial and law enforcement authorities.

The Vienna Convention in December 1988 was organized by the United Nations to address illicit traffic in drugs. One hundred states participated in this convention and it established internationally recognized offenses related to drug trafficking that were to be criminalized under domestic law. Five years later the Maastricht Treaty of 1993 stressed the need for intergovernmental cooperation on justice and home affairs, including fraud and drug addiction. This meeting led to the creation of Europol with a brief to make drug trafficking and money laundering its first priority.[9]

In 1991 the European Union passed a money laundering directive that became operational in 1995. Member states now agreed to legislate in order to enable the proceeds of drug smuggling and other serious crimes to be seized by national authorities. This was primarily addressed at credit and financial institutions, which were told to take steps to ensure that money laundering could be detected. A policy of "know your customer" was introduced. Banks, building societies, and other financial institutions were now required to maintain identification procedures and other internal controls directed at forestalling and preventing money laundering.[10] Europol, the European police initiative, now took responsibility for coordinating European cooperative action against money laundering.

In the United States legislation was introduced so that trading in dollars illegally in any part of the world was subject to prosecution under U.S. law. This meant that if a criminal tried to transfer the dollar proceeds of his or her crimes to a secret account in Switzerland via an account in New York, the transaction came within the jurisdiction of a New York court.[11] Europol's database greatly assisted the exchange of information on large-scale crime. Schengen, a group of countries that cooperated on border controls at common frontiers, had also created a database, SIS, which contained over three million files on individuals and stolen goods. This was intended to facilitate arrests and other police work within the European Union. The 1991 directive was the first legislative measure to be adopted by the European Commission and was follow-up legislation to the 1988 convention and to a 1990 Council of Europe convention on laundering and the confiscation of the proceeds of crime.[12]

A further weapon in the war against money laundering is the Financial Action Task Force (FATF). The decision to create this task force was made at the July 1989 Paris meeting of heads of state. Canada, France, Germany, Italy, Japan, the United Kingdom, the United States, and the Commission of the European Community all agreed to support this initiative and they were joined by seven other European countries and by Australia. It is now the only international body that fights against money laundering. The mandate of FATF is "to establish standards that can be endorsed by national authorities and applied internationally in order to prevent the utilization of the banking system and financial institutes for the purpose of money laundering." Its mission is to promote multinational antimoney laundering in all parts of the world. It does this by studying the trends and methods used to launder the billions of dollars flowing through laundering channels and to assess the potential for better international cooperation.

It began its task by focusing on drug trafficking syndicates and studying the most serious problems. These were criminal assets and their forfeiture, the criminal use of shell corporations and related organizations, and the regulation of electronic money transfers and of nonbank financial enterprises such as casinos and bureaux de change. FATF produced forty regulations to be implemented by each member country and by as many other countries as they could persuade to cooperate. FATF works closely with Interpol and carries out a comprehensive educational program to persuade more countries to join the antimoney laundering club. It also persuades its members to carry out rigorous self-assessments of their achievements and agree to periodic peer reviews from teams of at least three representatives from other member countries. Almost all countries have now recognized money laundering as a crime, although the majority limit their criminalization laws to drug trafficking.

Despite these developments difficult problems soon surfaced. The collapse of communism in Eastern Europe provided fertile opportunities for many criminal gangs who, it is now believed, own many of the new banks that have been established there. Russia emerged as a major factor in organized crime and as a big user of international money laundering with the Russian Mafia controlling its own financial institutions. When, in 1996, the Russian government claimed that its crime rate was declining, other European countries were fearful that this was due to the spread of crime into legitimate businesses. The British police were also concerned that the Russians were trying hard to get their money into London. If it was accepted there it would be accepted anywhere.

A new group of professional money launderers had now emerged to service the pro-laundering interests. These were often linked to corrupt banking, political, and economic interests.[13] These money "managers" and the drug traffickers learned from each other, and both worked together to circumvent the new measures governments were adding to banking and criminal laws.

In the 1980s, powers to confiscate the proceeds of crime and to combat money laundering were relatively new developments in the United Kingdom. England now had its own legislation, which was introduced by the 1986 Drug Trafficking Offences Act. This was amended several times to strengthen it and was then consolidated in the Drug Trafficking Act of 1994. This act covered offenses associated with the proceeds of drug trafficking, corruption, theft, and obtaining money by deception. It prohibited providing assistance to money launderers and created new powers to confiscate cash associated with the drugs trade. Failure to comply with these provisions could lead to prison sentences of fourteen years. In the United Kingdom, for legal reasons, banks placed less emphasis on the probity of the customer and more on watching for suspicious transactions. When a suspicious transaction occurred there was an obligation to notify the NCIS in London. The United Kingdom Treasury was also tightening and expanding its antilaundering penalties. In 1997 a package of new measures was proposed including the regulation of company formation agents who set up shell companies. These could conceal the identification of the funds' owner, make records difficult to access, and act on instructions from remote and anonymous owners.

The United States was also leading the way in efforts to combat money laundering. In 1994 President Clinton signed a Money Laundering Suppression Act. This introduced a system based on the idea of a "paper trail" in which every bank was required to file a Currency Transaction Report (CTR) for cash deposits of $10,000 or more. The aim of this was to trace drug money. Government agents monitored these reports for clues leading to the identification of drug trafficking customers. Unfortunately, this merely led to criminals placing their money through channels other than banks. Research also showed that the emphasis on drug money was misplaced. Up to 50% of the billions of dollars laundered in America were funds from customers and enterprises not involved with drug trafficking.[14]

The United States is continually reviewing its money laundering laws. In 1996, 2,000 people were accused of money laundering compared with 360 in 1991. Of these forty percent of the 1996 group were also charged with white-collar offenses such as bank and securities fraud. But, despite these efforts, the U.S. Financial Crimes Enforcement Network (FinCEN) created by the U.S. Treasury Department estimates that US$100 billion of drug-related money flows through the country each year. In addition there are the billions obtained from fraud and other illegal activities.[15]

Solutions are not yet in sight. Despite all these initiatives money laundering is becoming more extensive, complex, sophisticated, and internationalized with criminal groups forming strategic alliances. Even in remote parts of the world such as Afghanistan and Indochina sophisticated, Western-oriented, corporate money laundering structures can be found. As new regulations are introduced launderers find new loopholes and points of entry to the banking system. Money laundering is no longer the province of drug barons. It is now associated with general crime, the sale of arms, precious metals, and radioactive substances. It is being used for the purchase and sale of high technology equipment and, even more threatening, it can be used for investment in the legitimate economy through the privatization process. It can only be reduced through effective law enforcement agencies making it more risky, and through enhanced levels of international cooperation.

Much more still needs to be done. An editorial in the *European* in May 1997 stated: "The response from European Governments has been wholly inadequate. They have failed to give a lead in establishing a relationship between their national forces and the international bodies, Interpol and Europol."[16]

WHAT IS THE FUTURE?

Governments and police forces around the world are particularly worried about the development of the Internet and the assistance this will give to tax evasion and money laundering. More and more businesses are using the Internet for their commercial activities, with on-line banking as one example. There are also now Internet banks, many of which are linked with offshore banking. These have many advantages for criminals as they are difficult to investigate and money passing through them can avoid taxation. When offshore banking is accessible by Internet, payments can easily be made to a variety of accounts and illegal money spread around different countries.[17] Many experts believe that these kinds of problems will worsen when electronic transfers are made by thousands of businesses. Organized criminal groups can become Internet service providers and existing systems of regulation will prove to be of little protective value. This may make it difficult for governments to collect taxes, with as yet unknown consequences for society. It is also possible that unchecked money laundering could criminalize the global financial system and undermine development activities in emerging markets.

Money laundering problems, like those of illegal drugs and cyber crime, are not becoming easier to solve; they are becoming more difficult. With cyber crime and money laundering this is partly due to developments in technology. A feature of all three problem areas is that two powerful interest groups are involved everywhere—the criminals, who want crime and its results to be easier and better for them, and the rest of society, backed up by their law-enforcement agencies, who want protection and a reduction or cessation of the criminal activities. This leads to a battleground and to game-playing tactics in which each side continually tries to get one step ahead of the other.

Prosecutions for money laundering are few, and it is suggested that some of the reasons for this are:

- Difficulty in identifying the original offense that resulted in the need to launder its proceeds.
- Lack of information about the identity of the person or organization transferring money and the identity of its ultimate recipient. This problem is now being addressed by SWIFT (Society for Worldwide Interbank Financial Telecommunications), which is requiring more information when interbank money transfers occur.
- The failure of some organizations to report suspicious transactions.
- Lack of effective international cooperation.[18]

PROBLEM-SOLVING LESSONS TO BE LEARNED

Using our analytical categories of competencies, capabilities, and coordination it is clear that attempts to control or reduce money laundering will be most dependent on excellent *coordination*. This will be international and will involve collaborative research into the changing laundering situation with the growing use of the Internet as a subject of utmost importance. It will also involve the cooperation of different countries in the sharing of information and serious attempts to unify their differing legal rules and procedures. Common ways of monitoring the Internet will have to be developed and agreed upon.

This is easy to propose but tremendously difficult to achieve. Within the EC it requires the cooperation of wealthy Western European nations with impoverished eastern European countries. It also requires the abandonment of national attitudes, which prefer secrecy to the sharing of information and, for many, involves a major culture change. And it necessitates individual countries taking action against their own criminal groups. As these move into legitimate business this becomes increasingly difficult.

Everywhere it requires an appreciation of the new problem areas and a commitment to trying to address these in a meaningful and coordinated way. Most of Europe and the United States are dedicated to fighting the drug barons, but there is much less awareness of the problem associated with cyber crime and the Internet.

One way to reduce cyber crime and illegal drug trafficking is to remove the opportunities to launder money. This would mean that criminals could no longer hide their illegal gains and translate these into currencies and commodities that can be used without fear of identification or prosecution. It would not be impossible to do this if governments had the will. But it seems politically infeasible. Drugs and cyber crime money is now so entangled in legitimate business enterprises that no government will risk the commercial opprobrium that would result.

CHAPTER 13

The Challenges of Problem Solving

Problem solving is difficult yet too often it seems to be limited to a process of deciding to do something then following this with a series of actions that intuition suggests will achieve the desired result. This is similar to shooting in the dark. There is no way of knowing that the proposed actions will lead to a solution or even that the problem is soluble. The alternative is to create a well-thought-out, logical path to a solution. The aim of this book has been to provide some guidance on how to achieve this and to examine the difficulties when problems are complex rather than straightforward.

Effective problem solving requires the control of entropy. Entropy is a term used by physicists to describe energy that exists but is unavailable for productive use. When applied to problem solving it can be described as energy that is not being used to good effect. It is wasted on inappropriate strategies and actions that make little contribution. Too much energy of this kind can lead to chaos. The problem becomes increasingly confused and insoluble, and ideas on how to deal with it become more and more clouded.

COMPLEX PROBLEM SOLVING

Problem solving with difficult and complex problems requires a recognition of the interaction that is taking place between psychological, economic, technical, cultural, and political factors. Questions that need to be asked and answered are Who wants to solve this problem? Who will pay the costs of a solution? How can technology assist? What kinds of solutions will be culturally and politically acceptable?[1] Most major problems are affected by the positive or negative answers that are given to these questions. In the United States it is acceptable to describe the action against drugs as a "war" and to involve the military in the problem-solving processes. This approach is not favored in Europe, which prefers a softer approach. But European countries would not, at present, accept a strategy that involved legalizing or decriminalizing the use of drugs even though this would remove drug dealing from the control of criminals. Again, all countries are finding it difficult to introduce effective strategies against money laundering, the process that enables the drug and cyber criminals to realize their profits. This is because illegally acquired money is now becoming irretrievably mixed with money associated with legitimate economic activities.

A second characteristic of complex problems is that parts of them may be very resistant to any solution. Drug dealers when attacked do not go away. They either change their criminal area of interest or are replaced by a new group who continues running the old business. Similarly, hackers are almost impossible to eliminate. As one group is caught, another replaces it. The problem situations then create and maintain their own futures. The opposite is also true. Complex problems always have their vulnerable areas where progress can be made if there is the political will to do so. The removal of money laundering facilities would immediately remove the profits from drugs and cyber crime, and their criminal attraction would cease.

Another feature of complex problems is that they change over time. With drugs youth fashion has a major influence on who takes drugs and what kinds of drugs are used. With cyber crime developments in the business use of computers and in security technology affect the problems that have to be solved. Change here is more dynamic than with drugs because of the relationship between criminals and victims. There is a continual seesaw of competitive activity between the owners of the systems who are trying to protect them and the criminals who are trying to access them.

Most complex problem solving is a balancing act with problems being partially solved then returning in new forms, some of which may be as difficult or more difficult to solve than the original threat. Many solutions, which are politically attractive because they are cheap and acceptable to governments, can lead in the wrong direction. The early responses to mad cow disease provide many examples. Symptoms but not causes are being addressed. The answer here is understanding the social dynamics of the problem and identifying the pressure points where improvement can be secured.

One way of doing this is through identifying variables that are linked together and can be controlled as a single unit.[2] For example, if systems designers help users to play a major role in design, they can secure commitment, facilitate training, and ensure the new system is liked and used. Three problems will be solved through a single initiative. The more linkages that are identified, the more a single or a small number of actions can control them.

Designing a problem-solving program or strategy is communicating an ethical position, a set of values, and a series of practical operations designed to achieve a desired result. This communication stretches from those implementing the program to those benefiting from its results. If time is available a safe strategy is to proceed in stages so that each part of a program can be tested before the next is implemented. It can then be reversed if it has proven to be a mistake.[3] Another useful strategy is looking for "amplification," an amplifier being a device that, if given a small amount of something, will emit much more. A money amplifier would be an organization such as a stock exchange.

Good problem solving requires the avoidance of entropy or inappropriate or redundant activity and the amplification of efficiency and ethical design so that both of these increase as they are spread throughout the system.

MANAGING COMPLEXITY

Many very complex problems seem to have similar characteristics. They are pervasive, spreading unhindered into regions, countries, and economic activities that seem powerless to resist the invasion. They are difficult, it not impossible, to control without major changes in human behavior and government priorities, and those that serve illegal consumer markets are big money earners. Some receive tremendous attention, and there is a strong public pressure to remove or reduce them. This is true of health problems, particularly those caused by contaminated food where almost anyone in the community could be at risk. Some initially lack clarity as to their causes and effects, and there is uncertainty on how to approach them. These would include most environmental threats such as global warming. Other are almost invisible except to specialist groups. Cyber crime would come into this category as does the anticipated millennium computer bug that may cause systems to crash at the turn of the century if software has not been redesigned to prevent this.

In this book illegal drugs and cyber crime have been chosen as examples of complex problems, but there are many others that we are already having to deal with and some that we do not yet comprehend. In the health area we have the growing problem of new diseases for which cures do not yet exist. AIDS, CJD and the e-bola virus are three examples of these. Terrorism and armed conflict are other continuing sources of anxiety. The risk of major wars may be lessening as a result of international alliances and the development of weapons of total destruction, but local wars are increasing in number, often between groups living in close proximity to each other. While globalism affects large developed countries commercially, tribalism, religion, and nationalism are increasing in smaller nations leading to internal conflicts that can have devastating social and economic effects.

Many of these new problems are extremely complex and lack clarity. With AIDS there was initial confusion over whether it was primarily a problem for the gay community or whether heterosexuals were equally at risk. This affected decisions on which group to target with preventive measures. With mad cow disease (bovine spongiform encephalopathy or BSE) and its equivalent human complaint (Creutzfeldt-Jakob disease or CJD), it has taken time to discover its cause and to establish its ability to cross from animals to humans. These kinds of setbacks made the first steps in the problem-solving process, those of clarification and description, very difficult. There can be uncertainty over what kind of a problem has occurred, what has caused it, who is affected by it, and who is best qualified to address it. Many routes to a solution can be blocked because of lack of knowledge or through political, security, or financial constraints. With food contamination problems the solution is known to be better hygiene right along the food chain, yet, despite a proliferation of regulations, remedies are extremely difficult to apply.

There are also major environmental problems ahead, although the nature of these is not yet clearly understood. In the 1970s there were predictions of a new Ice Age. Today the threat is seen as one of global warming. Whichever is correct the consequences are likely to be tremendous upheavals for the human population, and, as with the global market, there will be winners and losers.

The changing structure of work is an example of a day-to-day activity with a potential for new and serious problems. The end of secure jobs for many groups that have become accustomed to them and the absence of jobs for young unskilled men could lead to greatly increased crime and social disturbance together with a major growth in the size of what today is called the "socially excluded" class. The global market, although hailed as a great opportunity, is unlikely to be a source of continuing social stability. Alliances between firms, industries, and countries will lead to successes for some, but disasters for others. There will be both winners and losers. Also, because the global production system is now so interlinked, a problem in one national area may easily spread to others. The 1997 over-investment problems in the Far East and their consequences for European industry illustrate this fact.

RECOGNIZING AND DESCRIBING PROBLEMS

An important competence for individuals and a necessary capability for their back-up organizations is the ability to recognize when a problem exists and to understand its nature. Many problems, such as those concerned with health issues, are immediately evident, while others, like certain kinds of cyber crime or money laundering, have to be sought out. In either of these situations there is a need to obtain as complete a picture as possible of the problem's nature, extent, and consequences. This is known as taking a "holistic" approach, and it differs greatly from traditional science approaches of dividing large problems into small sections and giving each part to a different group for solution. A holistic approach enables the spread of the problem, and its impact on different affected groups, to be seen as an interlinked whole. Although very complex problems are too large and intractable to be treated as single entities for problem solving, they need to be understood as linked systems with the likelihood that addressing one will affect some or all of the others.

One of the principal beliefs stressed in this book is that problems require careful initial analysis and description followed by the selection of strategies that are most likely to produce desired results. The actions associated with these are then prioritized. This kind of approach should reduce the amount of entropy in the problem situation. This sounds logical and neat and should certainly be attempted but, in reality, it may be difficult to achieve agreement on what aspects of a problem should be given priority and on the strategies most likely to succeed. Success may mean different things to different groups. Adults may regard a reduction of drug taking at raves and in clubs as highly desirable, whereas young people will see this as addressing completely the wrong targets.

It has to be recognized that many problems are not open and visible, they are often cloudy, complex, and uncertain. Much thought and discussion is required to agree upon the nature of the problem, the kind of solution that should be attempted, and the best means for achieving this. There must also be an assessment of the likely consequences of any selected strategy as its implementation may result in a whole new set of problems being released. Some of these may be as serious and difficult as those that have been successfully tackled. All decisions have consequences. If the police arrest a large number of drug dealers in an area without diminishing demand, the price of drugs will go up and there will be an increase in crime.

Sometimes problems arise as crises that have to be tackled immediately. There may be no time to proceed through a sequence of problem-solving steps and stages, immediate action will need to be taken. The techniques of "pattern recognition" used by physicians and surgeons may then be the best way forward. When a patient first arrives in the examination room the doctor asks questions but also looks for presenting physical signs and symptoms. These are then compared mentally with similar cases the doctor has encountered in the past. This approach can often provide a quick route to a diagnosis. The same technique can be used with other kinds of problems in situations where immediate action is required. The problem solver will ask the question Have I experienced a similar problem before or do I know of anyone who has? If the answer is yes he or she will proceed by taking the actions that produced a solution in that situation. This approach is now being used by emergency teams such as the fire service. To be successful it requires problem solvers with considerable experience of crisis situations.[4]

Obtaining a complete picture of a new, major problem is often not possible in the early stages of addressing it. This understanding may only arrive after a great deal of time and research. Nevertheless, if the situation is not a crisis, requiring immediate action, as full a picture as possible should be built at the beginning of any project, with all individuals and groups affected by it included in the discussion of a solution.

TOOLS FOR SOLVING PROBLEMS

In order to assist the understanding of the problem-solving process and how it is practiced a simple analytical framework has been used in this book. Problem solvers are seen as requiring certain competencies or skills that will help them to gain an understanding of the problem and make effective choices on how it can be solved. These will include understanding the total picture and taking a holistic approach; developing a broad overall strategy with clear ethical components; prioritizing subproblems, working together to achieve an agreed-upon system solution; implementing the system with care, caution, and an absence of victims; monitoring its operation and evaluating its success after twelve months.

The organizations or groups problem solvers are working for or with while solving problems are seen as needing certain capabilities, often of a resource nature, for example, information, time, equipment. Most important, problem solving today is rarely a solitary activity and almost always requires excellent coordination with other groups. This is often called networking. Certain psychological attributes are also seen as adding to problem-solving success. These are commitment to achieving a solution and, especially for law enforcement officers who directly confront criminals, considerable courage.

PROBLEM-SOLVING STRUCTURES AND PROCESSES

Groups that consist of individuals who come together to solve problems have to organize themselves to work effectively. A biological term for this self-organizing process when it is applied to the cells of living organisms is autopoisis. This describes the ability of these cells to behave cooperatively so that the system of which they are a part can maintain its stability and survive even when the environment is threatening. It is now being suggested that human groups can behave in the same way.[5] Like many of today's fashionable ideas this concept is not new. From the 1930s to the 1960s occupational psychologists have been inspired by the earlier work of anthropologists such as Bronislaw Malinowski to study group behavior.

Many experiments were carried out on how the members of groups work together and develop agreed-upon and accepted ways of behaving. Situations that were fluid and ambiguous with few accepted guidelines on how to behave followed the tradition of using Latin names and were called autokinetic. They were studied by psychologists interested in finding out how people behaved in conditions of considerable uncertainty.[6]

This early research suggested that newly formed groups without clear guidelines spent their first meetings establishing boundaries and agreeing upon the problem area they were going to focus on. This process was reciprocal with each individual seeking support from other members of the group. It was, however, influenced by status if certain individuals were seen as having more power and resources than others. A major function of groups of this kind was to maintain their stability and survival by protecting themselves from unwanted interference and to respond positively to environmental pressures that assisted the group's future success. In this way groups designed their own futures. If the group had an acceptable leader then this protective function was often a part of his or her responsibilities.

In the early days of occupational psychology this designing and survival process was called developing the group's informal structure. This contrasted with the formal structure in which roles and relationships were imposed by management. These informal relationships were not always benevolent. In situations where industrial relations took an adversarial form, the major objective of the informal structure could be to frustrate the production objectives of management. Today's problem-solving groups may have formal or informal structures or both. Formal structures occur when group members are given roles, instructions, objectives, and constraints by controlling groups such as government committees or senior police officers. This will reduce their ability to organize informally. When they are given a great deal of freedom on what to do and how to do it, they then have the task of developing their own structure and goals.

The well-functioning group, irrespective of whether it has a formal or informal structure, is believed to require a number of facilitating roles. Psychologists suggest that these include an expert, a mediator, a coordinator, and a morale builder.[7] These roles are not allocated but assumed by different members of the group at appropriate moments. Sometimes they may all be held by one person who moves from role to role according to the needs of the situation. More often each role is shared between one or two individuals with the expert role being given to the person or persons in the group who has the most relevant knowledge.

This book has emphasized the importance of problem solving moving through a number of different stages. These will not necessarily be in any particular order and may take place in parallel. Comparative studies have been made by the Catholic Institute for International Relations (CIIR) of peace processes in different countries, including Colombia. These studies have found that while every project has its own dynamic, all have certain patterns of action in common.[8] These include the facilitation of dialogue when armed conflict is ending, negotiations to establish new patterns of relationships, and peacekeeping and monitoring agreements. Finally, the causes of war have to be removed and socioeconomic and political changes implemented. Problem-solving groups are likely to do something similar. They too will need to collect information, share knowledge, discuss options, and decide on action. Their objective will also be to remove the cause of the problem or reduce its negative effects.

Certain of these phases are more open to intervention than others and are greatly assisted by the presence of facilitators. In peace programs these are often powerful and respected individuals who are seen as relatively neutral by both sides, and religious groups can also bring together groups for discussions and help keep them at the negotiating table. Similar roles and strategies can help bind together the different factions in other kinds of problem-solving groups. These are not at war with each other but may have different or diverging interests.

Effective dialogue is clearly critical at all stages of the problem-solving process and will be greatly assisted by a skilled facilitator or group leader. Agreeing upon the definition of the problem, where emphasis and resources are to be directed and initial actions to be taken, will require negotiation. Interpersonal conflict between different representatives in the groups will need to be recognized and the causes brought into the open, strategies for longer-term action will have to be identified, and their political and other consequences recognized and discussed.

NETWORKS

Many researchers and managers see networks as the organizational form of the future. These are described as groups that are stable, yet flexible, and have clear goals. They have the capability of resisting dysfunctional change yet accepting and welcoming positive change that is a response to a dynamic environment.[9] The power structure of these networks is based on flows, not hierarchies. The roles of individuals and groups acquire status because they have information that expedites the production of the product or service, not because of designated authority or title. Each network relates to other networks through excellent communication lines and a number of overlapping roles with each group needing the others to complete the total task effectively. Author Steven Rose describes this as "weaving." These characteristics enable networks to do things quickly because communication lines are short, necessary information is always available, and groups can expand or contract in size according to the needs of the situation they are handling.[10] Networks tackling the drug problem will include the military, police, customs officials, educators, therapists, and government committees.

Networks in industry are seen as being designed around work processes, with flat hierarchies, team management, and performance measured by customer satisfaction, the maximization of necessary contacts, availability of information, and multiskilled employees. Coordination and flexibility will be essential as is a "gatekeeper" role with individuals who manage the boundaries, overlaps, and interfaces in the networks. If networks are the best organization form for addressing complex problems, then at present it is the criminal groups that have these, not the law enforcement and other agencies. This model could easily describe the international drug-dealing Mafia. The difference between it and a legitimate company is that incentives are a mixture of financial rewards and life-threatening intimidation; customer satisfaction is getting drugs to the customer when required; and critical information is knowledge of the strategies and movements of law enforcement agencies.

DRUGS AND CYBER CRIME AS EXAMPLES OF COMPLEXITY

Will attempts to solve these problems ever prove successful? At present there is little room for optimism. Drug barons and international criminals continue to seek easy profits, and if financial success becomes difficult in one profit area they move to another. This is already happening with today's very high legal penalties persuading some barons to move from smuggling hard drugs to providing other illegal goods and services that are in demand. The Turkish Mafia, which, in the past, concentrated on smuggling heroin into Italy, is now transporting Kurdish nationals who wish to escape poverty and persecution in their home country.[11] Other criminal groups are smuggling weapons, radioactive materials, art treasures, and any other items for which there is a market.

Despite this lack of progress an important question is Are there still useful avenues to be followed that can help control or reduce the problem? For example, with drugs, can supplies be reduced through catching and prosecuting enough criminal dealers? Can potential future users be persuaded, by educational programs, to stay away from the habit, or can addicts be helped to give it up? With cyber crime an important question is can systems be so well protected that criminals find the effort of breaking in beyond their resources? If the answer to questions of this kind is no, then further questions have to be asked, such as, given these difficulties, can certain aspects of the principal problem or of subproblems still be usefully addressed so as to reduce some of the ill effects? Careful thought will also need to be given to the possible short- and long-term consequences of taking certain problem-solving routes.

With some problems, and these include illegal drugs and cyber crime, the solution is clear but difficult if not impossible to apply. The incentive for criminals to move into drugs and cyber crime is the possibility of large financial gain. But for this illegally acquired money to be used to further personal interests and objectives it has to be made legitimate and converted into a form that is acceptable to the institutions of international finance. It can then be used to take over established industries, to finance armies, and overthrow rival groups and to acquire all the trappings of wealth such as works of art, jewelry, large houses, and expensive forms of transport. Some of the Russian Mafia are reported as using part of their wealth to send their children to British public schools.[12]

Money can only be used in this way if it has been laundered so that it appears that it has been acquired honestly. This means that one of the most effective ways to reduce both the illegal drug trade and cyber crime is to remove or reduce money laundering facilities. Britain already has draconian penalties with the possibility of fourteen years' imprisonment and very large fines for money laundering and with all financial institutions required to have in place systems to deter money laundering and assist the authorities to detect money laundering activities. Directors and managers of banks, investment firms, and insurance companies who fail to comply can incur two years' imprisonment and unlimited fines.[13]

Offshore companies such as private banks are also coming under official pressure to monitor and expose money laundering activities. An estimated $300 to $500 billion is laundered offshore each year and many solicitors and accountants are expert at legitimizing laundering operations, frequently through the buying and selling of property. These organizations are now being asked to make serious inquiries about their customers or to run the risk of having to compensate the original owners of the money if they pay it to another party. Many are reluctant to do this because of the assurances of confidentiality they have given to their customers, while the efforts of those trying for reform are compromised by the increased use of the Internet as a means for transferring money and by the continuing willingness of many countries to provide money laundering facilities. Some experts are now suggesting that tougher controls and more policing are less effective than striving for market reforms and more ethical business practices. This point is made about Russia by John Lloyd in his book *Rebirth of a Nation: An Anatomy of Russia*.[14]

Drug barons are first-class managers who run complex international networks of collaborators with great efficiency using the powerful positive incentive of financial gain and the even stronger negative incentive of being murdered for noncooperation. Their enormous profits are greatly assisted by global money laundering facilities which, today, use electronic networks for transferring money from one country to another. These systems have some resemblance to a health virus spreading unchecked from one country to another with no known cure available.

FUTURE PROBLEMS

Yet if crime of this kind is not reduced there is a danger that global capitalism may become totally corrupted. Criminal activities will proliferate throughout the world leading eventually to a global criminal economy. Manuel Castells, an American sociologist of Spanish origin whose recent publications have greatly added to our understanding of how the world is changing, points out that global crime of the size, spread, and connectedness that we are experiencing today is a new phenomena that can profoundly change economies and cultures. He maintains that it is almost impossible to keep criminal activities separate from international trade and financial networks and that a combination of legitimate and illegitimate financial activities will be a continuing feature of the global economy and of the social and political dynamics of the information age.

He argues that, because of its acceptance of high risks, criminal capital follows, and amplifies, speculative turbulence in financial markets and then becomes an important source of financial destabilization.[15]

Some criminal groups have short histories. Their members come together for specific projects and then disband or end up in prison. Others endure over long periods. Many are embedded in national and ethnic cultures and have a long history of identification with these, which shows itself in codes of honor and bonding mechanisms. The Colombian and Italian Mafias are examples of this pattern. Their strategy is to base production activities in low risk areas where they have a great deal of control and to sell in areas where there is the greatest demand and the most money.

Castells points out that it is not the spread of crime that is new but the global linkages.[16] The scale and dynamics of the new criminal economy are now able to influence the economic and political aspects of international relationships. This could lead to the destabilization of countries that cannot protect themselves. The illicit trading that takes place is supported by a global system of money laundering, which enables the large profits that are made to be used to support further activities that can be either illegal or legal.

He sees the connecting of the criminal economy to legitimate financial markets as having a number of dangerous consequences for society. First, if the entire structure of a state is corrupted by criminal intervention, the ethical conduct of public affairs will be seriously threatened. Second, international relations between states will be greatly influenced by attempts to frustrate criminal activities. The strained relations between the United States and Colombia is an example of this problem. Lastly, the movement of criminally created money around the world can have unpredictable consequences for national economies.

INTERNATIONAL COOPERATION

The only means of addressing these dangerous and damaging problems is through good cooperation and coordination across national boundaries. This requires all countries to be willing to collect, provide, and share up-to-date information on criminal activities; to agree on and implement common legal processes and penalties; and to commit their security forces to work with those of other nations so that criminals can be tracked and caught as they move from country to country. If this cooperation and coordination is too slow, too late, or too little, perhaps because of an absence of will or because bureaucratic procedures get in the way, then very unwelcome change can take place. What, up to now, have been seen as good, ethical, well-controlled commercial practices can disintegrate and be replaced with systems that suit the objectives of the criminal community.

This could already be happening in Russia where the criminal economy is expanding to a size previously unknown in a major industrial country. A *London Times* article reported that Russian crime syndicates were now laundering money on a grand scale in London and other European capitals. The article suggested that this money was "legitimized" through property deals and that $26 billion of illegal money was being laundered through Europe and elsewhere. It also reported that Russian police figures revealed that 41,000 Russian companies were now run by Mafia groups as well as 50% of banks and 80% of the joint ventures with foreign capital.[17]

Castells suggests that global crime of this size brings with it a new culture that displaces the old with criminals becoming the role models of the younger generation.[18] This phenomena is described by Gabriel Garcia Marquez in his book *News of a Kidnapping*. He claims that the Colombian drug traffickers had a mythic aura. They enjoyed complete impunity and even a certain prestige because the Medellin cartel paid for charitable activities in poor neighborhoods. At the height of the cartel leader Pablo Escobar's popularity, people put up altars with his picture and lit candles to him in the slums of Medellin. He was a powerful shaper of public opinion yet in Marquez's view he was completely unable to distinguish good from evil.[19] Because the drug scene is so profitable, so international, and so easily infiltrated into existing national economics, it ranks as one of the most difficult and dangerous problems of our time.

Networking, flexibility, and coordination are three primary characteristics of the successful criminal organization. The Colombian drug traffickers have survived through modifying their organizations and decentralizing their structure. The Cali cartel has become a loose association of exporters with over two hundred independent groups cooperating in the production and marketing of drugs.[20] When threatened, flexible criminal networks find new arrangements, new power relations, and new forms of cooperation. They can easily adapt themselves to the control attempts of rigid, bureaucratic, nationally bound state institutions while their need to avoid police detection means they willingly form strategic alliances with other criminal groups.

Reducing the effects of crime requires countries to have similar flexible networks that coordinate the activities of customs, police, educational authorities, therapeutic services, and government committees, assisted by comprehensive shared electronic information systems. Countries also need to collaborate with one another in developing crime reducing strategies, including the prevention of money laundering. Without this it is unlikely that attempts to reduce illegal drug and cyber crime problems will make much headway. The creation of a pan-European body to coordinate strategies and action could greatly assist the moves toward a solution.

International bodies set up to reduce crime require mind-sets similar to that of the Mafia. They must develop innovative thinking and strategy, a knowledge of how the complex systems and situations with which they are interacting are changing, good feedback on their own responses to these changes, adaptability as a result of this feedback, flexibility to meet new problems, awareness of the consequences of decisions they are making, and action to ameliorate disadvantageous consequences. In addition they need to create structures based on equality, not elitism, and to keep their thinking and actions in step with public opinion. A culture of effective and ethical problem solving needs to be created.

Some moves toward this were incorporated in a new draft Treaty for Europe agreed upon by the fifteen counties of the European Union in October 1997. While unemployment was the number-one priority, security issues came next on the agenda. One part of the new treaty titled "Provisions on Police and Judicial Cooperation in Criminal Matters" focused on combating and preventing crime including illicit drug trafficking and fraud. This is to be achieved by closer cooperation between police forces, customs authorities, and other competent authorities through the European Police Office (Europol); closer cooperation between judicial and other competent authorities; and greater harmonization of rules on criminal matters in member states.[21] This seems to be an important step in the right direction if it can be implemented successfully.

LAST THOUGHTS

Tomorrow's problem solvers can gain much from examining the problems of the present and the past, but they will need great skills to tackle successfully new problems that are powerful in their impact and international in scope. Many of the methods and tools of the past, such as the careful testing of hypotheses and the systematic gathering of data, will still have a great deal to offer, but much more than this will be required. An essential skill will be the ability to understand and manage complexity as problems increase in scale and difficulty. Another is flexibility of thought and action so that strategies can be reformulated as rapidly developing problems and their environments change over time.

A lesson from cyber crime is that prevention is better than cure and that, in some areas, if the problem is not prevented it may prove impossible to find a cure. Another, is that technology can contribute to the prevention and solution of problems but will prove ineffective unless people know how to make use of it and are constantly vigilant to establish when and how it should be used. A further critical message is that reducing the rewards of crime can make a major contribution to the reduction of crime. The objective of most criminals is financial gain and if this can be reduced through ethical business behavior and a refusal to condone practices such as money laundering, then criminal activity will be greatly reduced.

The approaches described in this book will hopefully reduce the amount of entropy managers are faced with, but they cannot provide a total solution because events are moving too fast.

It seems that tomorrow's problems will be even more difficult than those of today. But it is people, not technology, who will solve them. They will require concerted effort from groups who can work together effectively. Cooperation, coordination, commitment, and networking at local, national, and international levels may help us toward finding some answers. But this will not be easy and it will require great creativity and imagination. As former U.S. Senator J. William Fulbright once suggested in a speech in the U.S. Senate.

> We must dare to think "unthinkable" thoughts. We must learn to explore all the options and possibilities that confront us in a complex and rapidly changing world. We must dare to think about "unthinkable things" because when things become unthinkable thinking stops and action becomes mindless.[22]

Notes

Introduction: Problem Solving and Uncertainty

1. Andrew Kopkind, "Are We in the Middle of a Revolution?" *New York Times* Magazine (November 10, 1968).
2. Zygmunt Baumann, *Post Modern Ethics* (London: Blackwell, 1993).
3. Peter L. Bernstein, *Against the Gods* (New York: Wiley, 1996).
4. Steven Overell, "Drugs at Work," *People Management* (February 5, 1998).
5. Alvin Toffler, *Powershift* (New York: Bantam Books, 1990).
6. John Kay, *The Business of Economics* (Oxford: Oxford University Press, 1996).
7. W. Ross Ashby, *An Introduction to Cybernetics* (London: Chapman and Hall, 1956).
8. Gilbert Ryle, *The Concept of Mind* (London: Hutchinson, 1949).
9. Kay, *The Business of Economics.*
10. John Harvey Jones, *Making It Happen* (London: Collins, 1988).
11. Manuel Castells, *The Rise of the Network Society* (London: Blackwell, 1996).

1. The Problem of Problem Solving

1. David Bayley, *Police for the Future* (Oxford: Oxford University Press, 1994).
2. Margaret Constanzo, *Problem Solving* (London: Cavendish Publishing, 1994).
3. Donald Schon, *The Reflective Practitioner* (London: Temple Smith, 1983).
4. C. West Churchman, *The Design of Inquiring Systems* (New York: Basic Books, 1971).
5. Ulrick Beck, *The Risk Society* (London: Sage, 1992).
6. Stafford Beer, *The Brain of the Firm* (Chichester: Wiley, 1972).
7. Tony Jefferson, *The Case Against Paramilitary Policing* (Milton Keynes: Open University Press, 1990).

2. Using Problem-Solving Methods

1. Nimal Jayartna, *Understanding and Evaluating Methodologies* (London: McGraw-Hill, 1994).
2. Michael Wilmer, "Information Theory and the Measurement of Detective Performance," *Kybernetes* 2 (1973): 225–231.
3. Peter L. Bernstein, *Against the Gods* (New York: Wiley 1996).
4. C. Kepner and B. Tregoe, *The Rational Manager* (London: McGraw-Hill, 1965).
5. Stafford Beer, *Diagnosing the System for Organizations* (New York: Wiley, 1985).
6. Enid Mumford, *Effective Systems Design and Requirements Analysis* (London: Macmillan, 1995).
7. Tudor Rickards, "Creativity Training," *Interfaces* 24 (November-December 1994).
8. Frank Watt and Patrick Tissington, "Making Decisions in Emergencies," *Intersec* 8 (January 1988): 13–15.
9. Gilbert Ryle, *The Concept of Mind* (London: Penguin University Books, 1973).
10. Richard Dawkins, *The Selfish Gene* (Oxford: Oxford University Press, 1989).
11. Geoffrey Vickers, *Making Institutions Work* (London: Associated Business Programmes Ltd., 1973).
12. Donald Schon, *The Reflective Practitioner* (London: Temple Smith, 1983).
13. Ibid.
14. Edward de Bono, *I Am Right You Are Wrong* (London: Penguin Books, 1991).
15. Chris Argyris, *On Organizational Learning* (Oxford: Blackwell, 1985).
16. De Bono, *I Am Right You Are Wrong.*

3. Problem Solving by Specialist Groups: Scientists, Doctors, Lawyers

1. Max Wertheimer, *Productive Thinking* (London: Tavistock Publications, 1961).
2. Bill Critchley, "A Gestalt Approach to Oraganizational Consulting," *Developing Organizational Consultancy*, eds. Jean Neumann, Kamil Kellner, and Andraea Dawson-Shepherd (London: Routledge, 1997).
3. P. Clarkson, *Gestalt Counselling in Action* (London: Sage, 1989).
4. David Deutsch, *The Fabric of Reality* (London: Allen Lane Penguin Press, 1997).
5. Chris Argyris, *Reasoning, Learning, and Action* (San Francisco: Jossey-Bass, 1982).
6. Karl Popper, *The Logic of Scientific Discovery* (London: Routledge, 1959).
7. William H. Calvin, *How Brains Think* (London: Weidenfeld and Nicolson, 1996).
8. William J. Goode and Paul K. Hatt, *Methods in Social Research* (London: McGraw-Hill, 1952).
9. Mitchell Wilson, *Passion to Know: The World's Scientists* (London: Weidenfeld and Nicolson, 1972).
10. W. B. Pillsbury, *Scientia* (1924).
11. Stafford Beer, *Diagnosing the System for Organizations* (Chichester: Wiley, 1985).
12. Edward Brech, Clive de Paula, and Norman White, *Management of Research and Development* (London: British Institute of Management, 1964).
13. Ibid.
14. Hugh Pennington, "Dining with Death," *London: Times Higher* (June 1997).

15. Margot Costanzo, *Problem Solving for Lawyers* (London: Cavendish Publishing, 1995); Simon Lee and Marie Fox, *Legal Skills* (London: Blackstone, 1991).
16. Costanzo, *Problem Solving for Laywers.*
17. David Kahneman, Paul Slovic, and Amos Tversky, *Judgment Under Uncertainty* (Cambridge: Cambridge University Press, 1982).
18. Argyris, *Reasoning, Learning, and Action.* (1982).
19. Costanzo, *Problem Solving for Lawyers.*
20. Richard Bomforth, Stuart Mason, Michael Swash, and Bailliere Tindall, *Hutchinson's Clinical Methods* (London: Hutchinson, 1975).
21. Reg Revans, "The Hospital as a Human System," *Physics in Medicine and Biology* 7 (1962).
22. Enid Mumford "Managing Complexity: The Design and Implementation of Expert Systems," in *Knowledge Based Management Support Systems*, eds. Goergios Doukidis, Frank Land, and Gordon Miller (Chichester: Ellis Horwood, 1989).

4. Problem Solving and the Police

1. Sheehy Report, *Report into the Inquiry into Police Responsibilities and Rewards* (CM 2280, I, II. London: HMSO 1993).
2. David Bayley, *Police for the Future* (Oxford: Oxford University Press, 1994).
3. T. A. Critchley, *A History of the Police in England and Wales* (London: Constable, 1967).
4. Rod Morgan and Tim Newburn, *The Future of Policing* (Oxford: Clarendon, 1997).
5. Peter Micheels, *The Detectives* (New York: St. Martin's Press, 1994).
6. John Douglas and Mark Olshaker, *Mindhunter* (London: Heinmann, 1996).
7. Ibid.
8. *Police Reform White Paper* (London: HMSO, 1993).
9. *Internal Police Report: Intelligence Development Recommendations to the West Yorkshire Command Team* (May, 1997).
10. Micheels, *The Detectives.*
11. Rod Morgan and Tim Newburn, *The Future of Policing* (Oxford: Clarendon, 1997).
12. Herbert Goldstein, *Problem Oriented Policing* (Philadelphia: Temple University Press, 1990).
13. Adrian Leigh, Tim Read, and Nick Tilley, *Problem-Oriented Policing.* British Home Office Policy Directorate (London: HMSO, 1996).
14. Brighton Police Department, *In Pursuit of Excellence: Applying Quality Improvement Principles to the Police Service.* (Internal Document, May, 1994).
15. Lord Scarman, *The Scarman Report: The Brixton Disorders 10–12 April 1981* (London: HMSO).

5. Drug Dealers and Drug Barons as Problem Solvers

1. Robert Gross, *Revenue Management* (London: Orion Business Books, 1997).
2. Howard Marks, *Mr. Nice* (London: Minerva, 1997).
3. Ibid.

4. Ibid., p. 327.
5. Ibid., p. 330.
6. Ibid., p. 332.
7. J. Thompson, *Intersec* 4, no. 5 (May 1994): 147.
8. W. Tupman, "Crime Patterns," *Intersec* 5, no. 4 (April 1995): 121–122.
9. Manual Castells, *End of Millennium* (London: Blackwell, 1998); Gabriel Garcia Marquez, *News of a Kidnapping* (London: Jonathon Cape, 1997).
10. Carl Wauben, "Drugs—the Caribbean Connection," *Intersec* 5, no. 3 (March 1995): 90–93.
11. Vincent P. Grimes, "USA Round-up," *Intersec* 7, no. 6 (June 1997): 213–214.
12. Garcia Marquez, *News of a Kidnapping*.
13. Ian Greig, "Latin American Security Problems," *Intersec* 5, no. 9 (1995): 307–308.
14. "Drugs, Latin America and the United States," *The Economist* (February 7, 1998): 69.
15. Castells, *End of Millennium*.
16. John Kay, *The Business of Economics* (Oxford: Oxford University Press, 1996).

6. Understanding the Drug Problem

1. Ken Duncan, "Drug Trafficking," *Intersec* 7, no. 9 (September 1997).
2. Paul Lockley, *Counselling Heroin and Other Drug Users* (London: Free Association Books, 1995).
3. Malcolm Ramsey and Andrew Percy, *Drug Misuse Declared: Results of the British Crime Survey* (London: Home Office Research Study, 151; Claire Gerada and Mark Ashworth, "Addiction and Dependence—Illicit Drugs," *British Medical Journal* 315 (August 2, 1997), 289–350.
4. Susan Greenfield, personal communication June 17, 1997.
5. Richard Webster, *Why Freud Was Wrong* (London: HarperCollins, 1995).
6. Matthew Collin and John Godfrey, *Altered States* (New York: Serpents Tale, 1997).
7. Ibid.
8. *European*, March 6–12, 1997.
9. Robert Holman Coombs, *Drug-Impaired Professionals* (Cambridge: Harvard University Press, 1997).
10. *The Big Issue* 273 (March 2–8 1998).
11. *New Musical Express* (February 15, 1997).
12. Philip Knightley, "The Drugs World War. What Do We Do Now?" *Independent on Sunday* (February 8, 1998).
13. Ian Roberts, Maggie Barker, and Leah Li. "Analysis of Deaths from Accidental Drug Poisoning in Teenagers," *British Medical Journal* 315 (August 2, 1997): 289.
14. "The Graduate Consumers Study" *Times* Higher Education Supplement (May 30, 1997).
15. *Independent*, September 17, 1997.
16. Irvine Welsh, *Trainspotting* (London: Minerva, 1993); Melvin Burgess, *Junk* (London: Penguin Books, 1996).
17. Burgess, *Junk*, p. 144.

18. Richard Lawrence Miller, *Drug Warriors and Their Prey: From Police Power to Police State* (Westport, Ct: Praeger, 1996).
19. *Independent* (February 16, 1997).
20. *Independent* (April 10, 1997).
21. Mark Edmunds, Michael Hough, and Norman Urguia, *Tackling Local Drug Markets* (London: Police Research Group, 1996).
22. Thomas Stuttaford, "Medicine Chest," *Times* (March 17, 1998).
23. Michael Evans, *London Times* (June 10, 1998).
24. John Lloyd, *Rebirth of a Nation: An Anatomy of Russia* (London: Michael Joseph, 1997).
25. Jason Bennetto, "Nigerian Crime Wave Sweeps Through Britain." *Independent* (February 2, 1998).
26. Philip Knightly, "How We Fought and Lost the Drugs World War," *Independent on Sunday* (January 25, 1998).
27. *Economist* (April 19–25, 1997).
28. *USA Today* (June 2, 1997).
29. Ibid.

7. Tackling the Drug Problem: Governments as Strategic Planners

1. Andrew Tudor, *Problem Solving* (London: Routledge and Kegan Paul, 1982).
2. "USA Round-Up," *Intersec* 5, no. 1, 3, 4, 5, 9, 10 (January, March, April, June, September, October, 1995).
3. "USA Round-Up," *Intersec* 7, no. 6 (June 1997).
4. Ibid.
5. Lee Smith, "The FBI Is a Touch Outfit to Run," *Fortune* 9, no. 21 (1989): 81–83.
6. Fenton Bresler, *Interpol* (London: Sinclair-Stevenson, 1992).
7. *European Parliament News* (February 1998).
8. Ibid.
9. Michael Forde, "International/EU Criminal Law," in *Justice Cooperation in the European Union*, ed. Gavin Barrett (Dublin: Institute of European Affairs, 1997).
10. Val Flynn, "Europol—a Watershed in Law Enforcement Cooperation," in *Justice Cooperation in the European Union*, ed. Gavin Barrett (Dublin: Institute of European Affairs, 1997).
11. *Times* (March 23, 1998).
12. Forde, "International/EU Criminal Law."
13. Val Flynn, "The Treaty of Amsterdam," *Intersec* 8, no. 1 (January 1998): 18–20.
14. Flynn, "Europol."
15. Dermot Gilroy, "Customs Cooperation in the Third Pillar," in *Justice Cooperation in the European Union*, ed. Gavin Barrett (Dublin: Institute of European Affairs, 1997).
16. Jason Lloyd, *Drugs, Addiction and the Law* (London: Elm Publications, 1995).
17. British White Paper, "Tackling Drugs Together: A Strategy for England 1995–98" (London: HMSO, 1995).
18. Ian Greig, "The Growing Menace of Intimidation," *Intersec* 4, no. 5 (May 1992).

19. "National Criminal Intelligence Service," *Intersec* 4, no. 9 (September 1994): 301–302.
20. *Sunday Observer* (May 18, 1997).

8. Operational Guidelines for Problem Solving

1. Stafford Beer, "The Viable System Model: Its Provenance, Development and Methodology," in *The Viable System Model*, eds. Raul Espejo and Roger Harnden (Chichester: Wiley, 1989).
2. Kenneth Schneider, *Destiny of Change* (New York: Holt, Rinehart and Winston, 1968).
3. Ibid.
4. Kevin Stringer, "Zurich: Microcosm of the International Drug War," *Intersec* 7, no. 9 (September 1997): 280–284.

9. Different Groups with Different Problems

1. Alistair Ramsey, "The Need for Good Drugs Education," in *National Drugs Conference: Final Report* (London: Association of Chief Police Officers, 1994).
2. Ibid.
3. Matthew Collin, *Altered States* (London: Serpents Tale, 1997).
4. Ibid.
5. "Address by the Rt. Hon. Michael Howard QC MP," in *National Drugs Conference: Final Report* (London: Association of Chief Police Officers, 1994).
6. Paul Lockley, *Counselling Heroin and Other Drug Users* (London: Free Association Books, 1995).
7. Ibid.
8. Paul Lockley, *Working with Drug Family Support Groups* (London: Free Association Books, 1996).
9. Personal communication.
10. Robert Holman Coombs, *Drug Impaired Professionals* (Cambridge: Harvard University Press, 1997).
11. *Independent* (May 23, 1997).
12. *Independent* (April 19, 1997).
13. "The Dutch Experiment," *New Scientist* 2122 (February 21, 1998): 30–31.
14. W. Ross Ashby, *An Introduction to Cybernetics* (London: Chapman and Hall, 1956).

10. Cyber Crime: A New Kind of Fraud

1. *European* (November 13–19, 1997).
2. Mark Mottershead, "Taking the Complexity out of Encryption," *Computer Bulletin*, no. 3: 12–14.
3. *European*, April 10–16, 1997.
4. Chris Sundt, "Security Problems of Electronic Data Interchange," *Intersec* 4, no. 1 (January 1994): 21–24.

5. Othmar Kyas, *Internet Security* (London: International Thomson Computer Press, 1997).
6. Joel P. Friedman and Frank Terzuoli, "Operating Risk in Financial Services," in *Risk Management: Problems and Solutions*, eds. William H. Beaver and George Parker (London: McGraw Hill, 1995).
7. Stephen Fay, *The Collapse of Barings* (London: Arrow Business Books, 1996).
8. Katie Hafner and John Markoff, *Cyberpunk* (London: Fourth Estate, 1991).
9. Alvin Toffler, *Powershift* (New York: Bantam Books, 1990).
10. Hafner and Markoff, *Cyberpunk*.
11. *Secure Computing* (May 1997). Editorial.
12. Othmar Kyas, *Internet Security* (London: International Thomson Computer Press, 1997).
13. Alan Routledge, "A Question of Responsibility," *Secure Computing* (June 1997): 38–40.
14. Neil Barrett, "Digital Crime: Policing the Cybernation," *Secure Computing* (November 1997): 21–24.
15. "Hackers for Hire," *Secure Computing* (December 1997): 22–28.
16. Clifford Stoll, *The Cuckoo's Egg* (London: Bodley Head, 1990).
17. Ibid., p. 104.

11. Addressing Cyber Crime Problems

1. Robert N. Charette, "The Mechanics of Managing IT Risk," *Journal of Information Technology* 11 (December 1996): 373–378.
2. Kalle Lyytinen, Lars Mathiassen, and Janne Ropporen, "A Framework for Software Risk Management," *Journal of Information Technology* 11 (December 1996): 275–285.
3. Gurpreet Dhillon and James Backhouse, "Managing for Secure Organizations: A Review of IT Security Research Approaches," in *Key Issues in Information Systems*, ed. David E. Avison (London: McGraw-Hill, 1997), 377–390.
4. Othmar Kyas, *Internet Security* (London: Thompson Computer Press, 1997).
5. Clifford Stoll, *The Cuckoo's Egg* (London: Bodley Head, 1990).
6. Fred J. Heemstra and Rob J. Kusters, "Dealing with Risk: A Practical Approach," *Journal of Information Technology* 11 (December 1996): 333–346.
7. Fred Piper, "Information Security," *Intersec* 5, no. 5 (May 1995): 192–194.
8. Judith Jeffcoate, "Security in the Internet Age," *Secure Computing* (September 1997): 60–61.
9. Dhillon and Backhouse, "Managing for Secure Organizations."
10. Martin Kettle and Owen Boycott, "The Age of the Digital Sleuth," *Guardian Newspaper* (December 12, 1997).
11. David Kahn, "Curiosity Code: Hackers Are Heirs to An Ancient Tradition," *Daily Telegraph* (July 1, 1997).
12. Chris Sundt, "Security Problems of Electronic Data Interchange," *Intersec* 4, no. 1 (January 1994): 22–24.
13. Vincent P. Grimes, "USA Round-UP," *Intersec* 7, no. 9 (September 1997): 304–305.
14. Peter Sommer, "Cyber Extortion," *Secure Computing* (April 1997); 41–43.

15. Bill Tupman, "Avoiding the Pitfalls of Fraud Investigation," *Intersec* 5, no. 4 (April 1995): 123–124.
16. Michael Hudson, "From Disaster Response to Business Recovery," *Intersec* 5, no. 7 (July 1995): 272–273.
17. Dhillon and Backhouse, "Managing for Secure Organization."
18. Richard Kusnierz, "Hunting for the Needle," *Intersec* 5, no. 5 (May 1995): 185–187.
19. Bryan Clough, "Computer Crime," *Intersec* 7, no. 10 (October 1997): 364–365.
20. R. Dixon and C. Marston, "Computer Fraud," *Journal of Management Accounting* 66, no. 9 (October 1988): 24–25.
21. John Cardin, "Welcome to World War Three," *Independent on Sunday* (February 22, 1998).

12. Money Laundering: Where Drugs and Cyber Crime Meet

1. Fenton Bresler, *Interpol* (London: Sinclair Stevenson, 1992).
2. William C. Gilmore, *Dirty Money* (Strasbourg: Council of Europe Press, 1993).
3. C. Hill, "Money Laundering Methodology," in *Butterworth's International Guide to Money Laundering Law*, ed. R. Parlour (London: Butterworth, 1994).
4. Helen Norman, "Tracing the Proceeds of Crime: An Inequitable Solution," in *Laundering and Tracing*, ed. P. B. H. Birk (Oxford: Clarendon Press, 1998).
5. Bresler, *Interpol.*
6. Stephen Moriarty, "Tracing, Mixing, Laundering," in *Laundering and Tracing*, ed. P. B. H. Birks (Oxford: Clarendon Press, 1998).
7. Paul Matthews, "The Legal and Moral Rules of Common Law Tracing," in *Laundering and Tracing*, ed. P. B. H. Birks (Oxford: Clarendon Press, 1998).
8. Gijs de Vries, "How Europe Fights the Mafia's Plague of Crime," *European* (May 8–14, 1997).
9. Gilmore, *Dirty Money.*
10. Norman, "Tracing the Proceeds of Crime."
11. Report of European Parliament (EP) News, June 1997.
12. Gilmore, *Dirty Money.*
13. Michael Fooner, "The Financial Action Task Force" *Intersec* 5, no. 6 (June 1995): 219–221.
14. Ibid.
15. Alistair Walters, "Money Laundering," *Independent* (February 4, 1998).
16. Editorial, *European* (May 8–14, 1997).
17. Nigel Morris-Cotterall, *Independent on Sunday* (August 7, 1997).
18. Walters, "Money Laundering."

13. The Challenge of Problem Solving

1. Jay Forrester, "Planning Under the Dynamic Influences of Complex Social Systems," in *Perspectives of Planning*, ed. Eric Jantsch (Paris: OECD, 1969), 237–256.
2. W. Ross Ashby, *An Introduction to Cybernetics* (London: Chapman and Hall, 1956).

3. Ibid.
4. Frank Watt and Patrick Tissington, "Making Decisions in Emergencies," *Intersec* 8, no. 1 (January 1998): 13–15.
5. Steven Rose, *Lifelines* (London: Allen Lane, Penguin Press, 1997).
6. Muzafer Sherif, *The Psychology of Social Norms* (New York: Harper, 1936).
7. Josephine Klein, *Working with Groups* (London: Hutchinson, 1961).
8. "Faith and Reason: A Proper Role at the Negotiating Table," *Independent* (January 10, 1998).
9. Rose, *Lifelines*.
10. Manuel Castells, *The Rise of the Network Society* (London: Blackwell, 1996).
11. Mark Porter and Julian Coman, "Kurdish Exodus Fuels Fears," *European* (January 1–7, 1988).
12. Michael Evans, "Russian Mafia Cash Washes into London," *Times* (January 10, 1998).
13. *Confiscation and Money Laundering: Law and Practice*, Home Office Publication (London: HMSO, 1997).
14. John Lloyd, *Rebirth of a Nation: An Anatomy of Russia* (London: Michael Joseph, 1997).
15. Manuel Castells, *End of Millennium* (London: Blackwell, 1998).
16. Ibid.
17. "Russian Mafia Cash Washes into London," *London Times* (January 10, 1998).
18. Castells, *End of Millennium*.
19. Gabriel Garcia Marquez, *News of a Kidnapping* (London: Jonathon Cape, 1997).
20. Manuel Castells, *The Power of Identity* (London: Blackwell, 1997).
21. Val Flynn, "The Treaty of Amsterdam," *Intersec* 8, no. 1 (January 1998): 18–20.
22. Speech in U.S. Senate, March 27, 1964.

Index